Cinema Novo *x* 5

hs, No. 60
an Studies
s at Austin

CINEMA NOVO *x* 5
Masters of Contemporary Brazilian Film

By Randal Johnson

 University of Texas Press, Austin

Library of Congress Cataloging in Publication Data
Johnson, Randal, 1948-
  Cinema novo *x* 5.

  (Latin American monographs; no. 60/Institute of Latin American
Studies, the University of Texas at Austin)
  Filmography: p.
  Includes index.
  1. Moving-pictures—Brazil. I. Title. II. Title: Cinema novo times five. III.
Series: Latin American monographs (University of Texas at Austin. Institute of
Latin American Studies); no. 60.
PN1993.5.B6J62   1984   791.43'75'0981   83-16685
ISBN 0-292-71090-9
ISBN 0-292-71091-7 (pbk.)

First Edition, 1984

Requests for permission to reproduce material from
this work should be sent to:
  Permissions
  University of Texas Press
  P.O. Box 7819
  Austin, Texas 78712

To my son, Paul Alexander,
and to Fred P. Ellison, friend and professor,
for his unending support and encouragement

Contents

Plates

Preface

This book deals less with Cinema Novo as a movement than with the films of the five most significant directors of modern Brazilian cinema: Joaquim Pedro de Andrade, Carlos Diegues, Ruy Guerra, Glauber Rocha, and Nelson Pereira dos Santos. That all five are also original participants in Cinema Novo is of course not coincidental, for Cinema Novo is the most important phenomenon in the history of Brazilian cinema. Besides the introduction, which provides a brief overview of the movement's contribution to the development of the Brazilian film industry as well as its relationship to the state film enterprise, Embrafilme, and the conclusion, I discuss Cinema Novo as such only in relationship to the films of the above-mentioned cinéastes.

By limiting the focus of this study to five directors, I have been forced to omit such Cinema Novo participants as Gustavo Dahl, Leon Hirszman, Arnaldo Jabor, and Paulo César Saraceni, documentarists such as Geraldo Sarno, Sérgio Muniz, and João Batista de Andrade, as well as younger filmmakers such as Ana Carolina Teixeira Soares, Carlos Alberto Prates Correa, Antônio Calmon, Héctor Babenco, Neville d'Almeida, Eduardo Escorel, and Bruno Barreto, all of whom merit attention. Although this self-imposed limitation makes it impossible to provide a full account of Cinema Novo and more recent developments in Brazilian cinema, it also, paradoxically, allows me to show that Cinema Novo as a "movement" is much broader and more diverse than is often thought. Such diversity is in my view best revealed through an analysis of the individuality of its most important participants. Studies concentrating solely on those elements that tend to unify Cinema Novo often result in impoverished and limiting definitions of the movement. Cinema Novo is much more than "bandit *cangaceiros*," "fanatical mystics," and "all-pervasive peasant suffering," as some would have it. It is, rather, the spirit of modern filmmaking in Brazil, a disposition to create a strong national cinema, a process of cinematic discovery and creativity. There is thus no contradiction in saying that, although Cinema Novo may no longer exist as a unified movement, the historical cycle of

Cinema Novo has not yet ended.

Since many of the films discussed have not yet been exhibited in the United States—or have been exhibited only in the major cities—I have chosen to use a more descriptive approach than would otherwise be necessary. Three of the filmmakers included here—Diegues, Guerra, and Rocha—have made films outside of Brazil, most of which have yet to be exhibited in the country. Because I have been unable to see all of these films, I have decided not to deal with any of them in great detail. The book thus treats films that have contributed to the development of Brazilian cinema.

I have also excluded the many short films that these directors have made. Single-director monographs—which they all deserve—would of course have to take their entire filmic production into consideration.

A short biographical sketch of the filmmaker is found at the beginning of each chapter. I provide original titles and English translations in this sketch. Thereafter, I use English titles for films in distribution in the United States (except those, like *Vidas Secas, Barravento,* and *Macunaíma,* that are known by their original titles).

My title is an homage to the 1962 student-produced *Cinco Vezes Favela* (*Five Times Favela*), on which three of the directors studied here collaborated. This study would have been impossible without the help of many people in the United States and Brazil. Some set up indispensable film screenings in Rio de Janeiro and São Paulo; others made research materials available; still others discussed different aspects of the films with me and provided helpful suggestions and constructive criticism. Special thanks must go, first of all, to Julianne Burton and Robert Stam for all of their comments, suggestions, and support. Acknowledgment is due as well to the following (in alphabetical order): Joaquim Pedro de Andrade, Sérgio Augusto, José Carlos Avellar, Luis Carlos Barreto, Jean-Claude Bernardet, Vera de Oliveira Brandão, Elenice de Castro, Carlos Diegues, Antônio Dimas, Eduardo Escorel, Michel do Espírito-Santo, Arnaldo Jabor, Telê Porto Ancona Lopez, Clóvis Loureiro, Jr., Aníbal Maccheroni, Hilda Machado, Jorge Peregrino, Jair Leal Piantino, Francisco Ramalho, Jr., Amaury Sanches, Luis Paulino dos Santos, Nelson Pereira dos Santos, Antônio Amâncio da Silva, Carlos Roberto Rodrigues de Souza, João Luiz Vieira, and Ismail Xavier. I would also like to thank the staff of the Fundação Cinemateca Brasileira (São Paulo), the Museu Lasar Segall (São Paulo), and the Cinemateca of the Museu de Arte Moderna (Rio de Janeiro). Photographs are from Embrafilme and the Fundação Cinemateca Brasileira. Above all I must thank my wife, Cida, for having supported and encouraged me throughout this project.

Parts of this book have appeared in other forms as "State Policy toward the Film Industry in Brazil," Technical Papers Series, Office for Public Sector Studies, Institute of Latin American Studies, The University of

Texas at Austin (1982); "Cinema Novo and Cannibalism: *Macunaíma*," in *Brazilian Cinema,* ed. Randal Johnson and Robert Stam (Rutherford, N.J.: Fairleigh Dickinson University Press, 1982); "Sex, Politics and Culture in *Xica da Silva,*" *JumpCut: A Review of Contemporary Cinema,* no. 22 (May 1980); "Carnivalesque Celebration in *Xica da Silva,*" in *Brazilian Cinema,* ed. Johnson and Stam; "The Cinema of Hunger: Nelson Pereira dos Santos's *Vidas Secas,*" in *Brazilian Cinema,* ed. Johnson and Stam; "*Vidas Secas* and the Politics of Filmic Adaptation," *Ideologies and Literature* 3, no. 15 (January-March 1981); "Toward a Popular Cinema: An Interview with Nelson Pereira dos Santos," *Studies in Latin American Popular Culture* 1 (1982); and "Film, Television and Popular Culture in *Bye Bye Brasil,*" *Journal of Popular Culture* (in press). All are used with permission.

Research was made possible by a grant from the Rutgers University Research Council.

Cinema Novo *x* 5

Introduction: Cinema Novo, the State, and Modern Brazilian Cinema

In February 1978, Bruno Barreto's *Dona Flor and Her Two Husbands* premiered at the Paris Theater in New York, thus initiating the most successful commercial run in the United States of any Brazilian film. *Dona Flor* was followed in October 1980 by Carlos Diegues's *Bye Bye Brasil*, then by Tizuka Yamasaki's *Gaijin: A Brazilian Odyssey* and Héctor Babenco's *Pixote*, which won the New York Film Critics' award for Best Foreign Film of 1981. Of the numerous things these films have in common, the most important is perhaps that they were all financed and distributed by the Brazilian state film enterprise, Embrafilme (Empresa Brasileira de Filmes). Embrafilme is in one way or another responsible for the best that Brazilian cinema has to offer. These four films are but the tip of the immense iceberg that is Brazilian cinema, a cinema now coming to full maturity as it consolidates its place in its domestic market and begins to make significant inroads in the American, European, South American, and African markets.

But the current success of Brazilian cinema is the result of many years of struggle by filmmakers determined to create a strong film industry in that country. At the forefront are those who participated in the Cinema Novo movement in the 1960s, the beginning of modern cinema in Brazil. Because of processes set in motion by Cinema Novo and because of its alliance with the state, Brazilian cinema has asserted itself as the premier cinema in Latin America and as one of the largest producers in the Western world, with some ninety to one hundred films per year. This introductory essay will outline the industrial development of Brazilian cinema and will trace the evolution of Cinema Novo's alliance with the state.

Cinema Novo arose in the late 1950s and early 1960s as part of a broad, heterogeneous movement of cultural transformation that involved theater, popular music, and literature, as well as the cinema. It evolved through a number of discernible phases, each of which corresponds to a specific sociopolitical conjuncture.

The seeds of Cinema Novo took root in the early 1950s, especially in two film industry congresses held in Rio de Janeiro and São Paulo in 1952 and

1953. It was in these congresses that filmmakers such as Alex Viany, Rodolfo Nanni, and Nelson Pereira dos Santos first articulated ideas for the creation of an independent national cinema.[1] The country had only recently seen the end of Getúlio Vargas's Estado Novo (1937–1945), and the process of redemocratization dramatically increased the level of political and cultural activity of Brazil's middle sectors. Vargas was reelected to the presidency in 1951 in the guise of a populist reformer who was attempting to mobilize support through, among other things, a nationalist discourse revolving around the creation of a state petroleum industry.

Despite Vargas's suicide in 1954, the nationalist euphoria he created continued and was strengthened with the election of Juscelino Kubitschek in 1955. Political stability (Kubitschek was the only president in the 1930–1964 period to remain in office, legally, throughout his designated term) and economic expansion and industrialization characterized Kubitschek's administration. The stability of his administration was due in part to his ability to rally the Brazilian people around a common ideology, known as developmentalism or developmentalist-nationalism.[2]

Kubitschek's developmentalism was, however, fraught with contradiction. Although it was a means of mobilizing support and guaranteeing the system's stability, it was also an effective tool for controlling social and political tensions. It toyed with the people's nationalist sentiments, but based its program of industrialization on foreign investment. By the end of his administration, this program provoked virulent opposition from the Left. Within this context, middle-class artists and intellectuals, such as those who created Cinema Novo, became increasingly politicized and sought to commit their art to the transformation of Brazilian society.

The first phase of Cinema Novo goes from 1960 to 1964, the year of the military coup d'état that overthrew President João Goulart, who had taken office after his predecessor, Jânio Quadros, resigned unexpectedly in 1961. The nationalist and developmentalist enthusiasm of the Kubitschek years continued in this period. With populists such as Quadros and Goulart in power, it was widely felt that the country was on the verge of a vast and radical transformation. The "national questions" were debated at every level of society, and the cinema attempted to contribute to the debate with films about the country's lumpen, often depicted in rural settings (dos Santos's *Vidas Secas* [*Barren Lives*, 1963], Guerra's *Os Fuzis* [*The Guns*, 1964], Rocha's *Deus e o Diabo na Terra do Sol* [*Black God, White Devil*, 1964]). The operative word in the films of this period was "alienation," as filmmakers hoped to raise the consciousness of a Brazilian people in the process of social transformation.

The second phase of Cinema Novo extends from 1964 to 1968, the year of the Fifth Institutional Act, which inaugurated a period of extremely repressive military rule. Although political liberties were restricted and censorship increased, there was still a degree of space available for discussion and debate. Paradoxically, in fact, sectors of the Left—including Cinema Novo—retained and strengthened their cultural hegemony during this period. But the focus of Cinema Novo shifted from rural to urban Brazil, from the lumpen proletariat to the middle class, as filmmakers turned their cameras, so to speak, on themselves in an attempt to understand the failure of the intellectual Left in relation to the events of 1964 (Saraceni's *O Desafio* [*The Challenge*, 1965], Rocha's *Terra em Transe* [*Land in Anguish*, 1967], Dahl's *O Bravo Guerreiro* [*The Brave Warrior*, 1968], dos Santos's *Fome de Amor* [*Hunger for Love*, 1968]). During this phase filmmakers also began to recognize that they were not reaching a sufficiently broad public, and many films began to be more commercially oriented (Hirszman's *Garota de Ipanema* [*Girl from Ipanema*, 1967], Oliveira's *Todas as Mulheres do Mundo* [*All the Women in the World*, 1967]).

A third phase ranges from 1968 until around 1972. During this period of extremely harsh military rule, habeas corpus was suspended for Brazilian citizens, censorship was tightened, and torture became institutionalized. It was difficult for filmmakers to express their opinions directly, and allegory became the preferred mode of cinematic discourse (Andrade's *Macunaíma* [1969], dos Santos's *Azyllo Muito Louco* [*The Alienist*, 1970], Jabor's *Pindorama* ([1971]). By 1973 Cinema Novo had ceased to exist as a coherent or unified movement, as the filmmakers began to follow individual paths in their cinematic expression.

Stylistic and thematic pluralism under the aegis of the state film agency, Embrafilme, has marked the period since 1973. And yet the historical cycle of Cinema Novo has not yet ended, for its major practitioners not only maintain intellectual hegemony within Brazilian cinema, but they also are the dominant force within Embrafilme and help determine the nature of state aid to the industry. Leon Hirszman's prize winner in Venice, *Eles Não Usam Black-Tie* (*They Don't Wear Black Tie*, 1981), has, in fact, been called "Cinema Novo de novo" ("Cinema Novo anew"). It was totally financed by Embrafilme, as was Glauber Rocha's last film, *A Idade da Terra* (*The Age of the Earth*, 1980).

To put Cinema Novo and its newfound alliance with the state in context, we must examine briefly the recent historical development of the national film industry.[3] Except for the brief period from 1908 to 1911, known as the "Bela Epoca," or Golden Age of Brazilian cinema, national cinema in Brazil has been a marginal factor in its own market. Unable to depend even on its own market for a return on investments, local cinema lacked the capital necessary to develop on an industrial scale. After World War I production became cyclical, often far removed from the country's cultural and economic centers. The only sustained production was that of newsreels and short documentaries about local events. Whenever such events transcended national interests—such as the visit of an American or European dignitary—foreign filmmakers relegated local production to a secondary place. Despite the efforts of some of Brazilian cinema's "pioneers" (Almeida Fleming, Luis de Barros, Gilberto Rossi, José Medina), the domestic market did not provide an outlet for whatever local production did indeed exist.

For many years the dream of Brazilian producers was to emulate Hollywood and build a national film industry based on large studios with expensive sets and contract stars. The advent of sound in the late twenties brought renewed optimism to such pioneers. They felt that foreign "talkies" would be unintelligible to Brazilian audiences and that local production would finally be able to develop without serious competition. The first two attempts at concentrated industrialization in the history of Brazilian cinema were Adhemar Gonzaga's Cinédia Studios, founded in 1930, and, in 1933, Carmen Santos's Brasil Vita Filmes. Between 1930 and 1945 Cinédia averaged two films per year, reaching a high of five in 1936. Brasil Vita was less successful, producing only thirteen films between its founding and 1958. The optimism of the Brazilian film industry was short-lived, as production dropped from twenty-seven films in 1930 to a mere five in 1935 (two of which were by Cinédia). Foreign cinemas once again strengthened their hold on the domestic market.

Other attempts at concentrated industrialization followed. In 1943 a number of producers founded what would turn out to be the most successful attempt at continuous production on an industrial scale in the history of Brazilian cinema: the Atlântida studios of Rio de Janeiro. Atlântida was particularly successful after Luis Severiano Ribeiro, owner of the largest exhibition chain in Brazil as well as of a major distributor, acquired it in 1947. His acquisition of Atlântida provided it with a vertically integrated system of production, distribution, and exhibition. Atlântida combined its advantageous position in the domestic market with a production geared toward and based on the commercial potential of that market to make a series of relatively inexpensive but immensely popular film genres (notably the *chanchada*, or light musical comedy). Between 1943 and 1977 Atlântida produced some eighty-five films. Its heyday was the period from 1945 to 1960. After that the growing influence of television caused the *chanchada* to lose appeal.

In sharp contrast to Atlântida were the Vera Cruz studios, founded in São Paulo in 1949. Members of São Paulo's industrial bourgeoisie (Franco Zampari and the Matarazzo group) created Vera Cruz and modeled it on the Metro-Goldwyn-Mayer studios in Hollywood. The idea was to create a "quality" cinema, much as the same group had attempted to create a "quality" theater several years earlier by founding the Teatro Brasileiro de Comédia (Brazilian Comedy Theater). "Quality," in both of these cases, meant an elegant form of artistic creation designed to show that Brazilians too knew how to make fine films and fine theater. It was to be an art form, as Augusto Boal puts it, "made for the rich by the rich." Vera Cruz imported top-quality equipment, contracted experienced European technicians to guarantee production quality, borrowed directors, scenographers, and actors from the Brazilian Comedy Theater, and invited Brazilian-born Alberto Cavalcânti—then in Europe—to direct the company. Cavalcânti stayed with the organization until 1951. Vera Cruz produced eighteen feature films, the most famous of which was Lima Barreto's *O Cangaceiro* (1953), double prize-winner in Cannes and a worldwide success.

The films of Vera Cruz, and of its "offspring," Multifilmes and Maristela, improved the technical quality of Brazilian films, increased capital investments in cinema, and incorporated into national cinema the "international cinematic language," with its panoply of conventional devices: sophisticated sets, classical framing, elaborate lighting, fluid cutting and camera movements, dissolves for the passage of time, and so on. The actors, the decor, the costumes, and the music often were chosen to evoke a European ambience.

Vera Cruz set up an expensive and luxurious system without the economic infrastructure on which to base such a system. Too ambitious, it tried to conquer the world market before it consolidated the Brazilian market. To reach the international market, it naively left distribution in the hands of Columbia Pictures, an organization more interested in promoting its own films than in fostering a vital Brazilian industry. In contrast to Atlântida, Vera Cruz drove production costs far above the lucrative potential of the Brazilian market and was finally forced to resort to temporary, but ultimately suicidal, palliatives to its problem of capital shortages: short-term, high-interest loans. Unable to recoup its investments in the domestic market successfully—only one of its films, *O Cangaceiro*, made a profit—and unable to reach the world market, Vera Cruz went bankrupt in 1954.[4]

The collapse of Vera Cruz sent shock waves through the industry and for many destroyed the perhaps unrealistic dream of developing a film industry based on the large-scale studio system. Such a system has only been truly successful in Brazil in one instance—the Atlântida studios. A small number of groups with large circuits of theaters historically has controlled exhibition. Their interests lie not with the development of Brazilian cinema, but rather with the guaranteed profits of American cinema. With the exception of Atlântida's distributor and foreign firms, no nationwide distributor for national films has existed until recently. The possibility of vertical integration based on a studio system grew increasingly remote after Vera Cruz folded.

The emergence of a new mentality among Brazilian producers coincided with the final years of Vera Cruz, however. They began to reject the artificiality and expense of the studio system in favor of an independent, artisan mode of production. This new mentality would later blossom into the Cinema Novo movement. Recalling the Vera Cruz period, Nelson Pereira dos Santos observed,

> Although all of us dreamed of entering Vera Cruz, we criticized everything it did. We wanted to participate in it in order to change its system. We did not know exactly how, we did not have a clearly defined alternative. It was something along the lines of neorealism, but the idea never entered our minds that that kind of film was incompatible with Vera Cruz's production scheme. . . .
>
> In short, what we were proposing was fundamentally a cinema free from the limitations of the studio, a cinema in the streets that had direct contact with the people and its problems. . . .
>
> We also proposed working with small crews. We combatted the American-style division of labor in Vera Cruz's production, and we demanded freedom of authorship for the director.[5]

The idea of a cinema independent of the rigid production system of Vera Cruz and other studios began to take form as early as 1951, when, in a round-table discussion organized by the Associação Paulista de Cinema (São Paulo Association of Cinema), director Rodolfo Nanni proposed the use of national themes and, given the unlikelihood of cooperation from the state or the large studios, the joining of small, independent production companies into large cooperatives.[6] They could thus use their collective resources to buy the equipment necessary to sustain independent production in São Paulo.

In the Primeiro Congresso Paulista de Cinema Brasileiro (First São Paulo Congress of Brazilian Cinema) in 1952, Nelson Pereira dos Santos presented a text titled "The Problem of Content in Brazilian Cinema" in which he discussed the creation of a free, independent, *national* cinema:

> But what does a free and independent Brazilian cinema mean? It means, first of all, overcoming economic problems deriving from the dependence of the Brazilian economy; it means breaking these bonds; it means freedom of production, the removal of all obstacles that impede the Brazilian film industry from becoming solidified; it means, finally, that national production be dominant in the domestic market. Brazilian cinema will be free and independent the day that, instead of one Brazilian film for every eight foreign films, the market functions in just the opposite proportion.[7]

With his last sentence dos Santos touched the crux of the matter: without being able to depend on even the domestic market for exhibition, Brazilian cinema cannot hope to develop freely and independently.

Cinema Novo's initial mode of production—low budgets, nonprofessional actors, independent production, natural settings, "a camera in hand and an idea in mind"—was the antithesis of Vera Cruz's. And yet there are points of contact between them. The goals of Vera Cruz and Cinema Novo—the development of a strong national cinema—were the same, but the conceptions of what that cinema should be were strikingly different. Nelson Pereira dos Santos, the only Cinema Novo filmmaker to begin his career during the Vera Cruz period, describes the impact of the São Paulo attempt at concentrated industrialization:

Cavalcânti's presence in São Paulo, participating in a film seminar, had enormous repercussions. After seeing and discussing [in film clubs] so many important films, after becoming familiar with the neorealists and understanding the importance of that type of cinema, Cavalcânti came to São Paulo, and in the film seminars we were told we would be taught to make films.

At the same time Vera Cruz appeared. Thus there were suddenly two extremely strong poles of opinion among those young people who wanted to do something and did not know exactly what, and who decided to make films: on the one hand, the cultural discovery of cinema with the film clubs, seminars, Cavalcânti, neorealism, discussions; on the other, the financial possibility of making films: the greatest São Paulo industrialist, Matarazzo himself, setting up a film production company. And the development of theater, with the Brazilian Comedy Theater, made us think that cinema would not be far behind.

Of course we criticized all of these things. Although Cavalcânti had been a fundamental part of this process of awakening our interest in cinema, for us he was no more than an "agent of imperialism. . . ."

When I say we fought *against* Vera Cruz, there is an important nuance: we did not struggle against Vera Cruz per se, but against its mode of action, against the kind of cinema it was making. But we thought the existence of a production center like Vera Cruz was very important. And whenever we felt that Vera Cruz was threatened, we struggled *for* Vera Cruz. Because in a certain sense it was not merely Franco Zampari's company, it was an achievement of us all, it was the possibility of making films in São Paulo. Vera Cruz was an achievement of Brazil, it was our first film industry, a collective achievement. So everyone fought for what they thought Vera Cruz should be, not over its existence as such. We did not question whether such a film industry and production center should exist or not. We wanted to preserve what Vera Cruz had, but to do things differently with its resources. Above all, we defended Vera Cruz as Brazilian cinema whenever we felt that it was threatened by the greater enemy, which was foreign cinema. It wasn't simply cinema that we wanted, it was Brazilian cinema.[8]

Thus although in one sense Cinema Novo reacted against Vera Cruz, in another it was a continuation of a collective struggle by filmmakers of all persuasions to develop the film industry in Brazil.

At the genesis of Cinema Novo, therefore, was a new attitude toward the structure the film industry should take. Influenced by Italian neorealism and based on the failure of Vera Cruz and the undermining of the *chanchada* by television, Cinema Novo correctly determined that the foreign-controlled Brazilian market could not provide an adequate return on expensive studio productions and opted instead for an independent, low-cost, artisan mode of production. This was the first time in the history of Brazilian cinema that such a mode of production was adopted by ideological and esthetic choice rather than by circumstance. Rather than being concentrated around large studios, production was atomized into many small production companies, which might each produce only one film per year (if that). To guarantee ideological and artistic freedom, directors frequently doubled as producers of their own films. When they did not, they associated themselves with producers such as Luis Carlos Barreto, who shared their goals.

Production financing has traditionally been problematic in the under-capitalized Brazilian film industry, and Cinema Novo represented no exception to this rule. Its directors therefore devised collaborative forms of financing in which all actors and members of the crew participated in a share system. They also adopted a pragmatic attitude toward financing, accepting the participation of capital from any source that did not make ideological demands on them. A number of early Cinema Novo films, paradoxically, were financed by the National Bank of Minas Gerais, owned by the family of Magalhães Pinto, one of the civilian conspirators in the 1964 coup d'état. The cinema lent a certain amount of cultural prestige to the bank, which, in turn, made filmmaking possible.

Like Vera Cruz, Cinema Novo initially made the mistake of assuming that simply producing a film was sufficient for it to be placed on the market. Directors and producers came to depend on distributors and even exhibitors for postproduction financing, which put them in the disadvantageous situation of often having to pay a larger percentage than usual for the distri-bution and exhibition of their films.

Exhibitors argued that Cinema Novo films were too intellectual for success in the market. The production of more popular films thus became imperative if Cinema Novo was to continue its cultural and political trajectory. As Gustavo Dahl once said, the making of popular films became the sine qua non of political action in the cinema. The struggle for the market became a priority.

Cinema Novo took a number of steps to ameliorate the problem of reaching a broad audience. First, together with producer Luis Carlos Barreto, producers and directors formed the distribution cooperative Difilme as a strategy for placing their films more easily in the multinational-controlled market. This step was important, since it is on the level of distribution that American cinema dominates the Brazilian market. In 1973 Embrafilme took up and expanded the idea of a central distributor for Brazilian films.

Second, they began to make films with more popular appeal. On the one hand they turned toward literary classics: Joaquim Pedro de Andrade's *O Padre e a Moça* (*The Priest and the Girl*, 1965) is based on a poem by Carlos Drummond de Andrade; Walter Lima, Jr.'s *Menino de Engenho* (*Plantation Boy*, 1965), on a novel by José Lins do Rego; Roberto Santos's

A Hora e a Vez de Augusto Matraga (*Matraga*, 1966), on a short story by João Guimarães Rosa; and Paulo César Saraceni's *Capitu* (1968) is based on Machado de Assis's masterpiece, *Dom Casmurro*. On the other hand, comedy became an acceptable mode of discourse, with such films as Nelson Pereira dos Santos's *El Justicero* (*The Enforcer*, 1967), Domingos de Oliveira's *Todas as Mulheres do Mundo* (*All the Women in the World*, 1967), and Roberto Farias's *Toda Donzela Tem um Pai que E uma Fera* (*Every Maiden Has a Father Who Is a Beast*, 1967).

By the late 1960s a tacit alliance began to form between Cinema Novo and the state in the struggle for the domestic market. Directors and producers felt that only the economic power of the state was strong enough to combat the highly organized foreign distributors. The state first turned its attention to the film industry in the 1930s, when Getúlio Vargas implemented the first screen quota for national films. That quota has now grown to 140 days per year of obligatory exhibition of Brazilian films in theaters throughout the country.[9] But it was only in the 1960s that the federal government began to intervene directly in the industry by providing it with financial incentives. In 1967 the newly created Instituto Nacional do Cinema (National Film Institute) initiated a program of production subsidies based on a percentage of box-office income. It was a democratic subsidy in the sense that it was paid to all national films exhibited, without regard to genre, social or cultural relevance, or even technical quality (of course, films could not be exhibited without proper approval from censors). At the same time, the institute established additional awards for "quality," based not on box-office income, but rather on the monthly minimum wage, thus freeing the subsidy from the dictates of the marketplace. Although Cinema Novo had virulently opposed the creation of the institute (Nelson Pereira dos Santos referred to it as a "fascist remnant of the Estado Novo"), its members were soon awarded the lion's share of the additional increment for quality films. This was important for the movement, since under military rule its participants had increasing difficulty financing their projects and were often forced to search for foreign coproducers for their films.

State intervention in the film industry expanded after 1969 with the creation of Embrafilme (the government film enterprise). Subordinated to the Ministry of Education and Culture, Embrafilme was created initially to promote and distribute Brazilian films abroad. A 1972 film industry congress proposed that the National Film Institute be transformed into a National Film Council with legislative powers and that Embrafilme be transformed from a mixed-ownership enterprise to a public enterprise with executive functions and administrative and financial autonomy.[10] In 1975 Embrafilme was reorganized, absorbing the executive functions of the institute, but it remained, at least in name, a mixed-ownership enterprise (the state holds a 99.9 percent share). Under its expanded powers, Embrafilme was authorized to act in all areas of cinematic commerce; it had already entered the production and distribution sectors. In 1976 the National Film Council (CONCINE) was created to serve as a legislative body in matters concerning the film industry.

Embrafilme initiated a number of programs of extreme relevance for the development of the film industry.[11] In 1973 it began its activity as a distributor and has since developed into the largest single distributor in Latin America, with over two hundred films at its disposal. It is the only distributor of Brazilian films organized nationwide and now accounts for some 30 percent to 35 percent of all national films distributed in the country. Since 1973 Embrafilme has engaged in three basic programs of financial assistance and investment in the film industry: (1) film financing, (2) advance on distribution, and (3) coproduction. In the financing program Embrafilme functions as a film bank and grants long-term, low-interest loans to production companies for the making of individual films. More traditional forms of bank financing are impractical because of the high risk and slow return of investment in the film industry (traditional bank loans speeded the bankruptcy of the Vera Cruz studios in the mid-fifties). This program has financed Joaquim Pedro de Andrade's *Guerra Conjugal* (*Conjugal Warfare*, 1975) and Carlos Diegues's *Bye Bye Brasil* (1980), among other Cinema Novo films.

The advance on distribution became available with Embrafilme's creation of its own distributor. The amount provided varies according to the film's stage of production and to its relationship to the enterprise. Embrafilme has distributed virtually all films by Cinema Novo participants since Leon Hirszman's *São Bernardo* (1973).

Finally, in 1973 Embrafilme initiated a program of coproduction financing in which it was to enter selected film projects with up to 30 percent of total production costs and receive in return a 30 percent share of profits. For a number of reasons this amount has increased in recent years, to 100 percent of a film's financing in some cases (Rocha's *A Idade da Terra* and Hirszman's *Eles Não Usam Black-Tie*). Between 1973 and 1979, Embrafilme signed contracts for the coproduction of 114 feature films plus 19 pilots for television series. These films were or are being made by eighty-nine different production companies. Among Cinema Novo films coproduced by Embrafilme are Nelson Pereira dos Santos's *O Amuleto de Ogum* (*The Amulet of Ogum*, 1974), Carlos Diegues's *Xica da Silva* (1976) and *Chuvas de Verão* (*Summer Showers*, 1978), Geraldo Sarno's *Coronel Delmiro Gouvéia* (1978), Walter Lima, Jr.'s *A Lira do Delírio* (*The Lyre of Delirium*, 1978), Rocha's *A Idade da Terra*, Hirszman's *Eles Não Usam Black-Tie*, and Joaquim Pedro de Andrade's *O Homem do Pau-Brasil* (*The Brazilwood Man*, 1982). Babenco's *Pixote* (1980) and Yamasaki's *Gaijin* (1980) were also coproduced under this program.

Embrafilme bases its decision to coproduce a film on a point system that considers the producer's or director's prior experience and activity in the film industry. The first three items on Embrafilme's list of priorities for coproduction and other forms of financing concern the number of prizes won in national and international festivals, including the National Film Institute's awards for quality. In the 1960s Cinema Novo dominated national festivals and the institute's awards for quality, and it won many prizes in international festivals, thereby bringing prestige value to Brazilian cinema. Therefore, the Cinema Novo group was favored in the very composition of Embrafilme's regulations for coproduction financing. The first film coproduced by Embrafilme was Nelson Pereira dos Santos's *O Amuleto de Ogum* (dos Santos has long been considered the "pope" of Cinema Novo; his production company, Regina Filmes, leads all others in the number of films or projects coproduced or financed by Embrafilme). The first film picked up for distribution by Embrafilme was Cinema Novo veteran Leon Hirszman's *São Bernardo*.

Cinema Novo directors have very quickly established hegemony within the state film enterprise, just as they maintain intellectual hegemony in Brazilian cinema as a whole. This hegemony was formalized in 1974, when President Ernesto Geisel took office and named Roberto Farias director of Embrafilme. Farias was the chosen candidate of Cinema Novo. Farias then named Cinema Novo participant Gustavo Dahl to head the enterprise's distribution sector. During Farias's tenure as director, all leading Cinema Novo directors and producers received film financing in one form or another from Embrafilme. In 1979 Brazilian president João Batista Figueiredo replaced Farias with career diplomat Celso Amorim. In the early 1960s Amorim had served as assistant director of two Cinema Novo films. It is relatively safe to say, therefore, that the original Cinema Novo group holds power within Embrafilme.[12]

Decisions to coproduce are made at the script level, and Embrafilme interferes at no other level of film production unless asked to render technical assistance. Intervention in the content of films does not occur. Only twice has the state enterprise developed programs designed to foster a certain kind of film: in 1973 it sponsored a contest for films based on literary classics by deceased authors, and in 1977 it sponsored research for some fifteen projects for historical films. Neither of these programs has been fruitful.

At the same time it is clear that Embrafilme reflects the regime to which it is subordinate, and it is just as clear that it will not, indeed cannot, finance films that directly challenge the regime. It has, however, both coproduced and distributed a number of films critical of the economic model military regimes have imposed since 1964. Ideological constraints come either before projects are submitted to Embrafilme—that is, constraints in the form of self-censorship, which is difficult to measure and assess—or after the film is completed, in the form of censorship, which has become less strict since the general process of political liberalization was initiated by President Geisel in 1975.

Through its financing programs, Embrafilme has tended to reinforce an atomized model of production. It has supported independent producers, that is, producers who also direct the films they produce. Such support has guaranteed Brazilian cinema a wide variety of styles and themes.

Economically, the state has had a significant impact on Brazilian cinema. Between 1974 and 1978 the screen quota for Brazilian films increased from 84 to 133 days per year, an increase of 58 percent. During the same period, the total number of film spectators doubled, from 30 million to 60 million. Total income of Brazilian films went from around 13 million dollars in 1974 to over 38 million in 1978, an increase of 288 percent. During the same period the gross income of foreign films increased at a rate of only 19 percent. Embrafilme has provided needed capital for film production and has stimulated capital accumulation in the private sector. It now accounts for some 35 percent of all national films distributed throughout the country, and most films that would be considered serious cultural products are linked to Embrafilme in some way, through financing, coproduction, or distribution.

Satisfaction with Embrafilme, however, is far from universal. Filmmakers from São Paulo complain of favoritism toward Rio de Janeiro. Documentarists claim that the enterprise's support of documentaries and short films has been inadequate. Joaquim Pedro de Andrade calls for Embrafilme's democratization, to give filmmakers a more direct say in its day-to-day operations. Others complain of cronyism and corruption. Filmmakers of all persuasions agree, however, that without state support and protection Brazilian cinema would be unable to withstand the power of foreign cinemas in the national market.[13]

1. Joaquim Pedro de Andrade: The Poet of Satire

> *Que importa a paisagem,*
> *a Glória, a baía, a linha do horizonte?*
> *O que eu vejo é o beco.*
>
> *Of what interest are the landscape,*
> *Glória, the bay, the horizon?*
> *What I see are the alleys.*
> —Manuel Bandeira, "Poema do Beco"

Like poet Manuel Bandeira, subject of his second short documentary, Joaquim Pedro de Andrade, a poet in the guise of filmmaker, is interested in the "alleys," in the sometimes dark corners of society and the human beings it comprises. Surface appearances are of interest only in the sense that they are demystified and shown to hide the deep contradictions of Brazilian society. Andrade prefers to see through the appearances—the "ideology," if this term is accepted as meaning the false values with which capitalist society justifies and defends itself—to critically examine that which lies below. His is a cinema of demystification. Whether dealing, directly or indirectly, with Carnival (*Couro de Gato*), soccer (*Garrincha, Alegria do Povo*), the impossible love of a priest in a small country town (*The Priest and the Girl*), national myths (*Macunaíma*), Brazilian history (*Os Inconfidentes*), or with sexual mores (*Guerra Conjugal, Vereda Tropical*), he maintains a consistent, coherent critical perspective throughout his filmic production. Yet, perhaps surprisingly, this consistency is revealed through several different cinematic styles and

Born in 1932, son of well-known Brazilian intellectual Rodrigo Mello Franco de Andrade, to whom *Os Inconfidentes* is dedicated. He was active in film clubs while studying physics at Rio de Janeiro's Federal University. In 1953 he made a short 16mm film entitled *O Mendigo e a Pintura* (*The Beggar and the Painting*) and shortly thereafter tried to get a job at the Vera Cruz film studios in São Paulo. In 1958 he served as assistant director for Geraldo and Renato Santos Pereira's *Rebelião em Vila Rica* (*Rebellion in Vila Rica*), the second color film made in Brazil. In 1959 he approaches, ranging from the documentary to the allegorical, from sober critical realism to biting satire, from Brechti to madcap comedy. As Andrade himself explains, "I make films about the problem of living in Brazil, and my understanding of this problem at different times generates very different kinds of films."[1]

Besides his consistent attitude of critical analysis, a number of other characteristics unite the (apparent) diversity of Joaquim Pedro de Andrade's films. All of his fiction films, for example, including the short *Vereda Tropical*, are based at least partially on literary works. This is a tendency evident in his choice of subjects for his first two short documentaries: sociologist Gilberto Freyre (who has often been accused of writing novels rather than sociology), and poet Manuel Bandeira. Cinema Novo arose in part from the national literary tradition.

But if early Cinema Novo draws primarily on the sociological novels of the Northeast, exemplified par excellence by Graciliano Ramos, whose *Vidas Secas* was filmed by Nelson Pereira dos Santos in 1963), Joaquim Pedro de Andrade stands out from this general tendency in that he draws more on the literary traditions of the first phase of Brazilian modernism (1922–1930). Such is apparent not only in his early work (Manuel Bandeira and Carlos Drummond de Andrade, author of the poem on which *The Priest and the Girl* is based, are both "modernist" poets), but also and more explicitly and profoundly in his work from *Macunaíma* to the present. *Macunaíma* is widely considered the prose masterpiece of modernism and the major work of the "Movimento Antropófago" (Cannibalist Movement), which arose in 1928. Cannibalism as a political and philosophical concept pervades all of Andrade's post-*Macunaíma* films, as they increasingly

---

directed two short documentaries for the Instituto Nacional do Livro, *O Mestre de Apipucos* (*The Master of Apipucos*) and *O Poeta do Castelo* (*The Poet from Castelo*). In 1961 he shot the short *Couro de Gato* (*Catskin*), finishing it in Paris after having been awarded a grant to study at the Institut des Hautes Etudes Cinétematographiques (IDHEC). While in Europe he was awarded a grant from the Rockefeller Foundation to study direction at the Slade School of Art in London with Thorold Dickinson. He then went to New York, where he studied direct cinema techniques with Albert and David Maysles. His *Couro de Gato* inspired and was incorporated into the feature-length *Cinco Vezes Favela* (*Five Times Favela*, 1962), produced by the student-led Centro Popular de Cultura. His filmography includes the documentaries *Garrincha, Alegria do Povo* (*Garrincha, Joy of the People*, 1963; feature-length), *Brasília, Contradições de uma Cidade* (*Brasília, Contradictions of a City*, 1967; short), and *Improvisiert und Zielbewurst* (*Cinema Novo*, 1968; short); the features *O Padre e a Moça* (*The Priest and the Girl*, 1965), *Macunaíma* (1969), *Os Inconfidentes* (*The Conspirators*, 1971), *Guerra Conjugal* (*Conjugal Warfare*, 1975), and the short *Vereda Tropical* (*Tropical Paths*, 1977), which is the final episode in the feature-length *Contos Eróticos* (*Erotic Tales*). In 1982 he completed a fiction film about the life and work of iconoclastic writer Oswald de Andrade, titled *O Homem do Pau-Brasil* (*The Brazilwood Man*).

come to reflect the influence not only of *Macunaíma's* author, Mário de Andrade, but also and perhaps more importantly, of the leader of the cannibalist movement, Oswald de Andrade. Joaquim Pedro de Andrade's most recent film is based precisely on the life and work of Oswald, thus representing the culmination of an interest evident since *Macunaíma.*

Andrade's "adaptations," however, are never simply transpositions of a literary work from one medium to another. Rather, he works with a process of inversion and dialogue, questioning, looking at the original text from a different angle, giving it an interpretation that may not be apparent at first glance. His critical strategy, especially since *Macunaíma*, is to invert—indeed, subvert—the values implied in the mode of discourse he chooses to utilize, whether it be the "official" version of history (*Os Inconfidentes*) or the erotic comedy (*Guerra Conjugal*). He thus ostensibly accepts the rules of the dominant ideology's game, only to invert those rules and turn them against their original purpose.[2] Satire, first used in *Macunaíma*, has become his favorite weapon in the carnivalesque inversion of established (or establishment) values, a weapon that reaches its level of perfection in *Vereda Tropical*. Joaquim Pedro de Andrade has indeed become the master and the poet of cinematic satire in Brazil, even though his first films would seem to point in other directions.

O Mestre de Apipucos (about Gilberto Freyre) and *O Poeta do Castelo* (about Manuel Bandeira) were made in 1959 for the Instituto Nacional do Livro (National Book Institute). Originally intended as two films in one, they have since been separated. Although the first film is of little interest today, the second establishes the director's cinematic artistry. It was linked to the first through a dissolve onto a book of Bandeira's poetry, but the film now opens with a shot of the book. Andrade's camera then follows the poet · on a street as he stops to buy milk and looks at the urban landscape around him. The voice-over narrator is the poet himself, reciting the lines of the epigraph to this chapter. A series of short shots illustrate the words' meaning and are quickly followed by high-angle shots of an alley covered with trash, as the poet says, "What I see are the alleys."

In both documentaries, the literary narration, an artistic, constructed reality, contrasts with the often banal and monotonous routine of the artist's day-to-day life. The loneliness of the poet, isolated in his small apartment, contrasts with the beauty and humanity of his art, a small portion of which makes up the narration.

The image we receive of the poet is an intensely human one, of an individual situated here and now, yet at the same time we are made to recognize the special quality of the artist and his work. Art transcends life, a fact the filmic discourse itself reinforces. Although in the diegesis art contrasts with the banality of the commonplace, the film's discourse tends to transform even the everyday into something perhaps larger than it in reality is. After Manuel Bandeira saw the film, relates Andrade, he "informed a great number of people that the act of buying milk . . . had none of the poignancy with which it appeared in the film. It was for him an action totally stripped of emotionalism."[3]

Andrade thus fuses and confuses art and reality. Even the documentary becomes another form of representation, an artistic construction. This dialectic between art and reality, between fiction and nonfiction, accompanies Joaquim Pedro de Andrade throughout his work.

Whereas *O Mestre de Apipucos* and *O Poeta do Castelo* deal with a sociologist and a poet, respectively, *Couro de Gato* articulates the art/reality dialectic into a synthesis of poetry and sociology. Filmed in Rio de Janeiro in 1961 and finished later the same year in Paris, it has been referred to variously as "documentary fiction," as an exercise in "lyrical realism," and as "the first poetic essay in cinema." Shot partially in Rio's slums (*favelas*), the short *Couro de Gato* inspired and was later incorporated, along with short films by Carlos Diegues, Marcos de Farias, Leon Hirszman, and Miguel Borges, into the feature-length *Cinco Vezes Favela*, produced by the Centro Popular de Cultura.

The films of *Cinco Vezes Favela*, except those of Joaquim Pedro de Andrade and Leon Hirszman (*Pedreira de São Diogo* [*São Diogo Quarry*]), often reveal an overly schematic, didactic, and paternalistic view of some of the problems faced by marginal elements of Brazilian society. The directors of *Cinco Vezes Favela* by and large made their individual films with a preconceived vision of society deriving more from their readings in sociology than from direct contact with the reality they set out to film. It was as if they were suddenly shocked and surprised by Brazil's underdevelopment and so romantically, and perhaps naively, attempted to change it through cinema. Andrade's *Couro de Gato* escapes such schematization—as well as the dramatic weakness of the other films— perhaps because it preceded the others and because his interests were as much cinematic and poetic as political (although the film *is* highly political in an understated way).

Couro de Gato, like Nelson Pereira dos Santos's *Rio 40 Graus* (1955), alternately focuses on several boys from a slum. The boys find, chase, and steal cats to sell to tambourine makers in the period preceding Carnival. The cats thus become part of Brazil's musical heritage. Music has structural importance in *Couro de Gato*, whether the rhythmic Carnival sambas played in the streets and hills of Rio de Janeiro, Carlos Lyra's tender Bossa Nova accompaniment to one boy's attachment to a stolen cat, or the free jazz saxophone that accompanies a wealthy woman's sunbathing in company with her beautiful white Angora. The music, in a certain sense, delineates and characterizes the various groups in the film.

Couro de Gato combines and synthesizes documentary and fictional modes of discourse. After an initial sequence showing the boys in different

Plate 1. *Couro de Gato (Catskin)*

situations—carrying water cans up the slum hills, selling peanuts near the beach, shining shoes in the city streets—a voice-over documentary narration tells of the cats' musical function. Besides this brief explanation, the film has no other narration or dialogue. It proceeds as a fiction film, alternately following one or another of the boys as they track down cats. Carnival and its rhythms, seen in a brief sequence following the voice-over narration, are a constant in the film's background.

Couro de Gato is an exercise in cinematic rhythm and timing, as the narrative develops through visuals alone, supported by the musical soundtrack. The boys' multiple paths through the city become one, as rapid parallel cutting combines their acts of theft and the chases that ensue. Their "collective destiny," so to speak, becomes embodied in the only boy who is successful in his hunt.

Though he arrives safely in the slum with his stolen white Angora, he falls in love with the animal. Several shots show him holding, caressing, and feeding the cat that he will eventually have to sell. "Whoever wants to love," say the lyrics of Carlos Lyra's accompaniment, "will have to suffer, will have to cry." The boy sells the cat, then walks down the hill with tears in his eyes, the inner conflict between wanting to keep it and having to sell it unresolved. Andrade has noted that the film, on a personal and political level, says that "the solution of sentimental problems depends in part on the solution of economic problems."[4]

But *Couro de Gato* is more lyrical than political. The use of the slum as scenario reflects a concern with marginal elements of Brazilian society, a concern shared by many if not most first-phase Cinema Novo films. The film, however, does not focus on the structural problems of poverty in Brazil nor does it exploit the misery of the slum dwellers: the slum and its problems are a given in the film's development. *Couro de Gato* prefers to focus on the sentimental conflict of one boy (even though he does embody the aspirations of the others) and the poignancy of his situation. *Couro de Gato*, like Nelson Pereira dos Santos's *Rio 40 Graus*, shows the boys' concurrent marginalization from and the integration in Rio de Janeiro society. They are marginalized from the mainstream of society's economy and yet integrated through the exercise of servile occupations (shoe shining, for example) and through the very act of hunting cats for use in Carnival. The film subtly reminds the spectator that it is society itself that marginalizes much of its youth and forces them to react to that marginalization in a perhaps less-than-desirable fashion.

After dealing in *Couro de Gato* with certain marginal elements of Brazilian society, Andrade made a documentary about the national passion, soccer, and one of its great stars, Garrincha. *Garrincha, Alegria do Povo*, produced by Luis Carlos Barreto, attempted to put into practice the direct cinema techniques Andrade had learned with the Maysle brothers during his brief stay in New York in 1961. The final result, however, is more of a documentary hybrid: part direct cinema, part cinema verité, and part traditional documentary based on newsreels and archive photographs.

Garrincha, Alegria do Povo can be divided into two parts: the first deals with Garrincha as a player and an individual; the second, with the phenomenon of soccer itself and its importance in the psychological life of the Brazilian people. This movement from the particular to the general is at the same time a description of the development of a myth, followed by an analysis of the myth itself. The film's focus moves from player to spectator, from the individual to the collectivity, as it attempts to analyze critically an important phenomenon in Brazilian society, a phenomenon as central to that society as the cat-hunters of *Couro de Gato* are marginal to it.

Joaquim Pedro de Andrade notes that, "through a primarily objective approach and a dramatic structure, *Garrincha* attempts to give an idea of the true psychological and sociological dimensions of soccer in Brazilian life. The film is conceived as a spectacle that attempts to direct the reactions of the audience, to suggest conclusions, to appeal to their reason, and to explain esthetic possibilities."[5] *Garrincha* is dialectical in conception and combination of modes of discourse, as the particular clashes with and melds into the general: movement becomes stasis; victory, defeat; reality, myth and back again. *Garrincha* combines analysis and synthesis, and shows how one man, from humble origins and with crooked legs, is transformed into a myth. He is used politically and is symbolically devoured by the collectivity as he is elevated from base to superstructure.

The film opens with a rapid series of stills from various soccer games, merging them into one. Despite the use of stills, the camera is never static, but always panning and zooming to isolate one element or another or to provide a sense of movement. An initial opposition is thus established formally through the juxtaposition of stasis and motion as the film brings to life that which is frozen in the past. Suddenly, Brazilian president Juscelino Kubitschek appears on the screen with Garrincha, and we are transported to the level of both politics and myth. Garrincha is no longer just the soccer player who appeared in the opening stills; rather, he has become a symbol of Brazilian nationality, a figure larger than life whom Kubitschek uses politically.

After the titles, the camera enters the players' dressing room as they prepare for a game and follows them as they go out onto the field. To this point there is no narration, merely the cold objectivity of the camera. Finally, a narrator describes Garrincha as a "little bird," as the "poet" of Brazilian soccer. The film thus works as well with a juxtaposition of praise and criticism. It admires that which is beautiful and graceful in Garrincha's art, yet criticizes the uses to which the dominant ideology puts it.

As the game begins, the camera becomes more participatory, concentrating on the movement and dexterity of the players' legs in an alternation of long and short shots. The sequence is so lyrical that one critic remarked that in *Garrincha* "soccer becomes ballet." Once again, as in *Couro de Gato*, we see that Andrade's concerns are as much esthetic as they are political. The filmed footage is intercut with stills, which are followed by a series of freeze-frames in sequence. All of this gives the impression of a soccer game in slow motion.

The camera then turns toward the crowd, the true subject of *Garrincha, Alegria do Povo*. A series of freeze-frames followed by slow motion footage as the composite game nears the end show crowd reactions. It is as though Andrade wants to suggest visually the letdown that inevitably follows the catharsis of spectator emotions.

After presenting the central elements of the drama—game/crowd, player/spectator, catharsis/letdown, reality/myth—Garrincha the individual becomes the film's central focus. We see him addressing the camera cinema verité style, follow him as he walks almost unrecognized through the streets of downtown Rio de Janeiro—a shot that seems to emphasize that the man, the individual, is forgotten in favor of the player, the myth—and finally accompany him to his hometown, Pau Grande, a small industrial town near Rio de Janeiro. After being presented to the myth, in other words, we see the man as he returns to his origins.

In Pau Grande we are the public at an amateur soccer match Garrincha plays with his old friends. Yet while his friends earn a minimum wage in the local textile mill, Garrincha, we are told, earns many times their wage. The salary differential underlines one of the basic inversions that occurs in the creation of a superstructural myth. The productive elements of society (Garrincha's friends) are exploited economically by their long hours and low wages while Garrincha (the myth) is exploited ideologically as part of the superstructure and receives much more. The film thus suggests his importance to the dominant ideology.

The core of the film, however, is the footage dedicated to the victories of the Brazilian team, led by Garrincha and Pelé, in the World Cup competitions of 1958 and 1962. Pain and joy are once again juxtaposed as newsreel footage from the games is interspersed with headlines announcing the victories in Brazilian papers, with a shot of Garrincha lying in pain on the field after being kicked by an opposing player, and with shots of a worried crowd. Stills of the euphoric crowd, of players embracing one another, of exuberant fans celebrating in Rio's streets, and finally, of the team being congratulated by Juscelino Kubitschek (in 1958), and by João Goulart and right-wing governor of Rio de Janeiro, Carlos Lacerda (in 1962) follow the victories. Once again politicians of all persuasions attempt to transform the euphoria of the moment into political advantage.

But the film soon bursts the euphoria as, through archive footage, it flashes back to Brazil's traumatic World Cup loss to Uruguay in Rio de Janeiro's Maracaná stadium in 1950. Through this chronological inversion, placing the 1950 loss after the victories of 1958 and 1962, Andrade attempts to put things in their proper perspective. "Soccer," he observes, "is really a battle that is never won, never permanently conquered." The euphoria of victory is illusory and transitory. An agonizing still of the opponent's ball in Brazil's net abruptly interrupts the certainty of victory. Silence engulfs the crowd, their tearful eyes fill the screen; all we hear is their collective heartbeat.

After the defeat, *Garrincha, Alegria do Povo* turns from the particular to the general, from the synthetic to the analytical, as it attempts to explain the immense power that soccer holds over the Brazilian people. The second half of the film lacks the strength of the first, since it depends less on visuals and more on narration. The film offers two reasons for soccer's power, one psychoanalytical, the other sociological. According to the first thesis, accompanied by close shots of worried faces and by solemn organ music, then by a fight on the field, the soccer ball is a symbol of the mother's breast, and for this reason is arduously pursued by the players and followed with such emotion by the spectators.

But the film quickly suggests that the other explanation is more plausible and proposes that soccer diverts human energy and passion from the frustrations of daily life. As the narrator explains, "The people use soccer to spend the emotive potential that accumulates through a process of frustration in daily life. . . . A game is the representation of a battle, and the gamelike universe of the stadium is more convenient than is life for the exercise of human emotions." In other words, soccer is an escape valve that alienates the people by helping them forget their socioeconomic marginalization and oppression rather than struggling to overcome that oppression. The film recalls that soccer is a brief cycle lasting only from whistle to whistle, as it shows the stadium emptying, trains heading home, and, finally, an aerial view of the empty stadium that suggests the game's ultimate emptiness. The final shot of the film, a freeze-frame of a player and the ball flying into the net, visually represents the alienating "trap" that is soccer.

Garrincha, Alegria do Povo, although praising the beauty of the athlete's art, stresses the negative social aspect of soccer as a factor in alienation. This perspective, looking at the phenomenon from the outside in a cold, objective fashion tempered by a preconceived notion of the game's significance, Andrade now admits, was perhaps overly distanced and sociological. Andrade has criticized this perspective in more recent interviews, observing that the sadness pervading the final portion of the film is a sadness imposed by him as director. Soccer, according to his self-criticism, is a unifying phenomenon that reaches all social strata. It is valid as an affirmation of a national talent that, instead of being merely a factor of alienation, can lead the people to a greater unity and greater self-confidence. The euphoria resulting from national victories (such as the World Cup victory in 1970, which occurred during the most repressive period of military rule in Brazil) can potentially be transformed and channeled into other areas of activity. *Garrincha, Alegria do Povo*, however, shares both the values and the shortcomings of the early phase of Cinema Novo by attempting to present a critical view of an important national phenomenon. The result, despite the faults pointed out here, is a film worthy of the sport itself.

In 1965 Joaquim Pedro de Andrade directed his first fiction feature, *The Priest and the Girl*, based loosely on a poem by Carlos Drummond de Andrade.[6] In an interview granted shortly after its release, Andrade explained in more detail the personal nature of his films and defined his conceptions of cinema:

I believe that a defined ideological position, a firm, general ideological position, the definition of a person in relation to the world, *a critical vision of the world*, oriented from a secure and well-situated perspective, implies the immediate solution to a number of secondary problems. The problem of form, for example, practically ceases to exist when a filmmaker takes such a position . . . [but] I am a person in constant movement, trying to understand things more completely, trying to place myself vis-à-vis the world by *the critical attitudes that I assume*; a person in

Plate 2. Paulo José and Helena Inês, *O Padre e a Moça (The Priest and the Girl)*

search of his values, questioning permanently the measuring scale of these values . . .
My only certainty is that I have the right to doubt everything and the duty to expound
these doubts in an effort to overcome them, or to act in order to overcome them, using
action as a process of knowledge.[7] [my emphasis]

Cinema, for Joaquim Pedro de Andrade, is a learning process based on a
critical questioning of the established values of society, a permanently
evolving critical vision, in short, of the ideological forms of that society, be
they explicitly political or not. Cinema is also, in his view, a form of praxis,
of action vis-à-vis these ideological forms.

Andrade chose as the subject of his first feature film a poem about a priest
who breaks his vows and falls in love with a young woman. But the director
observes that his intention in making the film was not sociopolitical, and *The
Priest and the Girl* would thus seem to be something of an anomaly, given
traditional political definitions of Cinema Novo.[8] In reality, however, the
film *is* political on an allegorical level and thus adds richness and depth to
the broad filmic "text" known as Cinema Novo.

The film's story is set in a small, isolated country town in the state of
Minas Gerais, where a young priest (played by Paulo José) arrives to

administer last rites to the old priest and to exercise his first official duties with the church. The town is inhabited by an aged population still searching for the diamonds that enriched its ancestors but that have long since been exhausted. The town lives in a past based on dreams that persist for its inhabitants, dreams having little to do with the desolate reality they live. But among these isolated, sad, somber people who are dying along with the village, lives Mariana (Helena Inês), a young woman who must hide her will to live from the jealousy and envy of the other townspeople.

The priest inevitably becomes involved with Mariana, who needs the company and support of other young people to survive. To emphasize the town's decadent, moribund quality, besides Mariana and the drunken pharmacist, there are no young people or children in the film. The priest's friendship with Mariana provokes the envy and ire of the other townspeople. Mariana lives with Honorato, a middle-aged diamond merchant who is convinced that the old priest was her lover. Honorato forbids Mariana to see the young priest and announces his intention to marry her, but Mariana leaves home late one night and goes to the priest's house. As she leaves there in the early hours of the morning, an anonymous figure sees and denounces her. Rejected and threatened by the townspeople, the priest takes advantage of Honorato's drunkenness and convinces Mariana to flee with him to a nearby town.

Walking along the dusty mountain road, Mariana confesses that she wants the priest "as a woman wants a man," and, despite initial resistance, the priest finally realizes that the road, no matter how long, eventually leads to her—to life—and not to the continuation of his vows. As they make love, his black cassock is superimposed on her white skin in the film's central visual metaphor. At daybreak, the priest once again begins walking, this time without apparent destination, and Mariana follows, receiving no answers to her hesitant questions. She finally realizes that he is returning to the small town from which they had fled. There the townspeople, led by old women who function as sort of sinister guardians of "morality," pursue them. Only the pharmacist protests. "I saw their love," he says, "and it is sacred." Both Mariana and the priest manage to escape their tormentors and flee together to a cave in the mountains. But the indignant and vengeful townspeople light a fire at the cave's entrance. The film ends with a shot of the priest and the girl, black against white, embracing each other as smoke fills the cave.

The Priest and the Girl is similar to *Garrincha, Alegria do Povo* in that its view of the priest, like the view of Garrincha, is an external one, although a much more personal view than in the previous film. The director is not interested, as is Robert Bresson in *Diary of a Country Priest*, in the spiritual struggle of the young priest, and, in fact, the role of religion is of secondary importance. We are given little information about the priest's background and little or no insight into his emotional or psychological motivations. The film's narrative and sparse dialogue are transmitted through what might be called a shorthand style, providing only the most important elements of the story and refusing to explain or expound on the moral or religious problems involved. The priest is a figure who denies himself and hides from the world and from life behind his cassock. That he is often filmed from behind, as if afraid to show his full face, reinforces this self-denial.

The same is true of the film's treatment of Mariana. As Andrade observes, "I did not want to provide information that would condition or explain her behavior." All we know is what we see and what we as creative spectators read into the film. The director leaves a great deal of space for spectator participation and conjecture. It is an open-ended narrative offering myriad opportunities for the viewer's own interpretation.

If the problem of the priest's religious vocation or his psychological motivations are of little interest in *The Priest and the Girl*, then the film's central theme is to be found on the level of allegory. The image of the black cassock superimposed on the woman's white skin—the central metaphor of both the film and the poem—is the key to its interpretation. The cassock represents, on the one hand, a visual barrier, understandable on an immediate level, between the priest and the world outside. On a deeper level, however, it represents much more. The priest's cassock is the symbol of a castrating ideology that is questioned by the film's discourse, not only religious ideology, but *any* restrictive, inhibiting ideology. The priest's struggle, albeit unconscious, is against the constraints imposed by this ideology, it is a struggle for life among the dead and the dying, a struggle against a suffocating pseudomorality, a struggle, ultimately, against the antiquated, false values of a decadent society. In this sense, *The Priest and the Girl* is indeed an exercise in demystification.

In contrast to the austere negativism of the priest dressed in black (traditionally a symbol of death), is the vital, open, youthful emotion of Mariana. Although her motivations are merely suggested, she is clearly on the side of those who want to live, who can no longer accept the restrictions society imposes. She is an almost diaphanous figure as, dressed in white, she walks through the town. She is desired, openly or not, by the townsmen. Mariana is the only figure in the film who is seen in motion, in contrast to the static, immobile "life" around her.

In *The Priest and the Girl* Joaquim Pedro de Andrade achieves a level of abstraction through artistic discipline and sensibility. The film is imbued with an almost dreamlike, poetic quality created by its exquisitely composed frames and use of natural lighting. Camera movements are slow, deliberate, and balanced. Little movement occurs in the film, and sparse dialogue reinforces this stasis. The town exudes an atmosphere of death from the initial sequences, when the young priest arrives to administer last rites to his predecessor. Children do not appear in the film, as if to reinforce the fact that the town and its inhabitants are dying. Omnipresent, however, are the *beatas*, old, pious women whose sinister vigilance guarantees observance of the antiquated morality they impose on the town.

If *The Priest and the Girl* is in some respects similar to *Garrincha, Alegria do Povo*, in others it is its antithesis. Whereas *Garrincha* sees involvement in collective emotion and joy as alienating from the struggle to create a better life, *The Priest and the Girl* considers such involvement absolutely necessary. The priest is an essentially negative personage because of his self-denial, because he accepts the inhibitions the cassock imposes. He is unable to transcend the barrier that he has helped raise between himself and the world. His consciousness is restrictive and not open to change. If *Garrincha, Alegria do Povo* is the thesis, then *The Priest and the Girl*, by negating what is denied in the first film, is the antithesis. The synthesis will come only in 1969 with *Macunaíma*.

The Priest and the Girl represents the end of what might be called the first phase in Joaquim Pedro de Andrade's filmmaking career, a phase marked by a seriousness of conception and realization corresponding to the director's introverted personality. It is a phase characterized as well by a concern with poetry, by a conception of cinema as esthetic balance and composition. The phase of cinema as poetry, or, in the case of *Garrincha*, of cinema as ballet, ends with *The Priest and the Girl*. A much more aggressive, biting, political conception of cinema and society, embodied in *Macunaíma*, characterizes Andrade's second phase.

Macunaíma, shot in 1968 and released in 1969 after the decree of the repressive Fifth Institutional Act, represents not only a turning point in Joaquim Pedro de Andrade's career, but also the culmination of the first three phases of Cinema Novo and the pacesetter for subsequent developments in Brazilian cinema.[9] Adapted from Mário de Andrade's modernist novel of the same name (1928), *Macunaíma* is perhaps the first Cinema Novo film to be formally innovative, politically radical, *and* immensely popular with the Brazilian public.

Macunaíma is in many respects the antithesis of *The Priest and the Girl*. It is as unrestrained as the 1965 film is restrained; as colorful and zany as the first film is solemn and subdued; as fast moving as the other is immobile. It elevates bad taste to an esthetic level, whereas impeccable taste characterizes *The Priest and the Girl*. The first film is concerned with careful composition within the frame, but *Macunaíma* seems to ignore the limits of the frame and creates what Andrade has called a film without a style. The hero Macunaíma, also played by Paulo José, is an exuberant free spirit who overindulges in the pleasures of life to the same extent that the priest denies them. *Macunaíma* is as extroverted as *The Priest and the Girl* is introverted.

In a 1966 interview, Joaquim Pedro de Andrade suggested that Cinema Novo filmmakers would do well to re-examine the Brazilian modernist movement of the 1920s in terms of the sociopolitical conjuncture of the

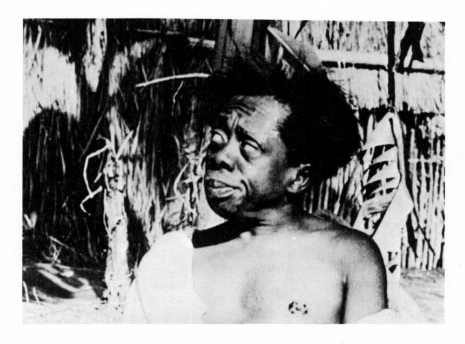

Plate 3. Grande Otelo as Macunaíma

country in the late 1960s.[10] Such a reevaluation burst on the Brazilian cultural
scene in 1967–68 with the tropicalist movement in theater, popular music, and
cinema. Cinema Novo is, in fact, deeply rooted in the problematic faced by
literary modernism. The movement had attempted to democratize Brazilian art
through a stance of cultural nationalism in favor of an interest in popular forms
of expression and the culture of native Brazilian peoples and a rejection of
acritical imitation of European models. Perhaps more than any other
modernist, Mário de Andrade (1893–1945) undertook extensive research into
music, dance, folk festivities and rituals as well as popular and indigenous
myths and legends. *Macunaíma*, widely considered his masterpiece, is the
esthetic apex of his attempts to fuse popular sources and erudite literary forms.

Mário de Andrade classifies his *Macunaíma*, written in one week in
1926, revised in 1927, and published in 1928, as a rhapsody (in the musical
sense), that is, a free fantasy "of an epic, heroic or national character." In
this work the author orchestrates popular and folkloric motifs to create what
has been called a compendium of Brazilian folklore. *Macunaíma* combines
popular expressions, proverbs, elements of popular literature and folklore
with indigenous legends German ethnologist Theodor Koch-Grünberg
collected in the headwaters of the Orinoco River in northern Brazil and

southern Venezuela between 1911 and 1913.[11] Through the combination of such heterogeneous elements, the novel attempts to synthesize Brazil. It negates the limitations of provincial regionalism by including, in its many enumerations, elements from all regions of the vast country (e.g., fish from the North and the South in the same body of water), by dissolving spatial limitations by placing Macunaíma, on his various journeys, in one part of the country at one moment and in another at the next, by suspending temporal limitations by allowing the hero to roam through Brazil's history, and by combining, in the *macumba* episode, elements of Afro-Brazilian religious cult ceremonies from several parts of the country.

The novel's Macunaíma is a composite of several heroes found in Koch-Grünberg's legends: Kone'wó, a courageous and astute hero; Kalawunseg, a liar; and Makunaíma, the tribal hero. Makunaíma as a hero is both good and evil, courageous and cowardly, capable and inept, characteristics that Mário de Andrade preserved in his hero. He subtitled the novel "the hero without a character," in fact. Linked to the folk tradition, *Macunaíma*, in its jocose examination of the Brazilian psyche, fuses symbols, satire, and free fantasy and melds the real and the fantastic into a unified fictional universe.

The film maintains the basic narrative structure of the novel. The narrative core of both works reduces, in accordance with the structuralist terminology of Vladimir Propp, to three basic functions: (1) the villainy (the "theft" of a talisman); (2) the struggle with the villain (Macunaíma vs. Venceslau Pietro Pietra); (3) the liquidation of the misfortune caused by the villainy (Macunaíma recovers the talisman). The filmmaker, however, introduces significant differences on other levels, including the characterization of the story's dramatis personae. The adaptation is not merely an attempt to express the ideas of the 1928 work in a different medium; rather, it is a critical reinterpretation and an ideological radicalization of Mário de Andrade's rhapsody, cast in terms of the social, economic, and political realities of the late 1960s.

Mário de Andrade's "hero without a character," like his model in Koch-Grünberg's legends, is a great transformer. He turns himself into a handsome white prince, into an ant, and, at the end of the narrative, into the constellation Ursa Major. He frequently transforms his brother Jiguê into the "telephone machine," to call a local cabaret to order "lobster and French women" or to curse the villain, Venceslau Pietro Pietra. He transforms an Englishman into the "London Bank machine" and, before returning to his homeland, he transforms the city of São Paulo into a giant, stone sloth. He dies several times, but magical agents revive him.

Joaquim Pedro de Andrade eliminated all magical transformations except two: Macunaíma becomes a handsome white prince and later turns white permanently. In neither case, however, is Macunaíma himself the agent of transformation: in the first case, Sofará (Jiguê's first companion) gives

Macunaíma a magical cigarrette that causes his transformation into a prince; in the second, a fountain magically appears that turns him white. The only other "magical" episodes preserved in the film are the "Currupira" episode (described later) and the scene in which Macunaíma uses *macumba* to give Venceslau a beating. In neither of these episodes, however, do magical powers emanate from Macunaíma, who is thus demystified as a hero. He has no more powers than any ordinary man. He survives largely by his own wits. At no time does Macunaíma, in the film, use magical agents of any kind in his face-to-face struggles with the villain. Furthermore, whereas in the novel the hero is characterized by both positive and negative traits, the director himself has observed that his Macunaíma is "a hero without purpose and without destiny."[12]

Ci, the "Mother of the Forest" in the book, has become Ci, urban guerrilla, in the film. Joaquim Pedro de Andrade's transformation of Ci into an urban guerrilla corresponds directly to the historical events of the period in which he made the film, when urban guerrilla warfare was one result of the military's closing of the political system in 1964. Macunaíma, after meeting and "conquering" Ci, becomes an object of desire for the dominating Ci, unlike in the book, where he becomes the "Emperor of the Virgin Forest."

The villain, Venceslau Pietro Pietra, is much the same in the film and the novel. The novel stresses that he is the cannibalistic giant Piaimã (once again a composite from indigenous legends and the imagination of the novelist), but in the film he is introduced as a giant of industry and commerce and as a champion of free enterprise. He is a wealthy industrialist, but one in a dependent relationship to the United States. As he shows reporters around his factory, he tells them that "all of these machines are new—second-hand American."

Joaquim Pedro de Andrade has transformed other magical, fantastic, animated creatures inhabiting the world of Mário de Andrade's narrative into the outcasts of Brazilian society. The director's basic strategy in the adaptation is to simplify and condense the book's narrative and to make concrete its magical and fantastic elements. The film develops a critical relationship with the novel. It renders explicit that which is implicit in the original and radicalizes many latent political aspects of the novel. Through this strategy Joaquim Pedro de Andrade makes the film relate more directly to modern Brazilian social, political, and economic reality. In this sense, the film represents a step toward realism vis-à-vis the novel; that is, the film is less fantastic and more realistic than the novel.

The textual system of a film is an integration of both cinematic and extracinematic codes, a productive practice. The codes of a text intermingle and interplay to create a multiplicity of meanings articulated across many different codes. The textual system of *Macunaíma* is one of the inversion, if not subversion, of established hierarchies, social mores, and spectator expectations. With its complex cultural coding, it is a radically subversive, carnivalistic text.

The narrative space of *Macunaíma* is one of incongruity, discontinuity, and non sequitur. Macunaíma is born full-grown, son of an old woman (played by a man). The family is racially mixed: one of his brothers (Jiguê) is black, the other (Maanape) is white. Although members of an apparently primitive and isolated Indian tribe, Macunaíma's mother uses an umbrella to keep from being urinated on by her son, who sleeps in the hammock above her. Sofará, Jiguê's girlfriend, wears a white sack dress with an Alliance for Progress emblem on it. There are bums who speak Latin, geese that defecate silver, trees with different kinds of fruit on the same branches, orgies, political speeches, street battles with police, transvestites, black magic, and a generous dose of bad taste. The director achieves temporal discontinuity precisely through the use of such disparate elements.

Macunaíma's central focus is apparent in its very first moments. The credits are set on a green and yellow background, obviously representing a jungle area. Green and yellow are Brazil's official colors and the colors of the flag. A patriotic march by nationalist composer Heitor Villa-Lobos, which seeks through its lyrics to glorify the heroes of Brazil, accompanies the credits. Before the initial shot of the image track, therefore, the film's basic theme is articulated across three distinct codes: a chromatic code (green and yellow with all their connotations of nationalism); a musical code (the patriotic march); and a linguistic code (the march's lyrics). The film links up immediately with the epic tradition, or more precisely, with the comic-epic tradition, as it proposes to deal with the problem of Brazil and the Brazilian hero.

If, in the novel, Macunaíma is characterized in folktale fashion by rapid growth, in the film he is born full-grown. An additional, grotesque charge in the film adapts the deformed, comic, fatherless birth of the novel. Macunaíma is born when he falls out from under his mother's dress and is, in a sense born of the earth. He tumbles onto the ground when he is born; his color is that of the earth. His mother is old and masculine (played by Paulo José, who later plays white Macunaíma). The ambivalent characterization of the mother (old age giving birth) is typical of a carnivalesque attitude toward the world, an attitude that, according to Mikhail Bakhtin, maintains a grotesque image of the body: "The grotesque image reflects a phenomenon in transformation, an as yet unfinished metamorphosis, of death and birth, growth and becoming. The relation to time is one determining trait of the grotesque image. The other indispensable trait is ambivalence. For in this image we find both poles of transformation, the old and the new, the dying and the procreating, the beginning and the end of the metamorphosis."[13]

The carnivalesque profoundly subverts the official, dominant ideology, since it abolishes hierarchies, levels social classes, and creates an alternative, second life, free from the rules and restrictions of official cultural life. Macunaíma's humorous and grotesque birth serves to subvert the ideology suggested by the theme song and background colors of the credits. The film deals with a Brazilian hero, but not the kind envisioned by the dominant ideology. The use of actor Grande Otelo (who, together with Oscarito, epitomizes the *chanchada* in Brazilian cinema) as Macunaíma-child creates an immediate empathy for the character, an identification important for the success of the film as a political statement.

Whereas Mário de Andrade's rhapsody satirizes foreign influence and cultural dependence, Joaquim Pedro de Andrade denounces cultural and economic imperialism. The director transmits much of his criticism of imperialism, capitalism, and modern Brazilian society through a subcode or subtext of cannibalistic imagery. The film is replete with cannibals: an ogre (the Currupira) who cuts off a piece of his leg for Macunaíma to eat; an Italo-Brazilian industrialist (Venceslau Pietro Pietra) who tries to persuade Macunaíma to join—literally—their cannibalistic banquet; the villain's wife, who refers to the captured hero as a "duck" and begins preparing him in a large pot before he manages to escape; and the Uiara, an encarnation of a Brazilian folk legend, a "mermaid" who devours Macunaíma at the end of the film. Cannibalism pervades both works, but gains importance in the film as the guiding force behind its message. It is synonymous with exploitation, especially the international capitalist system's exploitation of underdeveloped Brazil. In a text written as a presentation of the film for the 1969 Venice Film Festival and later included as a preface to the version of the film distributed in the United States, the director observed, "Every consumer is reducible, in the last analysis, to cannibalism. The present work relationships, as well as the relationships between people—social, political, and economic—are still basically cannibalistic. Those who can 'eat' others through their consumption of products, or even more directly in sexual relationships."[14]

Throughout the film an erotic code interweaves with the film's political code, almost always within a broader context of the director's concept of cannibalism. Early in the film, for example, Macunaíma and Sofará go into the woods to set a trap for a tapir. After setting the trap, Sofará takes a magical cigarette out of her crotch (erotic code) and gives it to Macunaíma. When he takes a puff, he immediately becomes a handsome white prince. Sofará and Macunaíma then run deeper into the woods for a sexual romp to the sound of an old Carnival march entitled "Peri e Ceci." Peri and Ceci are characters in José de Alencar's famous romantic novel, *O Guarani*. Peri is the noble savage with whom the young European (or Europeanized) girl, Ceci, falls in love. An opposition develops, on the level of a musical/linguistic code, between the native Peri (Macunaíma) and the foreign Ceci (Sofará).

The filmmaker's characterization of Macunaíma-prince differs from the novel's Macunaíma, who, through his own powers of transformation, becomes a "fiery prince." Macunaíma's transformation into a prince in the film, however, is only superficial. His clothes are made of gaudy crepe paper, and he soon reverts to the black "baby" who amuses himself by sucking on a pacifier and eating dirt. He is no more than a paper prince.[15]

The trap that Macunaíma and Sofará set is successful, and we soon see Jiguê dividing the cooked tapir among the members of the family while the hero boasts of his exploits. All that Macunaíma receives of the tapir he trapped are the intestines.

Most critics have overlooked one detail in these two episodes: Sofará is wearing a sack dress with an Alliance for Progress emblem on it. On a deeper level, then, it is the Alliance for Progress (representing North American imperialism) that gives Macunaíma (representing Brazil) an appearance of development; but when the goods are divided, all Macunaíma receives is tripe. Just as Sofará/Ceci wants to consume Macunaíma/Peri sexually, American capital attempts to consume Brazil economically. The political allegory is clear, albeit only superficially outlined here.

Cannibalistic imagery continues after a devastating flood leaves Macunaíma's family hungry. The hero had hidden some food, but refuses to share it with his brothers. His mother therefore abandons him with the admonition, "You stay alone here and don't grow any more, stupid!" Shortly thereafter, Macunaíma comes upon the Currupira who, from the narrative point of view, serves as a hostile donor who tries to trick the hero in order to eat him. In Brazilian folk legends, whence Mário de Andrade borrowed the episode, the Currupira is a god who protects the forests. After cutting off a piece of his leg for the hero to eat, the Currupira shows Macunaíma the wrong way home, and a chase ensues. As the hero flees, the ogre yells to the flesh from his leg, now inside Macunaíma's stomach. The meat indicates the hero's route to the ogre. Finally Macunaíma realizes what is happening and vomits the meat into a mud puddle.

The last shot of the sequence shows the puddle, with the meat still trying to respond to the Currupira's calls, but in reality only gurgling in the muddy water. The puddle, as filmed, forms, together with the film's frame, the design of the Brazilian flag: a rectangle enclosing a diamond shape, within which is a globe with stars on it. The frame represents the flag as a whole: the puddle is diamond-shaped; and the meat, gurgling and making concentric circles, is the globe. The connotations and implications are multiple. The image is at once a comment on the state of Brazilian politics under the military regime and a cannibalistic image, as Brazil (here, the earth and the flag) devours part of the Currupira. In this sense the image echoes earlier scenes in which Macunaíma had attempted to "consume" Sofará under water while the family bathed together in the river and foreshadows the consumption (again in water) of Venceslau Pietro Pietra later in the film. The muddy flag also foreshadows the final shot of the film, in which Macunaíma dies while his green jacket spreads over the water like a flag.

After their mother's death, Macunaíma and his brothers depart for the city. They soon come upon a magical fountain that turns the hero white again. An old, romantic song entitled "Sob uma Cascata" ("By a Waterfall"), the Brazilian version of a song Lloyd Bacon used in his *Footlight Parade* (1933), ironically accompanies the transformation. The cultural code thus refers on one level to American musical comedy (and to the Brazilian version of the genre, the *chanchada*), and on another, to cultural imperialism.

On arriving in the city, where Iriqui (Jiguê's second "companion") becomes a prostitute, Macunaíma faces another problem: he is unable to distinguish men from machines. After much contemplation, he determines in high carnivalesque fashion that the men are machines and the machines are men, a wry comment on the alienation of modern man in technological society.

Macunaíma soon encounters Ci as she battles the police. Like many other elements in the film, the episodes involving Ci represent an inversion of established values and social hierarchies of patriarchal Brazilian society. Macunaíma is interested in Ci sexually, but Ci in reality dominates and determines their relationship. In their initial struggle, Ci soundly defeats Macunaíma. Later, Macunaíma, not Ci, prostitutes himself for money. Six months after their first encounter, Ci gives birth to a black baby (once again played by Grande Otelo), but it is Macunaíma who must rest. The clothes he wears while in Ci's house (a purple robe with male genital organs designed on it) and the colors that his part of the house, the bedroom, is painted (pink and other shades of red) reinforce Macunaíma's role as a sex object. Ci's part of the house is green, yellow, and blue (Brazil's colors). While Ci goes out to fight the forces of repression, Macunaíma, the antihero, stays home to rest. But Ci herself, a dominant agent in relation to the object Macunaíma, also becomes an object—an object for mass consumption, a pop song, a poster on the wall. Later she literally self-destructs, blowing up with her own bomb, thereby participating in what Joaquim Pedro de Andrade refers to as the "self-cannibalism" of the Left.

Before her death, Ci had promised to leave Macunaíma a precious stone, the *muiraquitã*, as an inheritance. The talisman is lost in the explosion of Ci's bomb. After her death, Macunaíma learns that an Italo-Brazilian industrialist, Venceslau Pietro Pietra, has found the stone. The film's narrative core revolves around Macunaíma's attempts to recover the stone. The final battle between Macunaíma and the giant of industry takes place only after several preliminary rounds and other misadventures: in a *tour de force* of carnivalesque inversion and ambivalence Macunaíma goes in drag to Venceslau's house and is almost "devoured" by the giant; the hero uses *macumba* to give Venceslau a beating; he is captured, in a scene that re-creates a shot from the *chanchada Carnaval Atlântida* (1953), and is almost eaten by Venceslau's wife; he gives a patriotic speech in a public plaza; he chases an invisible cavy through the stock market; he attempts to get a scholarship to pursue the giant, who is in Europe convalescing from the beating; he is tricked by a bum into smashing his testicles ("sic transit," remarks the bum); he is tricked into buying a goose that "defecates silver"; he takes a walk in the local leper colony, playing "kick the can" with a leper's lost hand.

Finally, invited by the giant to participate in a *feijoada* commemorating his younger daughter's marriage, Macunaíma returns to the villain's mansion for the final confrontation. The *feijoada*, in a large swimming pool, is a cannibalistic feast in which the traditional sausage, dried beef, and pork ends have been replaced by human bodies, intestines, and appendages—a far cry from the pools used for synchronized swimming in Bacon's *Footlight Parade*. After much peril, Macunaíma finally defeats Venceslau, who falls into the pool of food. Before he goes under, however, he yells, "It needs salt!" Macunaíma's victory is complete.

But what is Macunaíma's victory? Looking at the film to this point, one might be tempted to see the struggle between Macunaíma and Venceslau Pietro Pietra as a rather bizarre allegory of class struggle, with the industrial bourgeoisie defeated by the disinherited masses. Such an interpretation is simplistic, however, and is soon undercut by subsequent events. Macunaíma, his brothers, and Princesa (the hero's new companion) leave the city with a wagon filled with electrical appliances: fans, televisions, stereos, blenders, electric guitars. His dress gives him away. He is wearing a green and yellow (symbolic of Brazil) buckskin cowboy suit and hat (representing U.S. cultural imperialism). Taking back to the jungle with him products of multinational corporations and dressed as he is, Macunaíma has been incorporated by consumer society and co-opted by American cultural domination. In the jungle all of his electrical appliances will be useless.

Upon arriving at his birthplace, Macunaíma refuses to help the others find food, preferring instead to sleep. They soon abandon him. One hot day, the hero awakes "with a new feeling in his muscles" and goes to the river to swim. There he encounters the cannibal Uiara in the form of a beautiful, nude woman (Maria Lúcia Dahl). He jumps in the river. The last shot shows his green jacket afloat with blood gushing from under it, as Villa-Lobos's patriotic march once again begins. In the novel, Macunaíma, mutilated by piranhas, tires of living on earth and is magically transformed into Ursa Major. The final shot echoes all of the earlier scenes of cannibalism, including Venceslau Pietro Pietra's death at the *feijoada*. The patriotic march continues through the final credits, set once again on a green and yellow background, until the screen becomes black. The black screen accompanied by the music continues for several seconds before the film ends. Blackness—death—therefore surrounds the film (before the first shot of the image track the screen is black).

Throughout the film Macunaíma undergoes a process of demystification. His generally anarchistic attitude must certainly offend the dominant ideology, but at the same time he is not the kind of hero those who oppose the dominant ideology envision. Through his own laziness and egotism, Macunaíma largely defeats himself. He becomes, in fact, his own antagonist. Despite his tremendous energy and madcap humor, he is a failed hero. The director has frequently observed that *Macunaíma* is a film about a Brazilian devoured by Brazil, but, since Macunaíma frequently represents Brazil itself, one can say that the underlying theme is that of "auto-cannibalism": Brazil devours its citizens through poverty and underdevelopment; its citizens devour Brazil; and so Brazil, consequently, devours itself.

Despite the tremendous critical and popular success of *Macunaíma*, a truly radical film in both political and cinematic terms, the cinema of Joaquim Pedro de Andrade reaches its high point, in my view, in *Os Inconfidentes*, which takes as its subject an unsuccessful revolt against the Portuguese Crown by a group of intellectuals in the late eighteenth century. The leader of the revolt, Tiradentes (Joaquim José da Silva Xavier), is now revered as a national hero, and his birthday, April 21, is a national holiday. Made during the darkest period of repression in military-ruled Brazil and during a period in which the government film enterprise, Embrafilme, was supporting and encouraging the production of films on historical topics— films, that is, that transmitted the "official" version of Brazilian history— Andrade's film challenges that version. Ironically, though, *Os Inconfidentes* challenges the official version of history by using the official documents of that history. All of the film's dialogue comes directly from the court records of the conspirators' trials (the *Autos da Devassa*), from the neoclassical poetry of the intellectual conspirators themselves, or, in a few cases, from *O Romanceiro da Inconfidência*, a book of verse by Cecilia Meireles, one of Brazil's most important modern poets. The result, by Andrade and Eduardo Escorel, is one of the most beautifully complex scripts yet written for Brazilian cinema. The idea, according to the director, was to make a film about the contemporary political conjuncture, a film challenging the ideology of the military dictatorship, by using virtually *uncensorable* material: the words of one of Brazil's national heroes; the poetry, long consecrated by critics, of those who wished to free Brazil from the yoke of Portuguese colonialism. As Andrade observes, *Os Inconfidentes* "sambas out of step in the school of the historical film."[16]

Os Inconfidentes is complex not only as a script, but also visually. The film synthesizes the "austere negation" (to use the director's words) of *The Priest and the Girl* and the explosive vitality of *Macunaíma*. It is a film that

Plate 4. *Os Inconfidentes (The Conspirators)*

"recovers the expressive limits of the frame" and that is highly Brechtian in its composition. It prefers the sequence shot to montage and uses the close shot as the dominant mode of discourse. The film creates a closed, almost abstract space, as it attempts to analyze the motives of the conspirators. At one moment they espouse the ideals of democracy and freedom and at the next deny all involvement in the conspiracy and swear allegiance to the queen of Portugal, Dona Maria I. *Os Inconfidentes* also creates and develops intersecting planes of space and time, both intra- and intertextually, both within the diegesis and between the film and the modern spectator. It is, in short, a film about history and about the present filmed with a perspective critical of the dominant ideology and with a biting, yet sometimes humorous, sense of irony.

The film's first sequence—precredits—is typical of the director's aggressive irony. In the first shot a large piece of red meat, swarming with flies, covers the screen. Only later does the spectator learn that the meat is supposedly Tiradentes' body, which was drawn and quartered as part of his sentence for leading the conspiracy. This shot in itself represents aggression toward the spectator.

The second shot shows, in an extremely close low-angle, one of the conspirators, Cláudio Manuel da Costa (played by Fernando Torres, who with his full grey beard looks remarkably like Karl Marx), tying a rope around his neck and hanging himself. The third shot is of poet-conspirator José de Alvarenga Peixoto (Paulo César Pereio) wasting away in a cholera-infested jail in Mozambique. The fourth conspirator, poet Tomás Antônio Gonzaga—the Arcadian Dirceu—then appears on a deserted beach in Mozambique, a yellowed manuscript in hand, where he reveals an advanced stage of madness and talks of returning to Brazil. As Gonzaga runs across the beach toward the water, followed by his wife and son, the film's musical soundtrack softly plays Ari Barroso's "Aquarela do Brasil" ("Brazil" in the American version). As the music gains force, a picture postcard view of the colonial mining town, Ouro Preto, where the conspiracy took place, replaces the shot of Gonzaga. The irony could not be more perfect: after four aggressive shots of death, exile, and madness, a beautiful establishing shot of a baroque mountain town to the tune of a song that is almost synonymous with an idealized, overoptimistic vision of the country. A tremendous difference and disjunction exist between appearance and reality, between the "official," glossed-over version of history, and the historical events themselves. The juxtaposition of reconstructed historical events and twentieth-century popular music also reinforces the fact that Andrade's principal concern in *Os Inconfidentes* is not the conspiracy itself, but rather the current political conjuncture. A disjunction thus exists between the time of the narrative (eighteenth-century Brazil) and the time of the narration (twentieth-century Brazil).

By reversing the order of most historical dramas dealing with national heroes, Andrade first shows the failed result of the Minas conspiracy— banishment, death, and madness—before turning to the conspiracy itself, as revealed through a series of flashbacks from the time frame of the first sequence. This strategy inevitably brings to mind a more recent political failure: the failure of the Left, and more specifically of the intellectual Left, in confrontation with the military in 1964. In the next few sequences, *Os Inconfidentes* formally introduces its historical actors: Peixoto, a weak, indecisive man with a perhaps exaggerated sense of class, dreams of royalty and of making his wife a queen and his daughter a princess; Cláudio Manuel da Costa, a tortured, self-doubting man who eventually kills himself after denouncing his friends; Gonzaga, the sensitive preromantic poet who dreams only of his approaching marriage to Marília; and finally Tiradentes himself, the revolutionary from a lower class who calls the people "stupid" because they do not want to overthrow the colonial regime. The other figures involved in this historical drama are Padre Carlos Corrêa de Toledo, vicar of São José (a composite of several religious figures who were to some extent involved in the conspiracy), Lieutenant-Colonel Francisco de Paula Freire de Andrade, José Alvares Maciel, the traitor Joaquim Silvério dos

Reis, and, finally, the governor of the capitania, the Visconde de Barbacena.

The other conspirators, who consider themselves superior to Tiradentes, refer to him as a "fanatic" and as a man of "little talent." Despite his contradictory relationship with the lower classes (political concern tempered by outright scorn), Tiradentes is the only conspirator with true revolutionary convictions. Although Tiradentes was forty years old when the conspiracy occurred, Andrade chose a young actor (José Wilker) to play the role, as if to emphasize his inner youth and spirit.

The most immediately apparent contradiction in the conspirator's actions is that they are all slaveholders discussing the possibility of freedom—for themselves, not for their slaves (in this sense they are not unlike American revolutionaries such as George Washington and Thomas Jefferson). Even Tiradentes is a slaveholder, and it is purposefully ironic that his hangman later in the film is black, as if in revenge for Tiradentes' having marginalized blacks from the "revolutionary" process. At one point in the conspiracy, the problem of slavery is discussed openly:

Maciel: The number of black slaves is greater than that of whites. If we revolt the blacks will also revolt, and then it will be worse than before.

Peixoto: The problem is easily resolved: giving the slaves their freedom, they will be on our side.

Maciel: If we free the slaves, who will work the land, take gold from the mines? No. In my view the only way to make the uprising work is to kill all the Europeans . . .

The irony of Maciel's last line is not lost on the spectator (Maciel and the other conspirators *are* culturally European), but the contradiction remains unresolved. The planned revolt, by a group of intellectually inclined aristocrats, is to be from the top down, without the participation of the people, who are *politically* absent from the official version of history and, as such, *visually* absent from the film.

The *inconfidência*, according to the version offered by Joaquim Pedro de Andrade, was planned by four different groups of people representing three distinct, but perhaps interrelated, motivations. First of all, the intellectuals (Gonzaga, Peixoto, Cláudio Manuel da Costa) were "revolutionary" on a cultural level because of the imported ideals with which they had become familiar (the ideals of the French and American revolutions). Others, notably the traitor Silvério, were hurt by taxes levied by the Crown. Yet others, like Tiradentes, saw colonialism itself as the greatest barrier to the country's development. Lieutenant-Colonel Francisco de Paula, on the other hand, seemed to be more interested in personal power than in anything else. The conspiracy was variously motivated and heterogeneous, a fact that perhaps explains the Machiavellian accusations and counteraccusations that occurred after the conspiracy was discovered.

Scenes of the conspiracy taking form alternate with scenes of the conspirators being interrogated by the Visconde de Barbacena and with shots of the various conspirators in jail. In one of the film's most humorous sequence shots, Silvério betrays his fellow conspirators and tells the visconde of their plans, convincing him that his will be the first head to roll. The visconde is taking a bath when Silvério enters and immediately invites, then orders, Silvério to enter the tub with him. Their entire dialogue takes place as Silvério washes the visconde in the small bathtub. The hint of homosexuality and the utter ridiculousness of the sequence not only reflect the pusillanimity of Silvério but also are a wry comment on the nature of power itself.

In rapid succession, the conspirators go before their accusers. Tiradentes is tortured as he denies Silvério's accusations (an obvious reference to the military regime's systematic torture of political prisoners): "I have neither the figure, nor the courage, nor the wealth to be able to persuade such a great people to do such a stupid thing." During his second interrogation, later in the film (which, historically, took place nearly a year after the first), Tiradentes admits his guilt and assumes responsibility for the conspiracy:

Yes, it is true that I was preparing the revolt and that I was the one who originated the idea, without anyone instigating or inspiring me in any way. I had been passed over four times in the regiment. No matter how well I did, they only gave me the riskiest missions. They gave promotions and increases to others, either because they were more handsome or because they had better relations than I did. I was desperate and was the first to talk about the revolt. The others followed and approved, but without ever becoming the leader.

Andrade thus preserves a portion of the official version of Tiradentes as the leader of the *inconfidência* while at the same time casting doubt on his motives. This ambiguity, or even parody, of the official version, is perhaps the key to the film.

Finally, after the conspirators' interrogations and Cláudio Manuel da Costa's suicide, all the remaining conspirators appear together in a jail cell. The space surrounding them has decreased throughout the film, thus reaching its maximum (or minimum) limits. In the one creative "betrayal" of history, Queen Maria I, who never went to Brazil, arrives to listen to the conspirators' pleas and to read their sentences, with Gonzaga's Marília at her side. All of the conspirators except Tiradentes are condemned to perpetual banishment. Tiradentes, who, instead of repenting, declares that "if I had ten lives, ten lives would I give," is condemned to hang until death, then to have his body quartered and displayed along the road for all to see. His house is to be destroyed and the ground salted. His descendents are disgraced to the fifth generation.

In a series of shots similar to the opening sequence, Gonzaga departs for

Africa, reciting poetry to his beloved Marília. Peixoto appears again in jail, and preparations are made for Tiradentes's execution. But as he is hanged, the film cuts from a low-angle shot looking up at the gallows to a reverse high-angle shot of children in modern-day Brazil who applaud as the historical drama reaches an end. Black and white newsreel footage of a military parade in Ouro Preto alternates with the film's initial sequence of red meat (Tiradentes's body) being cut up by a cleaver. Once again, the irony of the juxtaposition is not lost on the spectator, as Andrade comments on the tremendous distance between the ideas, however contradictory, of the national hero, and the ideology of military rule. Freedom, the film seems to be saying, is still a long way off for the Brazilian people. The film ends on a shot of the meat, once again to the sounds of Ari Barroso's "Aquarela do Brasil."

Perhaps more interesting than the historical reconstruction and interpretation itself is the way in which it is conveyed. *Os Inconfidentes* was produced by and for Italian television (RAI) and was made with direct sound (as are all of Andrade's features). Both the screen size and the choice of sound reproduction affect the film's mode of discourse. A film about a conspiracy, its action occurs in closed spaces, normally interiors, that, through a process of abstraction, give an idea of both the opulence and austerity of the conspirators' lifestyle. Decoration is sparse, unlike in most historical dramas, to emphasize the dialogues, which are often whispered and usually poetic. The film comprises a mere forty-two sequences, each one presenting a new bit of information about the conspirators and about the development and later negation of their democratic ideals. Exteriors are rare. Gonzaga recites poetry to Marília among the flowers and later on a boat leaving for Mozambique, but even in this shot the framing is very tight and closed and gives no natural dimension to the exterior. Another exterior shows Tiradentes and Maciel walking in a nearby meadow. But the natural setting is not important except, in the case of Gonzaga, for reinforcing personal characteristics.

Os Inconfidentes renders both time and space abstract; different spatial and temporal planes intersect at different times within the narration. The space of the jail—of repression—gradually expands throughout the film as the characters' freedom of movement diminishes. The balanced space that the film's careful composition represents, a space that the ideals of the elevation of man represent, contrasts with the closed, tight space of degradation and once again reinforces the distance between ideas, ideals, and reality.

As already noted, the film begins with the result of the conspiracy and flashes back to the events leading up to it. Within the historical reconstruction itself there is little concern with a linear narrative, as the film cuts from the conspiracy to the interrogations and back again. There are even flashbacks within the shot, as one character moves to the background while another takes over the foreground in a different time frame. The same thing occurs spatially, as, in one sequence, Tiradentes begins his interrogation in the visconde's office, and through a Brechtian jumpcut continues in an exterior as he walks with Maciel.

The influence of Brecht is more visible in this film than in any other by Joaquim Pedro de Andrade. Personages consistently direct their lines to the camera, as if to create a direct, conspiratorial relationship between the film and the public, between the diegesis and the theater, between history and the present, and most importantly between a historical *myth* and a contemporary political reality: history inserted in the present; the present, a result of history. The ironic provocation that develops in the sequences where the conspirators collectively plan their revolt makes the political significance of the link between past and present clear. In one such meeting, Lieutenant–Colonel Francisco de Paula says that it is of little importance whether the people revolt or not, since the arms are "well kept with my regiment. Since I command the regiment, the arms are in my hands." Padre Toledo, in an aside to Peixoto, looks at the camera and says, "This is what we have to avoid in the future, that everything remain in the hands of one man. Especially in the hands of a military man." The meaning for contemporary Brazil could not be clearer, especially when the conspirators go on to conjecture that under their regime there can be no role for professional soldiers. Although set in the past, *Os Inconfidentes* is talking about the present, about the military regime's abuse of power, and about the role of intellectuals in a situation of revolt and, subsequently, repression.

Despite the creative fidelity to historical and literary documents, the basic mode of *Os Inconfidentes* is not realistic, unless one accepts that term in the Brechtian sense of not "reflecting" reality, but rather of revealing the true ("real") relationships underlying the appearances of that reality. A distancing effect is used throughout, whether by personages directing themselves at the camera, by the "creative" interpretation of history, or by the use of poetry (in this case, eighteenth-century neoclassical verse) as dialogue.

Realism also breaks down in a number of sequences involving the poet Gonzaga. While in jail, Gonzaga imagines himself sewing Marília's wedding gown. A blond angel suddenly appears in the window behind him. Then, as he imagines their wedding and wedding night, he and Marília appear in a large bed, she still wearing her veil. Surrounding them are a group of nude children, laughing and throwing flowers on the newlyweds. On the soundtrack João Gilberto sings Augustín Lara's "Farolito lindo." Even when Gonzaga is seen on the bow of a small boat, a symbol of his departure for Mozambique, the take is nonrealistic, since all we see is Gonzaga himself framed against the sky and rocking with the motion of the waves.

The allegorical language of *Os Inconfidentes*, much more than that of *The Priest and the Girl* and *Macunaíma*, is an invitation to the spectator to reflect. But *Os Inconfidentes* goes beyond the earlier films in terms of its political analysis. Like *The Priest and the Girl*, it was filmed in Minas Gerais and is characterized by a certain solemnity of language; but more like *Macunaíma*, its language incorporates structures of aggression designed to provoke the spectator. In both *The Priest and the Girl* and *Os Inconfidentes* key personages take steps that are far beyond their capability for successful action, and in both cases they suffer disastrous consequences: death or exile. But unlike *The Priest and the Girl*, which starts with a particular situation and evolves to a level of abstraction, *Os Inconfidentes* begins with a certain level of abstraction—the ideals behind the planned revolt—evolves to the particular situation of each participant, then relates their situations to a concrete, contemporary political conjuncture.

In *Guerra Conjugal*, Joaquim Pedro de Andrade continues the "subversive" tactic used in *Os Inconfidentes*. As he observes, whereas "*Os Inconfidentes* sambas out of step in the school of the historical film, *Guerra Conjugal* is the black sheep of the erotic comedy."[17] In the early 1970s, a flood of vapid erotic comedies (*pornochanchadas*, which in reality are neither "pornographic" nor *chanchadas*) imitating the well-worn Italian genre, rushed into the Brazilian market to fill the partial vacuum left by the political censorship of more serious films. Taken together, these films offer a cinematic portrait of the sexual alienation of the Brazilian petite bourgeoisie; they exalt the good bourgeois life of fast cars, wild parties, and luxurious surroundings and offer the voyeur titillating shots of breasts and buttocks.[18] More recently, with the easing of censorship, some of them have incorporated scenes of explicit sexual activity.

Just as he used the historical formula in *Os Inconfidentes* to challenge the official version of history, in *Guerra Conjugal*, Cinema Novo's first "response" to the *pornochanchada*, Joaquim Pedro de Andrade uses the erotic comedy formula to invert its own values, revealing them to be rotten under the flashy surface. Speaking of the *pornochanchada*, Andrade notes,

What we see is the appearance of a kind of hypocrisy; that is, people working in cinema are prohibited from dealing truthfully with a number of themes. Thus a false morality arises, completely out of touch with the practical urban morality of the very class that consumes these films. And this fact destroys their cultural and even commercial vitality. If these films were made with the irreverence that implies contesting values that are evidently rotten and falsified, they would gain another kind of life and interest.[19]

His own *Guerra Conjugal*, like *Macunaíma*, possesses just the irreverence and critical perspective to which he refers.

With *Guerra Conjugal*, Andrade once again turns to a literary source for the basis of his film, this time to the modern master of the Brazilian short story, Dalton Trevisan, also known as the "Vampire of Curitiba." But the interesting thing about *Guerra Conjugal* (which is the title of one of Trevisan's books) is that it is not adapted from a single work, but rather from sixteen short stories chosen from seven different volumes of Trevisan's work. The short stories, dealing with different characters in diverse yet similar situations, are organized into three basic groups, each unified around a single character (or, in one case, a couple): Osiris, an unscrupulous lawyer who uses his profession to seduce his women clients; Nelsinho, a sinister young man looking for the ultimate pleasure; and Joãozinho and Amália, an elderly couple who argue constantly. Although organized syntagmatically with no apparent pattern, each group of episodes develops its characters with a certain linearity. The episodes of the different groups interact and reflect each other, since, like Trevisan's short stories, they all belong to the same general universe. In one case, the director divides one of the short stories into two separate episodes. In general each episode is autonomous, separated by a simple cut from the others, as if each were in itself a short, anecdotal film.

Andrade's camera focuses constantly on the characters themselves, emphasizing their words and gestures. The cinematic language of *Guerra Conjugal* is straightforward and simple. The scenography is determined largely in function of the personages: Osiris's gaudy office; Joãozinho and Amália's decadent, run-down house; the kitsch and bad taste of the bordello and other scenarios frequented by Nelsinho. The bad taste of much of the scenography reflects the "bad taste" of the personages' moral character.

With *Guerra Conjugal*, however, there is no attempt to invert or subvert the original text. As Andrade noted when asked why he decided to film Trevisan, "It was a case of identity. . . . Dalton destroys complacency and has a fine sense of hypocrisy. I identify with that."[20] The director described *Guerra Conjugal* as "an intersection of both of us imagined by me."[21]

According to the film's press book, *Guerra Conjugal* "illustrates curious cases of amorous psycho-pathology in a coat-and-tie civilization, still very much alive in the mythological and ubiquitous city of Curitiba, where plastic flowers grow and red porcelain elephants may appear at any moment." Like Brazilian playwright Nelson Rodrigues, Dalton Trevisan and Joaquim Pedro de Andrade portray a world of carnal and moral decadence, a morbid and sordid world of inverted values. And, as for Rodrigues, sickness and disease become symbolic of society as a whole in *Guerra Conjugal*.

As *Guerra Conjugal*'s credits proceed, the background, accompanied by romantic piano music, evolves from a heart shape surrounded by pink flowers to a circle surrounded by blue flowers. At the end of the film the same music is repeated, but with a gaudy, purple wreath surrounded by insects, wasps, ants, and cockroaches. As we have seen throughout

Andrade's filmography, the pretty, pleasant surface of things hides something terribly rotten underneath. *Guerra Conjugal* deals with the putrid reality beneath the sexual mores of the petite bourgeoisie: the cult of *machismo*, women as sex objects, repression of homosexuality, the avoidance of divorce at all costs. The combatants of this conjugal war reflect an atrophied and oppressed sexuality marked by what one of Osiris's victims calls "the commerce of kisses," that is, sexuality as a commodity to be exploited. The film deals, ultimately, with the everyday violence of human relationships in a society that reifies human beings. It is, in short, a film about the ugliness and cruelty of the conjugal war in which, directly or indirectly, we all participate.

In the film's initial sequence, Joãozinho (played superbly by Jofre Soares) wakes up in the middle of the night at his wife's side, gets up, mumbling and complaining about Amália's cooking, and goes into the kitchen to take some bicarbonate of soda. His only consolation, he grumbles, is that she will die before he does (she does not). As he goes back to bed his wife says, "Joãozinho, you haven't kissed me in years." He suddenly remembers their long-past wedding day, when his brother kissed Amália as a form of wishing her well. But Joãozinho does not see it that way and explodes in jealousy: "Your kiss rotted on his lips." Obsessed with death, he goes on to describe how some corpses' stomachs explode as they decay.

Such is the level, often humorous but just as often grotesque, of *Guerra Conjugal*. It presents us with a universe filled with jealousy, passion, betrayal, and any number of anomalies—swollen livers, cancer of the head, alcoholism, blindness, obesity, deforming arthritis, asthma—all of which serve, as has been suggested, as symbols of the moral decadence of Brazil's petite bourgeoisie.

We accompany Joãozinho's often unequal war with Amália as he complains of her "stupidity," of her food, of the fact that she always sits on the edge of the chair; as he accuses her of trying to poison him by putting green pepper in his food, of not respecting him; as he tells her to leave him and go live with her mother if she does not like the way he treats her. When she reminds him that her mother is dead, he accuses, "Ah, but if she were alive you'd abandon me, right?"

But Amália finally gets her revenge, first by telling her husband that he makes her sick by the way he slurps soup—she will clean his house, wash his clothes and cook his food, but she will not sit at the table with him. Later, as Joãozinho lays dying ("I fought with God," he agonizes), he asks his son not to let Amália kiss him after he dies. Amália's victory comes when he dies before she does and she can be exultant when talking to her neighbor. Amália can finally put on her spring dress and smile for a change.

A fundamental ambivalence structures the sequences concerning Joãozinho and Amália. Life (for Amália) occurs only through death (Joãozinho's), human companionship (represented by Amália's friend, who only appears at Joãozinho's funeral), through solitude. This ambivalence, in fact, structures the entire film.

The lawyer Osiris is just as sinister as Joãozinho, albeit in a different way. Osiris's function as a lawyer is to save social institutions (paternity, marriage) in which he himself does not believe. He is more concerned with solving his own sexual problems at his clients' expense, and he too has the tables turned on him in the end. We first see him in his office greeting a young, attractive client named Maria. She has been "dishonored" by her boyfriend, João. When she told him she was pregnant, he fled. In reality she was not pregnant at all; her liver was merely swollen.

But João is planning to marry a blond, and Maria wants to know what the lawyer can do to help her. The only solution she sees is to enter a convent. Osiris has an immediate (and self-serving) plan for her revenge. Through insinuations—asking about her sex life, talking about her body—he tries to convince her to move over to the couch with him. It is only then that she says she is tired of couches and the "commerce of kisses." She finally succumbs as Osiris says, "Nobody has pity on Marias."

In later episodes Osiris begins an affair with Olga, who has been beaten by her husband because of her many lovers. "Every man who is weak in bed," Osiris tells her, "is strong out of it." Olga's husband, João, consults Osiris as well, saying that he suspects that she is unfaithful. Osiris then begins frequenting Olga and João's house, making love to her in the afternoon before having dinner with the couple in the evening. His relationship with Olga advances to such a point that she wants to make love in the kitchen while her husband finishes dinner in the dining room. Osiris finally realizes that João knows about and approves of her affairs. The culmination of this relationship with Olga comes, however, when he arrives at her house in the afternoon and finds her husband sprawled out on the couch, victim of a heart attack. In an act of what the director calls "voyeuristic necrophilia," Olga forces Osiris to make love to her in front of her dead husband.

Osiris pays for his sins, however, in an episode based on the short story "The Thousand Eyes of a Blind Man." In this story he visits a high school friend who now admits that he has always desired Osiris, whom he remembers running around in his tight little shorts. "Between João and Maria," he remarks, "I prefer João." As Osiris becomes increasingly uneasy, his friend talks of women as "rotten flowers" and says that touching them is like picking up a frog. He speaks in misogynistic disgust of their "frightful breasts" and their "blue legs filled with varicose veins." Osiris squirms as he is asked if he has ever kissed a man on the lips and as his friend runs his hand up and down his leg.

The most sinister of all is Nelsinho, whose first act in the film is to kick a sickly dog sleeping on the steps of a girlfriend's house. He enters the house, talks to the girl's blind mother, and gives her a bottle of beer in an effort to stimulate her growing alcoholism. As he and his girlfriend go into the next room, he suggests that she put ground glass in the old woman's food, or that she put the woman in the attic, where chances are good she will fall down the stairs. He refuses the young woman's kisses because she is eating peppermint candy, and then forces her to swallow it. He makes her take off her clothes, but at that moment the old woman enters the room. After a few brief words, Nelsinho and his girlfriend continue their foreplay in the blind woman's presence.

The second time we see him, he rejects another girlfriend, saying that she is too old for him, after forcing her to take off her dress. He then goes down the hall, but instead of going out the door, he walks through a gaudy blue bathroom into a large bedroom where the girl's obese mother is lounging and eating bonbons. Ninety-nine kilos of flesh just for him. As they start to make love, his girlfriend bangs on the door in despair.

In the final sequence of the film Nelsinho visits a bordello. Walking past all the young prostitutes, he finally arrives in the back of the house where a seventy-year old prostitute awaits him. After having sex with her, he walks out the door saying, "Now I can go home, embrace my wife, and kiss my children. Now I feel good." Redemption through the excess of sin? The triumph of prostitution over old age? A Freudian search for the mother? The film ends on this ambiguous note, but leaves a bitter taste in the spectator's mouth. The music at the film's end, although the same as at the beginning, now has a totally different meaning. The pink flowers of the credits have indeed been replaced by wasps and cockroaches. Degradation, cruelty, and aggression accumulate throughout the film into a brilliant climax.

Joaquim Pedro de Andrade's study of "amorous psycho-pathology" is in reality a frontal assault on the hypocrisy of the sexual mores of the Brazilian middle class. In this sense the film is at least as political, if not more so, than either *Macunaíma* or *Os Inconfidentes*. *Guerra Conjugal*'s grotesque realism hits the public much closer to home than does the more allegorical language of the two previous films. As critic José Carlos Avellar has observed, the film shows "how the political system is assimilated by the individual, and how people begin to lie, be aggressive, torture, and live in a state of war" in their relationships with other people.[22] *Guerra Conjugal* is a film about the daily, personal violence of middle-class society, a violence distinguished by a false etiquette imposed by the conventions of that society. It is a film about what Avellar has called "whispered violence" and about egotistical catharsis through this violence. Metalinguistically, *Guerra Conjugal*'s black humor ideologically assaults the conservative and moralistic values of the *pornochanchada* and its love for shiny surfaces.

"The chronicle of a gentle perversion" containing the "denunciation of the genital vocation of vegetables, the intelligence of budding young women, the freedom of games played in bed, the sympathy of deviation . . . liberating and educational" is how Andrade describes his next film, *Vereda Tropical*, the final episode in the four-episode feature *Contos Eróticos*. The feature was thought up and produced by the Brazilian men's magazine *Status*. The idea was to have four well-known directors choose among the prize-winning erotic short stories in a contest sponsored by the magazine. The other directors were Roberto Santos, Roberto Palmari, and Eduardo Escorel. The story chosen by Andrade, written by Pedro Maia Soares, consists of little more than an interior monologue. The director, by situating it in time and space and adding a female character (played by his wife, Cristina Aché), gave the story life.

Andrade also situates his adaptation ideologically, continuing his critique of the *pornochanchada*. This time, though, he uses a lighter form of parody than that in *Guerra Conjugal*. The film's title immediately recalls the tropicalist movement of the late sixties. Cultural meaning saturates the setting (Paquetá Island, near Rio de Janeiro), as the romantic, bucolic, and "idyllic" site of innocent love in such nineteenth-century novels as Joaquim Manuel de Macedo's *A Moreninha*. The theme song, "Vereda Tropical," a bolero crooned by Carlos Galhardo, brings into the film the cultural universe of the *chanchada* of the 1950s.

Vereda Tropical tells the story of Cláudio (played by Cláudio Cavalcânti), a graduate student and professor who is writing a thesis entitled "Collateral Parentage among Northeastern Migrants in Rio de Janeiro's Civil Construction Industry" (a good-humored jab at academic "seriousness"). It so happens, however, that Cláudio prefers watermelons to women. He tells Cristina,

Oh, I've had girlfriends, but they always caused problems and made things complicated. They were either too conventional or I didn't have enough patience. I don't know. Anyway I usually didn't have enough money to go out with women, or to pay, if that were the case. . . . With watermelons it's different. You just go out and buy one. I can't say that I'm addicted, because it's not the kind of thing that creates a great dependence. It's just good. Healthful, fresh, natural. I got used to it.

Cláudio first appears riding his bicycle, a watermelon tied on behind, along the bucolic streets of Paquetá. He juggles the melon as he opens the door, enters the house, and takes off his clothes. Cut to the shower, where he gently washes the melon. After the bath, he lovingly dries and puts talcum powder on the melon before taking a butcher knife and slowly inserting it through the green skin, the white rind, and finally into the red meat. He carves out an elongated orifice, then trembles as he slides down his pants and begins to penetrate the melon, only to fall back into the chair: "Premature ejaculation!"

Cláudio, as male protagonist, is the central element in Andrade's parody of the *pornochanchada* and its most sacred "value," *machismo*. He is, in fact, exactly the opposite of what one has come to expect from the male characters in that genre. Rather than a strong, masculine character, he is effeminate and speaks with a lisp. Unlike the macho, he suffers sexual problems (e.g., premature ejaculation). His gestures and demeanor, and his "relations" with the watermelon emphasize his latent homosexuality. At one point the melon "forces" him to perform fellatio on its stem. The melon is, as the Museum of Modern Art's program notes observe, "polymorphously perverse" and takes on both masculine and feminine roles. Whereas the *pornochanchada* macho is typically wealthy, drives fast cars, lives in a luxury apartment, and dresses in the latest fashion, Cláudio rides a bicycle, lives very modestly with obvious financial difficulties, and is decidedly *démodé*. Whereas the macho chases and seduces myriad voluptuous women, Cláudio is limited to watermelons, though he does admit to having experimented with other fruits and vegetables. The only woman to appear in the film is, in fact, thin, brainy, and bookish—certainly not the "ideal" of the *pornochanchada*.

Andrade also parodies the cinematic language of the *pornochanchada* and its until recently unattainable (for reasons of censorship) model, the hard-core pornographic film. The smooth curves of watermelons take the place of titillating shots of breasts and buttocks. The camera is alternately participatory and objective. In a *tour de force* Andrade crosses the barrier that the pornographic film cannot cross: he films the sexual act *from the inside* by having the camera take up a position inside the melon and filming (supposed) penetration from that perspective. The film also discusses and criticizes the misogynist violence inherent in pornographic films, as, at one moment, Cláudio takes out his knife and "kills" his melon.

The film, which is shot in natural settings throughout, ends with singer Carlos Galhardo surrounded by beautiful women on an artificial tropical set and singing the final strains of "Vereda Tropical." The setting is that of a typical 1950s *chanchada*, an innocent and "pure" ambience. Although *Vereda Tropical* ostensibly deals with "abnormal" behavior, its emphasis is on gentleness, harmony, and the reconciliation of conflictive elements. Cristina, for example, does not censure Cláudio for his sexual preference, but agrees to join him in a fruit and vegetable/male and female orgy. "Normality" is thus resolved in "abnormality" as Joaquim Pedro de Andrade offers a carnivalesque view of sexuality in a world governed by what Bakhtin would call "gay relativity." In this sense *Vereda Tropical* is a truly liberating film.

When *Macunaíma* appeared in 1969, concrete poet Décio Pignatari described it as being "Mário de Andrade [the author of the novel] revised by Oswald [de Andrade, none of them related]."[23] Oswald de Andrade was the

Plate 5. The Two Oswalds and Branca Clara, *O Homen do Pau-Brasil (The Brazilwood Man)*

rebellious, irreverent, and sometimes revolutionary spirit behind the modernist movement of the 1920s whom the concretists have praised for his radical formal solutions to questions of literary techniques and for his generally iconoclastic attitude toward social mores and artistic conventions.

Joaquim Pedro de Andrade's most recent film, *O Homem do Pau-Brasil (The Brazilwood Man)*, continues the discussion of modernism begun in *Macunaíma* by creating a fictional biography of the life and work of Oswald de Andrade. The film's punning title (*pau* in Portuguese means both "wood" and, in slang, "penis") derives from Oswald de Andrade's 1924 manifesto and volume of poetry titled *Pau-Brasil*. Oswald based the "brazilwood" manifesto and the "movement" he claimed to have initiated on the concept of a native originality that combined elements of Brazilian popular culture (which the academic discourse of Brazil's literary establishment had marginalized) with elements of modern technological society as a means of synthesizing the foreign/national dialectic of Brazilian modernist art. The movement attempted to be "modern" without rejecting the best of Brazilian traditions.

In 1928 Oswald de Andrade re-elaborated and radicalized the "brazilwood" manifesto in the "Manifesto Antropófago" ("Cannibalist Manifesto"), published in the first number of the *Revista de Antropofagia* (*Cannibalist Review*). Using the cannibal as symbol, this manifesto recognizes the need for taking advantage of positive influences wherever they may come from and adapting them to Brazilian reality as a way of assimilating and organizing elements already saturated with cultural meaning. Imported cultural influences must be devoured, digested, and critically re-elaborated in terms of local conditions.

Lévy-Bruhl's concept of the primitive mind as being at a prelogical stage and Keyserling's idea that modern, civilized man, alienated by technology, rather than primitive man, is the true barbarian influenced Oswald de Andrade's anthropophagous program. Oswald accepts the advantages of technological society but rejects the analytical consciousness that it entails. His program expresses the utopian desire for a return to a mythical golden age of primitive, matriarchal society, when enemies were eaten rather than enslaved. He calls such a return the Caraíba Revolution. His cannibal is not the romantic ideal of the noble savage, but rather corresponds more to Montaigne's cannibal, who devours enemies as a supreme act of vengeance.

O Homem do Pau-Brasil is not merely a panegyric to one of the great figures of modern Brazilian literature; rather, it assumes much of its subject's irreverent, critical, "cannibalistic" attitudes in its intertextual discussion of his life and work. It alternately approaches and backs away from the object of its discourse, criticizes that which is frivolous in Oswald de Andrade's ideas while retaining their essense. The film takes the idea of the Caraíba Revolution to its ultimate conclusion as the phallus is finally transferred from man to woman.

The film is a collage of Oswald de Andrade's texts, ranging from the Week of Modern Art in São Paulo (1922) to his manifestoes, from his novels *Memórias Sentimentais de João Miramar* (1924; translated as *Sentimental Memoirs of John Seaborne*) and *Serafim Ponte-Grande* (1933; translated as *Seraphim Grosse Pointe*), to his dramas of the 1930s (*O Homem do Cavalo* [1934; *The Horseman*] and *O Rei da Vela* [1937; *The Candle King*]), and to the philosophical treatises of his later life in which he returned to and expanded his utopian philosophy based on the idea of a return to matriarchal society.

But these excerpts do not rigidly follow the chronological sequence in which they were produced. The film's Week of Modern Art, for example, which is shown to be a much more timid event than literary history would have it, includes excerpts from Oswald de Andrade's poetry and from the "brazilwood" manifesto, which was written two years later. Joaquim Pedro de Andrade's "unfaithful" attitude toward his subject develops a creative, intertextual tension between Oswald de Andrade's life, his writing, and the film itself.

As João Luiz Vieira has so perceptively pointed out, Joaquim Pedro de Andrade was also "unfaithful" to the genre of fictional biography.[24] He in no way helps the viewer identify, in historical terms, the major characters of his drama. Scholars of Brazilian modernism will immediately recognize and understand the role of such figures as Mário de Andrade, Paulo Prado, Graça Aranha (Aranha sem Graça in the film), Blaise Cendrars, and Oswald himself, but the film itself provides little biographical information, focusing instead on the ideas of the period.

Just as the director is unconcerned with a "realistic" reconstruction of Oswald de Andrade's writing, so too does he reject a conventional view of Oswald the man. In a *tour de force*, Oswald de Andrade is played by two actors, one male (Flávio Galvão) and one female (Itala Nandi), normally appearing in scene simultaneously. In this sense, Joaquim Pedro de Andrade takes Buñuel's character doubling of *That Obscure Object of Desire* a step farther. The duplication of Oswald de Andrade not only serves as a source of the film's humor and as a distancing device, but also, and more importantly, as a visualization of his philosophical concept of a matriarchal society. With regard to humor, the doubling of the character frequently combines with the double entendre of the film's title for ironic effect, as Oswald-female speaks of her "erection" and of her "brilliant idea of buggering Martins Fontes."

His romantic involvement with a series of women marks the intellectual phases of Oswald's life. Initially, Oswald lives with Lalá, whom he excites sexually by reading Freud. At the same time, he is infatuated with the underage, neophyte dancer Dorotéia (played by Cristina Aché). Later, his passion turns toward Branca Clara, the filmic representation of painter Tarsila do Amaral (played by Dina Sfat, Ci of *Macunaíma*). In the period when he elaborates his esthetic and cultural ideas, he travels to Europe with her on the ship *Rompe-Nuvem*, decorated in art deco luxury. In Paris they become involved with the European avant-garde, notably with Jean Cocteau and Blaise Cendrars (Blaise Sans Bras in the film). The latter returns to Brazil with them to make a "100 percent Brazilian film." The appearance of Grande Otelo (black Macunaíma in the earlier film) brings out wonderfully the European infatuation with primitivism in this segment of the film. In Branca Clara's studio, the Grande Otelo figure, Fillet, looks at the painting *A Negra* (1923) and says, between bites of his banana, "C'est vovó!" ("It's grandma!") On board the ship returning to Brazil, Oswald invents the "cannibalist movement" while dining on frog legs.

Back in Brazil, Oswald becomes infatuated with Rosa Lituana (Patrícia "Pagu" Galvão, played by Dora Peregrino), whose influence leads him to join the Communist party. He temporarily abandons his aristocratic life-style, but his irreverence and anarchistic humor cannot accept the rigors of party discipline. He then hijacks the yacht of the millionaire Capone and travels to a deserted island to install his immaculate revolution. But his involvement with the Communist party had convinced Rosa Lituana and his female half of his affirmation of patriarchal society, and they revolt against him. In the film's ending, Oswald-male's erect penis (the "pau" of the title is finally realized) is commandeered by Oswald-female, who embarks on the path of the matriarchal revolution.

In its construction, *O Homem do Pau-Brasil* adapts less the facts of Oswald de Andrade's life than its spirit. It is irreverent, iconoclastic, sarcastic, and, above all, carnivalesque. The vulgarity of the characters' dialogue constantly undercuts much of the film's elegant *mise-en-scène*, thus Joaquim Pedro Andrade rejects bourgeois values of good taste.[25] In Oswald de Andrade, Joaquim Pedro de Andrade has found his perfect match. Both have managed to develop critical views of Brazilian social and sexual structures, and both have managed to do so while preserving a keen sense of irony and an intelligent use of satire.

2. Carlos Diegues: *Alegoria, Alegria*

> *Cinema is not the reproduction of reality. It implies
> the creation of a parallel, alternative, and verisimilar
> universe. This verisimilitude nourishes itself more
> on the spirit and ideology of the spectator than on
> his or her daily experience.*
>
> —Carlos Diegues

Of all the Cinema Novo directors, Carlos Diegues is perhaps the most intensely personal in his approach to filmmaking. His films consume his energy and emotions as they successively occupy the center of his creative life. Since he has given so much of himself emotionally and psychologically to his cinematic production, it is not surprising that over the years he has become, with the obvious exception of Glauber Rocha, the most controversial of the Cinema Novo directors. His films provoke virulent debates that reflect the increasing polarization of different sectors of Brazilian cinema. One example is the polemic that raged when in 1976 he denounced what he called "ideological patrols," that is, certain leftist critics who expect, indeed demand, that he and other artists follow what the Left has decided to be the "correct" political and ideological line. Carlos Diegues has always defended a cinematic and cultural pluralism, the freedom of the artist to express himself or herself as he or she sees fit. In this sense he has properly opposed authoritarianism of both the Right *and* the Left, and for this he has been harshly criticized by both sides.

Born on 19 May 1940, in Maceió, the capital of the northeastern state of Alagoas. After moving with his family to Rio de Janeiro, he completed a degree in law at the Catholic University, but decided to take up filmmaking. He worked as a journalist for several years and was active in film societies both at the Catholic University and at Rio de Janeiro's Museum of Modern Art, where many of the original participants of Cinema Novo met each other. He made his first short film, in 16mm, in the late 1950s. An active participant in student politics, Diegues's first professional film,

Diegues is one of Cinema Novo's major theoreticians and has explained its significance and changes throughout its trajectory. He was one of the first to define Cinema Novo and one of the first to declare it moribund. He was also one of the first to protest the mythification of Cinema Novo, even calling into question its very existence as a collective movement.

Diegues's own early definition of Cinema Novo is perhaps the best clue to understanding the movement as a whole and his own filmic production. In an article written in 1962 for the National Students' Union magazine, *Movimento 2*, he noted that the purpose of new Brazilian cinema was "to study in depth the social relations of each city and region as a way of critically exposing, as if in miniature, the sociocultural structure of the country as a whole. To take the people as theme, to give human form to fundamental conflicts, to make the people the center and master of the cinematic universe."[1] Cinema Novo, he continued, is a socially committed cinema, a critical cinema turned toward the problems of Brazil and its people. But this critical cinema is made by individuals, and the individuality of each film and filmmaker must be defended, because "Cinema Novo is above all freedom. Freedom of invention, freedom of expression. . . . Cinema Novo is not a *school*, it has no established style."[2]

Throughout his filmmaking career, Cacá Diegues reveals a concern with freedom, a concern that goes beyond a mere freedom of expression for the *auteur* to become one of the major thematic threads running through his production: freedom from slavery (*Ganga Zumba* and *Xica da Silva*), from economic marginalization (*The Big City*), from foreign domination and neocolonialism (*Joana Francesa* and *Bye Bye Brasil*), freedom to love, regardless of age (*Summer Showers*).[3]

Equally central to the director's theory of filmmaking is a concern with the relationship between the film and the spectator, that is, with how a film is perceived and understood by the spectator and what form of cinematic discourse is most conducive to that understanding. Such a concern has led Diegues to experiment with different cinematic styles and modes of

---

Escola de Samba, Alegria de Viver (Samba School, Joy of Living, 1962), was made as part of the CPC-produced *Cinco Vezes Favela*. He directed his first feature, *Ganga Zumba*, in 1963. His filmography includes the features *A Grande Cidade (The Big City*, 1966), *Os Herdeiros (The Heirs*, 1968), *Quando o Carnaval Chegar (When Carnival Comes*, 1972), *Joana Francesca (Joana the Frenchwoman*, 1974), *Xica da Silva*, (1976), *Chuvas de Verão (Summer Showers*, 1978), and *Bye Bye Brasil* (1980). He is currently working on a sequel to *Ganga Zumba* about the slave Republic of Palmares. In 1970 he made a film for French television, *Un Séjour*, which has yet to be exhibited in Brazil. With eight features, he ranks behind only Nelson Pereira dos Santos as the most prolific director of the Cinema Novo generation. He has also been a productive writer as one of the major spokesmen of modern Brazilian cinema.

discourse, ranging from the slow, deliberate realism of *Ganga Zumba* to the carnivalesque exuberance of *Xica da Silva*; from the "non-Cartesian," nonlinear *The Heirs* to the musical comedy *Quando o Carnaval Chegar*; from the political didacticism of *Escola de Samba, Alegria de Viver* to the "Hollywoodian" *Bye Bye Brasil*. This preoccupation with spectacle is often internalized as the films self-reflexively discuss modes and forms of representation. One might even say that the central theme of all of Diegues's films is Brazilian cinema itself in its multiplicity of themes and styles. Diegues is thus a director in search of a style, or a director whose style is stylistic pluralism itself.

The search or quest, whether for a style or for freedom, is a major motif in many of Diegues's films, and it often takes on an allegorical form, whence the title of this chapter (*alegoria* ["allegory"], *alegria* ["joy"]). Freedom is often synonymous with joy or happiness, even though several of his films would seem at first glance to be extremely pessimistic. His films, taken as a single text, represent an allegorical quest for that freedom (or happiness), although freedom (and happiness) may be conceived differently in different films.

This allegorical quest, moreover, is eminently political. In discussing his use of allegory—"fable," in his words—in *Ganga Zumba*, Diegues explains that he believes "in the fable as an example, as a means of communication between a petit-bourgeois filmmaker and a public that in its great majority has not yet acquired a consciousness of its own problematic in objective terms."[4] The idea is that the spectator will take the "fable" as presented and develop analogies with his or her own socioeconomic situation. The use of allegory thus presupposes a high degree of spectator participation. It is not the filmmaker's duty to transmit didactic "lessons," but rather to involve the spectators in the act of communication and allow them to make the proper connections.

Diegues's concept of joy and happiness is also political. He correctly attacks the humorlessness of much of the Left's criticism and filmmaking in a more recent interview: "A more just and free society means a more joyous one as well. An intellectual perversion places pleasure on the Right, suffering on the Left. Celebrating failures, deploring victories. Placing reason to the left of dreams; emotion to the right of intelligence."[5]

Diegues's first professional film, *Escola de Samba, Alegria de Viver* reflects the populism and romantic political enthusiasm of the earliest phase of Cinema Novo, when filmmakers felt that the mere denunciation of a situation was enough to change it and that a call to action by middle-class artists and intellectuals was sufficient to cause the "people" (seen in mythic terms) to rise up and transform society. *Escola de Samba*, as part of *Cinco Vezes Favela*, is flawed by an overly paternalistic vision of one of the most important popular phenomena of Brazilian society: the samba schools that

Plate 6. *Escola de Samba, Alegria de Viver (Samba School, Joy of Living)*

are spontaneously organized by slum dwellers to permit their collective participation in Carnival activities. Based on a story by CPC director Carlos Estevam Martins and edited by Ruy Guerra, *Escola de Samba* depicts the economic problems one samba school confronts in the period preceding Carnival. The film features late Brazilian playwright Oduvaldo Vianna Filho (one of the founders of the CPC) in the lead role.

Escola de Samba is weak in conception and flawed in its realization. Its sound is particularly uneven throughout. It is a view from the outside looking in, and rejects popular culture in favor of a paternalistic, populist view of the people. It fails to recognize the samba school as an important collective activity, but sees it merely as a form of alienation. The slum dwellers, the film seems to say, should be more concerned with union organizing than with Carnival. It shares the negativism of Joaquim Pedro de Andrade's *Garrincha, Alegria do Povo*, which sees soccer as an alienating phenomenon. Both films, ironically, use the word *"alegria"* ("joy") in their titles, yet neither recognizes the people's true joy and happiness in their participation in soccer and Carnival.

Like Andrade, however, Diegues later realized the paternalistic nature of his early film. "In a certain sense," he says, "it is a naive film, like the others made at that time, still perplexed by our discovery of Brazil's misery. . . . The social and political problems were not felt, but rather rationalized through a preconceived ideology and world view."[6]

Implicit in *Escola de Samba* is an interest in black culture, but Diegues develops this interest fully only in his first feature, *Ganga Zumba*, made at age twenty-three. It is often said that Brazilian culture is the result of the mixture of European, African, and indigenous cultures; yet, until recently, blacks and Indians have been represented only sparsely in Brazilian cinema and even then, frequently, stereotypically. Cacá Diegues's declared purpose in *Ganga Zumba* was to make not only a film about the black struggle in colonial Brazil, but also a film relating that struggle from the blacks' point of view and giving black culture value in and of itself.

Like many of Diegues's films, *Ganga Zumba* deals with history. But the dominant ideology writes history and often ignores what might be called the dominated ideology. According to the official version of history, such as that propagated by sociologist Gilberto Freyre, master-slave relations in Brazil were more "cordial" than, for example, in the United States, since the Portuguese were supposedly less brutal than their American counterparts. For this reason, and because of the relatively high degree of miscegenation in the country, Brazil has long claimed a mythical racial democracy, a myth that there is no racism in Brazil and that slave revolts were minor events in Brazilian history. But as historian Richard Morse once remarked, the dead of Brazil's "cordial" past are doubly dead: they not only died physically, but also have been eliminated from the official version of history.

In *Ganga Zumba* Diegues attempts to give an idea of the forgotten side of history, to show the brutality of master-slave relations and the slaves' struggle for freedom. Based on historical events, black myths, and a novel by João Felício dos Santos titled *Ganga Zumba, Zumbi dos Palmares*, the film tells of a slave revolt on a sugarcane plantation in Brazil's Northeast in 1641. It opens with a series of etchings recounting the black experience in Brazil as a voice-over tells the story of the Republic of Palmares, a *quilombo* (free community) set up in the mid-seventeenth century by runaway slaves in what are now the states of Alagoas and Pernambuco. Palmares lasted nearly half a century before being crushed by Portuguese troops. It comprised ten to twelve villages inhabited by nearly twenty thousand escaped slaves. It had its own system of government and a diversified agriculture, in contrast to the monoculture of sugar the Portuguese implanted. The novel on which *Ganga Zumba* is based not only deals with a slave revolt on a plantation, but also follows Palmares until its tragic end. Because of financial and technical limitations, however, Carlos Diegues utilized only the first half of the novel in his film.

After the etchings and the narration, but before the credits, the film focuses on a group of slaves moving slowly in the dark toward the camera. The shot begins at an extreme distance, which gradually lessens as the group nears the camera. Before any explanation of the identity of these people, the film cuts to a shot of another group standing near the door of the plantation house, with the first group's music—a *candomblé* (syncretic Afro-Brazilian religion) chant—in the background. An audiovisual opposition thus develops immediately between the two groups, the slaves and the masters, and it is only then that we see the object of the slaves' attention: a person chained to a stake. At first we see only the person's back, then a series of close shots of the mourners as they move in and out of focus. There is a cut to a close of shackled hands, then the hand-held camera tilts to show a woman in chains. Then the film cuts to the master's house, showing the effect (the woman in chains) before the cause. After a series of shots of sorrowful yet defiant black faces, of African drums, of wrung hands, of the woman in chains, the film cuts to a close of Antão, *Ganga Zumba*'s protagonist, in tears, then to a two-shot of Antão and Aroroba, the slave leader. In opposition to them, we once again see the master's house. This precredits sequence synthesizes *Ganga Zumba* thematically: the brutality of slavery, the sadness and defiance on the faces of Antão and Aroroba, and the vitality of African culture in Brazil despite the violence imposed on it. It also synthesizes *Ganga Zumba* visually: the use of hand-held camera, the alternation of extreme long and close shots, the development of ideological and political oppositions through montage. Stylistically, the film combines Eisensteinian montage sequences with sequences reminiscent in tone of neorealism.

Ganga Zumba presents a sort of case study of what educator Paulo Freire has called *conscientização* (consciousness-raising). It is through the transformation of the protagonist's consciousness from naive to revolutionary that the film's allegory operates. Antão (played by Antônio Pitanga) is Ganga Zumba, son of Zambi, the king of Palmares, but he is unaware of his own history until midway in the film. Zambi, who does not appear in the film, takes on mythological significance as the symbol of black liberation, as does Palmares. Antão, though, seems to be more concerned with women and playfulness than with the slaves' struggle for freedom. Initially, he is a child-like figure, but he gradually matures into a leader. The overseer's brutality is constant in the background as he mercilessly flogs one slave or another.

Cipriana brings Diegues's concern with representation and self-reflection into the film. As the overseer is distracted, two slaves slip off into the cane to receive orders from Zambi. The overseer sends Antão, apparently oblivious to all of this, after water. He meets the woman Cipriana near the river, and in extreme long shots they romp and play in the water. The tremendous distance of the camera reinforces the irreality of their playing. The film cuts to a medium shot as the two of them begin to act out the drama of "overseer and slave," with Cipriana pretending to whip Antão. Their playacting repeats the action of the film itself and stresses that the film is no more than a *representation*, an imitation of a very painful reality, and that the true struggle lies with the spectators themselves.

As they lie down, Antão threatens to kill the overseer. Only then do we realize that he too is concerned with Palmares, where "people don't have to hide to make love," where "there are no masters or slaves." But Cipriana is more skeptical. "Whites are also slaves of whites," she says in obvious reference to Brazil's current economic conjuncture. "Aroroba wants to cease being a slave of whites in order to be a slave of blacks. Going to Palmares we will only change shanties and overseers. We have to be our own boss."

Her individualist thesis counterpoints the collective desire for freedom shown by the slaves and the need for individual freedom and individual choice (a major thesis running throughout Diegues's filmic production). As he himself noted on the occasion of *Ganga Zumba*'s release, "The words are the same for everyone: love, freedom, war, suffering, faith, etc., but in each spirit they have a different meaning. People are victims of their own history until each one chooses his or her own path."[7] Within the collectivity, individual decisions and options must be made; the individual is responsible for the collectivity. As Antão says in response to Cipriana's skepticism, "We have to risk it." Later in the film, Cipriana acts on her own ideas and abandons the group going to Palmares; instead, she decides to stay with a fisherman, himself an escaped slave. There are many roads to freedom, the director seems to be saying.

The rest of *Ganga Zumba* tells of the slaves' plan to escape to Palmares, of their victories and defeats, of their struggles with the overseer. When the day of escape arrives, however, Antão does not appear and, dangerously, keeps the others waiting. He had stayed behind to carry out his threat to kill the overseer. Cipriana had agreed to seduce the overseer, and once he was distracted, Antão would kill him. He not only kills him, but also cuts out his heart and delivers it to Aroroba. This action is reminiscent of Fanon's idea that freedom from slavery or colonialism will come only through violence against the master and that only violence will cleanse the slave of the stigma of slavery.[8] As Glauber Rocha writes, "Only when confronted with violence does the colonizer understand, through horror, the strength of the culture he exploits. As long as they do not take up arms, the colonized remain slaves; a first policeman had to die for the French to become aware of the Algerians."[9]

The culture of the slaves gains in importance throughout the film. The precredits etchings present an already-codified visual representation of black culture in Brazil. The precredits sequence that follows the etchings introduces African religious chants, which are repeated throughout the film. The musical soundtrack, composed by a black, Moacyr Santos, develops African themes into more stylized compositions. *Candomblé* is present throughout, in the slaves' chants and rituals, and in the amulet Aroroba gives Antão when he tells him he is Ganga Zumba. As they plan for escape, the slaves silently practice *capoeira*, an African art of self-defense banned by the Portuguese. An Eisensteinian sequence presents an African *samba de roda*, thereby giving value to the different elements that make up this traditional form of dance. Afro-Brazilian culture is pictured as somehow transcendent, destined to overcome any temporary situation of political repression.

Speaking of the film shortly before the military coup of 1964, Carlos Diegues explained its analogical nature. His purpose was "to develop a fable, to try to find the link that connects consciousness and the spontaneous culture of the masses in a higher degree of a critique of reality . . . which can serve as an example of other forms of analogous and fundamental behavior . . . in the modern world."[10] Although perhaps overly simplistic and didactic (at one point Antão looks at the camera and yells, "We have to do something"), especially in its Manichaean view of social relationships, *Ganga Zumba* is one of the first Cinema Novo films to give value to Afro-Brazilian culture per se, without seeing it merely as a source of alienation. In *Ganga Zumba* Afro-Brazilian religion serves as a unifying activity that gives strength to the collectivity.

Ganga Zumba shares with other first-phase Cinema Novo films a commitment to realism as the privileged mode of cinematic discourse. Although I have termed some sequences "Eisensteinian," those sequences lack the didacticism of Eisenstein, but instead reveal through montage the multiplicity of elements and emotions making up African rituals and dances. The film attempts to portray on screen the legends and myths of the black struggle for freedom in Brazil. Its predominantly slow, deliberate rhythm, counterpointed by rapid cutting in the *candomblé* sequences, is also typical of the general text of first-phase films. The style changes dramatically in Diegues's second feature, *The Big City*.

Carlos Diegues describes *The Big City* as an "urban fable," but unlike his earlier fable, *Ganga Zumba*, which developed a realistic narrative from history and myth, *The Big City* starts from the painful reality of the modern urban drama—more specifically the problem of internal migration—and works toward the mythological. *The Big City*, in this sense, is the converse of *Ganga Zumba*. It is a film in which realism as such breaks down, giving way to a discontinuity of representation and an almost surreal *mise-en-*

Plate 7. Anecy Rocha, *A Grande Cidade (The Big City)*

scène. It is a drama not so much integrated into the city as it is played out
against it. Its protagonists—Calunga, Luzia, Inácio de Loyola, and Jasão—
are all marginal elements who have at one time or another migrated to the
urban center, which becomes a stage for their actions.

The Big City provides continuity with first-phase Cinema Novo, but not
so much with Diegues's own contribution to that phase as with films such as
dos Santos's *Vidas Secas,* Guerra's *The Guns* (1964), and Rocha's *Black
God, White Devil* (1964), all of which concern problems related to drought
in the Northeast. In the first two films, there is a movement south, as
peasants are forced to flee in order to survive. *The Big City* shows what
happens when they arrive.

Subtitled "The Adventures and Misadventures of Luzia and Her Friends,
Come from Afar," *The Big City* is a mosaic of situations, types of behavior,
and frustrated dreams. Each of the central characters is a type whose actions
are conducive to the maintenance of the stereotype. Luzia is the innocent
woman lost in the big city; Inácio de Loyola, as the name suggests, maintains
traditional religious and moral values and longs to return to the *sertão*
(northeastern backlands) where, according to him, things are more orderly
and traditions are revered; Jasão represents the transferral of *cangaceiro*

(northeastern bandit) violence from the *sertão* to the city. But Calunga (played by Antônio Pitanga) is the central figure of *The Big City*. He serves not only as a foil to the naïveté of Luzia and the ingenuous religiosity of Inácio de Loyola, but also as the *meneur de jeu* of the film itself, a kind of one-man chorus who guides the other characters, creates situations, and comments on the action.[11]

The Big City continues and deepens *Ganga Zumba*'s concern with modes of representation. It opens with a postcard view of Rio de Janeiro over which is superimposed a quotation from Padre Simão Vasconcelos about the beauty and wonders of the locale. This seventeenth-century quotation lends an ironic tone to the film's discourse.

Calunga suddenly appears, overlooking the city. In discontinuous jump cuts he appears in a park, on a street, taking an informal poll about the lives of "average" citizens, asking them how much time they spend at different activities. He then looks at the camera and asks us as spectators what we are doing at the movies. The cinema, he says, is "a temple of magicians, a dream factory, a source of memory. . . . I have laughter and tears to give you," he continues, "but not forgetfulness." His apparently spontaneous definition of the cinema corresponds to that of Carlos Diegues: a form of entertainment filled with "laughter and tears," but one with a social responsibility that cannot be forgotten.

Cinematic self-referentiality pervades the film, which borrows and "quotes" from traditional cinematic genres: romantic comedy, police drama, western, silent comedy. *The Big City* also quotes indirectly, in the oneiric *cangaceiro* sequence, Glauber Rocha's *Black God, White Devil*, in which it was prophesied that "the *sertão* will become the sea, the sea, *sertão*."

Calunga's world, like that of cinema itself, is one of fantasy; his Rio de Janeiro is the stereotypical vision of eternal playfulness, but his spontaneity contrasts sharply with the problems the other characters confront. Although he refuses to become directly involved in their drama, he is drawn, almost in spite of himself, into it as he helps Luzia in her search for Jasão. His vision of the city is, in this sense, revealed to be false.

The Big City is divided into four segments, each of which carries the name of the character whose "drama" colors it. The first block concerns Luzia (played by Anecy Rocha), her arrival in the city, and her initial contact with Jasão. It is in this block that the film's conflicts are introduced. The city serves both as Calunga's playground and as Jasão's turf, as a cause of Luzia's hope and fear and as a stage across which Inácio de Loyola must pass before returning to the *sertão*.

The initial block also introduces the film's dominant style: a synthesis, of discontinuity (through jump cuts) and the documentary (stills and newsreel footage), that contrasts the personal drama of the four characters with the harsh, objective reality of the city. Although much of the film's discourse is realistic in nature, the film ultimately rejects realism as a form of cinematic representation. In some sequences, for example, the fantasies of Inácio de Loyola, who longs to return to the *sertão*, it even approaches the surreal.

The second block deals with Jasão and his life of crime in the city. Jasão was to marry Luzia in the Northeast, but economic difficulties forced him to leave for the city. After initially rejecting Luzia in the city, he sends her a message via Calunga. As the two of them talk, the camera zooms back from a medium to an extreme long shot, as if to emphasize the growing distance between them and the impossibility of love in the city. Jasão and Luzia are finally reunited, and their personal history is told in a brief flashback. Jasão promises Luzia that he will leave with her after one more job, the assassination of a senator. Luzia learns of the crime through a newspaper, which also brings news of the military government's decree of the Second Institutional Act, which further limits the rights of Brazilian citizens. History thus serves as a backdrop to the film's story.

The third block carries Inácio's name, but opens with a discussion among intellectuals (with director Arnaldo Jabor in the role of an American novelist) in a house where Luzia works as a maid. As she serves them, they talk about the relationship between art and reality and about Vaqueiro (Jasão), who is on the front page of all the newspapers. The sterility of their discussion shows the great distance between "elite" culture and the people, and thus reflects and criticizes the relationship between first-phase Cinema Novo and its (absent) public.

Inácio de Loyola represents a conservative ideology of resignation to and maintenance of traditional values.[12] He believes in the values the transistor radio he carries transmits, values reflective of the holders of economic power. Inácio speaks of a division of power, but feels that things are as they should be. His ideology is a contradiction in terms of his own class. Capitalist society has marginalized him, but he does nothing to struggle against his marginalization. He longs for the "order and respect" of Pedro II's empire (which ended in 1889). His is an ideology that looks toward the past, never to the future, except in idyllic terms. He has idealized the Northeast as a terrestrial paradise, but the discourse undercuts and criticizes his vision: a series of stills showing the misery of the region accompany his talk of returning.

The documentary mode of discourse reaches its most important moment in this section of the film. As Inácio de Loyola and Luzia take a bus to a distant beach and talk of the *sertão*, the camera tracks, in a simulated newsreel sequence, along military vehicles and equipment displayed along the beach road. Political repression accompanies people like Inácio de Loyola and ensures their economic repression. The film's "surreal" discourse also peaks in this segment, as Inácio imagines himself running into the sea and Vaqueiro as a *cangaceiro* riding into the wind. Projected in negative, this sequence lends an eerie tone to the dialogue and points out the dreamlike quality of Inácio de Loyola's arguments and Luzia's hopes.

During Carnival, Inácio de Loyola and Luzia go to church. Inácio longs for a society that does not permit such "decadence" as Carnival. Calunga appears with a message for Luzia to meet Vaqueiro near the ferry boat. Calunga then disappears into the Carnival festivities. But he has made the mistake of giving Luzia Vaqueiro's message in the presence of Inácio de Loyola, who inadvertently reveals its contents to a police informer. Calunga is thus indirectly responsible for the tragedy that follows and, despite himself, is drawn into the action. And this occurs precisely in the segment that carries his name. It is impossible for him to remain uncommitted and marginal to the conflicts and problems of society.

After Jasão and Luzia are gunned down by the police, Calunga runs through the streets of the city, oblivious to the festivities around him. His flight ends in a circular arena in which he mimes the events he has just witnessed. In the tradition of folk theater, reality becomes art as he re-creates the action, just as art (the film) becomes reality. Calunga no longer guides the action but rather follows it. His failure as a *meneur de jeu*, however, is consistent with the failure of the other characters to find what they had searched for in the city.

Jean-Claude Bernardet has perceptively observed that *The Big City* is a mosaic in which disparate elements are juxtaposed and played off against each other. It mixes the documentary and the fictional, modes of representation linked to the *cordel* ("popular poetry") and to comic strips, naturalistic sequences with surrealistic ones. The soundtrack obeys the same strategy, mixing rock and samba, Villa-Lobos and Bossa Nova, Roberto Carlos and classical harpsichord. Rather than being realistic, the film is spectacle presented as spectacle.[13]

The Big City marks an important step in Carlos Diegues's search for an original and effective form of cinematic communication. He has at least temporarily abandoned the realistic mode of *Escola de Samba, Alegria de Viver* and *Ganga Zumba* and the didacticism of those films. As Diegues himself observes, he is "not concerned with making purely social works nor with transmitting messages, because that is Western Union's job. But, of course, by being interested in the problems facing my country and the world, trying to understand them, it is evident that this concern will appear in my work."[14]

By the time he made *The Big City*, Diegues no longer saw cinema as an instrument of political mobilization. Rather, to him cinema is valid as an instrument of liberation to the extent that it reflects the historical moment and opens new perspectives for its public.

Carlos Diegues granted an extensive interview to Rogério Sganzerla after completing *The Big City*. It is perhaps a key to understanding not only

Diegues's filmic production but also the general evolution of Cinema Novo in the period from 1964 to 1968. He begins by saying (and this in 1966) that there is no longer any reason to speak of Cinema Novo, since the movement, or "club" as he ironically calls it, has been diluted into Brazilian cinema as a whole. Although it originally had a common goal (to make Brazilian cinema), common tastes (those of Eisenstein, Welles, Rosselini, Antonioni, Godard), and a collaborative system of production, each director has by this time followed his own personal path. The goal remains the same—to make Brazilian films about Brazilian problems—but the tactics and strategies have multiplied, as has the number of cinéastes who share this goal. Cinema Novo, he suggests, should be no more than a historical reference point.[15]

By 1966, Diegues continues, Cinema Novo is freeing itself from the youthful prejudices of its initial phase: "For romantic and moral reasons . . . we made a certain type of committed cinema that became inevitably paternalistic. Any type of complexity was condemned as intellectualism and schematic solutions were thought of in terms of a mobilization that revealed itself to be inviable, in terms of a certain militancy that would finally become an alibi." Glauber Rocha's *Black God, White Devil* freed Cinema Novo from such paternalistic schematicism and allowed it to see its true task, that of being "the witness of a time and a world that is not consumed merely in the social relations of work, but that interrogates the very consciousness of man in his multiplicity and alienation."

Diegues repeats that all styles are possible and must be chosen by the individual filmmaker. He is interested in creating a new form of spectacle from "the ashes of intimist realism," a "spectacle that mixes politics and humor, Shakespeare and the *modinha de viola* [a form of folk music], the Beatles and Jorge de Lima, Pelé and Brecht, Maria Bethânia and Godard." In other words, Diegues calls for a breakdown of stratified, classical forms of cinematic discourse, and thus values the work of Godard, who "made two films in three weeks," over Antonioni, who "has spent months in Pinewood filming *Blow-Up*." Godard, camera in hand, "waits for reality on the corner, interpreting it in 'bistros,' questioning it and film as well." Godard's cinema is modern, says Diegues, whereas Antonioni's is "a museum piece."

The filmmaker is above all opinionated and critical and thus cannot live without also being political. But the true political work is to be left to politicians. The artist must be free to question and to serve as witness to his or her generation and the problems of society. Nobody is interested, Diegues observes, in the personal anguish and doubts of a filmmaker, and didacticism has no place in Third World cinema. "A delirious cinema, ideologically positioned, can be much more effective than a thousand films about nutrition, iron, or the fall of kings."

In his next film, *The Heirs*, Diegues attempts to create a Shakespearian climate in a Brechtian structure, though he is quick to note that modern cinema has more to do with Shakespeare than with Brecht,

primarily with regard to the conflicts and contradictions (at times paradoxical) of his themes. Politics as an existential tragedy and not as a speculative science: the fatalism of certain personages and situations (but not the "deus ex machina" of Greek tragedy, which in Shakespeare is substituted by History); the division of the central theme into infinite variations; the experience of the grotesque and the oneiric . . . but primarily the humanism of great artists, a humanism with dirty hands, the great tragedy of the impossibility of Good and Evil, the reconstruction of the world starting from its formidable defects.[16]

A humanistic cinema in which all of the contradictions of humanity may be expressed without resorting to ready-made formulas or cinematic strategies is Carlos Diegues's concern as he prepares the shooting of *The Heirs*, a film that takes the antirealism of *The Big City* a gigantic step forward.

The Heirs is intended as a mural of Brazilian political and cultural history from 1930 to 1964, seen through the trajectory of a single, bourgeois family. The family's trajectory parallels as well the political progression of Getúlio Vargas. Vargas rose to power in 1930 on the wave of a liberal revolution that resulted in part from the coffee crisis and the decadence of the rural oligarchy. In 1937 he decreed the corporativist "Estado Novo," linked in spirit to European fascism of the same period. Overthrown in 1945 by, once again, "liberal" generals and politicians, Vargas was reelected to the presidency in 1950 as a populist reformer. In 1954 he committed suicide, leaving an anti-imperialist, "socialist" message for the people. Such a trajectory—from liberal to fascist to populist—is of course fraught with contradiction, which Carlos Diegues attempts to reveal in *The Heirs*.

The film is divided into six blocks, each accounting for a specific moment of the political and cultural history in question: (1) 1930, the coffee crisis and the revolution; (2) 1940, the political struggle against the Estado Novo; (3) 1945, Vargas's overthrow; (4) 1954, Vargas's speech warning against the denationalization of the economy, and, eventually, his suicide; (5) 1960, the construction of Brasília; (6) 1964, the overthrow of João Goulart by the military.

Throughout this historical development, *The Heirs* follows the career of Jorge Ramos, who moves from idealistic young Communist pamphleteer to reactionary senator and member of the ruling elite. His major characteristic is the ability to betray anyone and everyone to maintain his hold on power. He spends his life attempting to rationalize or otherwise justify his "original sin," his initial betrayal. Arrested by the police for Communist agitation during Vargas's repressive Estado Novo, Ramos denounced his best friend, David, who died under torture. Sent by his newspaper to rest on a nearby coffee plantation (São Martinho), Jorge makes friends with the plantation owner, Joaquim de Almeida. Almeida, fearing the loss of his wealth at the hands of the "revolution," convinces Jorge to marry his daughter. The marriage should give him an heir and guarantee continuity in the plantation's administration. After linking up with the ruling class, albeit with a decadent sector of that class, Jorge Ramos's career follows the oscillations of Vargas's own political career.

In 1945 Ramos returns to his job with the *Diário Nacional*, whose owner is convinced that Vargas will one day return to power and who plans to support him in the newspaper. Vargas does return to power in 1950, and Jorge Ramos rises with him. A series of scenes concerning the National Radio, which functioned as a source of publicity for Getúlio Vargas, narrates Ramos's "city period." The subtitle of this block of the film is, in fact, "The Radio of the People, August 1954." Critic Sérgio Augusto suggests that *The Heirs* is "a political and cultural history of Brazil as we, contemporaries of Carlos Diegues, learned and accompanied it through the magic filter of the National Radio," which was "the exclusive channel of information and the cultural formation of the Brazilian people" during the period in question.[17]

By 1960 Ramos is a powerful senator considered in certain circles to be the spiritual heir of Vargas. He participates in the inauguration of Brasília, the symbol of populist, developmentalist ideology, and prepares a presidential campaign after having made a secret pact with his enemies. But by this time a new generation has risen, and his two sons, Joaquim (named after his grandfather, the plantation owner) and David (named after Ramos's murdered best friend) enter the scene. Joaquim denies and, by becoming active in the opposition, contests the very class to which he belongs and assumes the role of a member of the radical Left. David, Ramos's favorite son, is assassinated. Like Vargas, Ramos commits suicide. Joaquim quickly abandons his opposition and takes up his upper class values again.

According to Carlos Diegues, *The Heirs* is a film about forty years of national history and the "imprecise image of this strange, violent and sentimental, baroque and surreal, sincere and subtle country, this country whose passion torments [Diegues] more than anything else."[18] *The Heirs*, he says, is witness of his passion for Brazil. It is a film with multiple styles, "the result of a universe of contradictions and imprecisions—the political history of Brazil. But it is also a history of customs, behavior, a history within History. Each shot contains within itself the maximum of possible information going in different directions. These diverse levels intersect each other, complete each other, absorb each other, or collide with each other, forming a large mural of forty Brazilian years."[19]

Betrayal is the key in this film about a political heritage that changes hands but not its nature, about a political class that speaks in the name of the people to keep the people from assuming power, about, in short, the political development of Brazil over the last four decades. Although it is a film about politics—and more specifically about political betrayal—it goes far beyond traditional political analyses to discuss not so much the events themselves as the way in which these events have been interpreted. The historical events are not re-created in the film; rather, they are evoked allegorically through parallel actions of the principal characters and through the *mise-en-scène*.

Diegues develops this political and cultural history of Brazil in a strikingly original manner that does indeed combine Brecht and Shakespeare, Godard and Maria Bethânia (in the form of her brother, Caetano Veloso). In its six major blocks, everything corresponds to a style that reflects the period in question. The actor who plays Getúlio Vargas, for example, impersonated Vargas in musical reviews in the 1930s, so, when he appears on the screen, "his contemporaries do not see only an actor representing Vargas, but rather the whole atmosphere of a past in which this episode occurred."[20] Representation and history, art and reality, once again mix.

The setting and the mode of representation are highly synthetic. Although scenarios are designed to capture a specific atmosphere (a coffee plantation in a rapid process of decay, Rio de Janeiro's Municipal Theater, where the elite gathered, the Colombo confectionery, the open spaces of Brasília), the dominant mode of representation is Brechtian in its breakdown of realism and its symbolic use of gestures. As Diegues observes, "The action [of each block] begins in a very realistic manner and is gradually exacerbated, entering into conflict with itself, until it reaches a poetic synthesis in which time and action itself no longer have any relationship with the *real* of each sequence."[21]

Exemplary of this disintegration of realism is the use of inner-shot editing in the National Radio sequence. The sequence begins with a shot of two radio actresses recording an episode of a serial. The camera pans left until it focuses on Jorge Ramos, then farther to the left until it encompasses a singer (Odete Lara) and her band. It then tracks forward to a close of the singer's face before moving back once again to reveal a nearly empty scenario in which only Jorge and the singer appear. The band and the radio actresses have disappeared, leaving only the most important elements of the sequence's diegesis.

Synthesis is the most important technique in *The Heirs*. Diegues presents the elements of the equation schematically, and the spectator must connect them. In this sense the film is very much an open one (in Umberto Eco's usage of the term).[22] Examples of the film's synthetic nature abound. Jorge Ramos first appears passing out revolutionary pamphlets. Neither the people to whom he distributes them nor the police who later arrest him appear on the screen. Ramos distributes pamphlets to the air and, at the sound of approaching horses, flees to a cabaret where a transvestite Carmen

Miranda sings. The fact that the masses do not appear emphasizes Ramos's distance from them. The "people," in fact, rarely appear in the film at all, which indicates their marginalization from the Brazilian political process. As soon as a voice announces his arrest, a huge screen covered with a portrait of Vargas lowers before the camera while Jorge's off-camera screams at the hands of his torturers are heard.

The inauguration of Brasília offers another example of synthesis. Jorge Ramos in a tuxedo standing in the open spaces in front of the presidential palace while Jean-Pierre Leaud proffers a revolutionary discourse in French represent the official ceremonies. As critic José Carlos Avellar suggests, Carlos Diegues "rejects the simple illustration or narration of a naturalistic character in order to pursue an image between allegory and dreams capable of acting with a critical synthesis superior to that of an image situated on a realistic plane."[23] Diegues, moreover, observes that his intention is to "reveal the ghosts" of the past, ghosts that exist on a level that the naturalistic representation of historical events cannot capture.

On another level, *The Heirs* attempts to exorcise the myth of the Father, a myth virtually incarnate in the figure of Getúlio Vargas. Beginning with a quotation from *Hamlet* ("I am thy father's spirit"), Diegues attempts to analyze this father figure and his significance for modern Brazilian society: "The role of the Father is strongly related to the social, political, and also religious behavior of the Brazilian. In all the great mass phenomena of Brazil, the idea of paternalism is always understood. Fathers decide among themselves the destiny of the people, and the people obey. They even call Vargas the father of the poor. The idea of paternal protection is very deeply rooted in Brazilian history."[24] The symbolic death of the Father— through the double suicides of Vargas and Jorge Ramos—is a road toward the people's liberation. As long as the Father figure exists and rules, the people will never be free to determine their own destiny.

The Heirs has rightly been referred to as a "political opera," and Elia Kazan has praised its use of music and dance.[25] The film's principal musical theme is Heitor Villa-Lobos's "Invocação em Defesa da Pátria" ("Invocation in Defense of the Fatherland"), composed at the request of Vargas to honor the Brazilian soldiers who were leaving to fight in Italy in World War II. Villa-Lobos's "Segunda Sonata-Fantasma" ("Second Phantom-Sonata") for violin and piano is also used. Each historical block, furthermore, is accompanied by music representative of the period, drawn from the theater, radio, cinema, and television, including such foreign singers as Bing Crosby, who had a marked influence on Brazilian musical culture. *The Heirs*, like *The Big City*, is a politico-cultural mosaic of modern Brazil.

Dedicated to Cinema Novo, *The Heirs* perhaps closes for Carlos Diegues the historical cycle of that cinematic movement, a cycle of experimentation with cinematic form and political expression through cinema. A collage of many different styles, it, like *Macunaíma*, is a film without a style, a film that returns to a "degree zero" to open doors to the future:

> It is not a melodrama, but it uses melodrama. Sometimes critically, other times not. It is not realistic, but it is; it is not romantic, but it is. . . . When Cinema Novo began, we were inventing Brazil in cinema, or a cinema for Brazil (which is the same thing). Afterwards, we began to think about the destiny that we were fulfilling. And this almost led us to impotence. I made *The Heirs* to close the cycle of reflection. At least my reflection. From now on, only creation—action—is valid.[26]

In his next films, Diegues attempts to move toward a greater affinity with the Brazilian film public through the use of more traditional (and more commercially oriented) forms of cinematic discourse.

Ways of seeing and representing, the history of cinema, and the nature of popular spectacle continue to concern Carlos Diegues in *Quando o Carnaval Chegar*. With this film, the director returns to the form of the *chanchada*, the light musical comedy that was tremendously popular in Brazil between 1935 and 1960, when the genre began to die out because of the increasing importance of television. Cinema Novo, it might be remembered, was in part a reaction against the *chanchada* and its idealized vision of Brazilian society. *Quando o Carnaval Chegar* is the second musical comedy by a Cinema Novo director (the first was Leon Hirszman's melancholic *Garota de Ipanema* [*Girl from Ipanema*, 1967]).

According to the press book for *Quando o Carnaval Chegar*, it is "the first Brazilian musical within a new era of national cinema: after the *chanchada*, after Cinema Novo arises the cinema of the seventies, joyful, musical, relaxed, debauched, and colorful." *Quando o Carnaval Chegar* takes to the extreme Carlos Diegues's perhaps not very original idea, expressed by Calunga in *The Big City*, that cinema is "the temple of magicians" designed first and foremost to entertain. The film is carnivalesque in its very conception and plays with an idea that the director is to develop further in films such as *Xica da Silva*: one cannot underestimate the joy and festivities of the people as a liberating force. The fiesta is wherever the people are and derives from them rather than being imposed on them.

In *Quando o Carnaval Chegar* the gangster Anjo (Angel) contracts a musical troupe to perform at the "festa do rei" (festivities of the king). After several adventures and misadventures, the members of the troupe decide one by one that they do not want to perform in the festivities, thereby leaving the manager (played by Hugo Carvana) to deal with Anjo (José Lewgoy). Finally, even the manager joins in the troupe's refusal and rides off with them in their colorful bus. The plot is very simple, as were those of the *chanchada*.

Just as the *chanchada* used popular stars and the hit songs of Carnival, so too does *Quando o Carnaval Chegar* take advantage of the popularity of musicians such as Chico Buarque, Nara Leão (the director's wife at the time), and Maria Bethânia, who, together with the manager and Antônio Pitanga (Calunga in *The Big City*) compose the troupe. The selection of actors recognizes the film's intended audience, the middle-class, since the three singers appeal primarily to that class. The *chanchada*, on the other hand, used truly popular artists such as Grande Otelo. Chico Buarque, who composed much of the film's music, is perhaps best known for his consistent political opposition to the military regime and for songs that deal with the problems of the urban proletariat (e.g., "Pedro Pedreiro"). Nara Leão is one of the most important singers of the Bossa Nova period, and Maria Bethânia first became known through her participation in the politically oriented "Opinião" show in 1964, which attempted to unite middle-class and popular musicians.

Like *The Big City, Quando o Carnaval Chegar* is a collage of musical and cinematic references. The film opens with shots of dancers on a nightclub stage (à la Carmen Miranda musicals), then cuts to a street where preparations for Carnival are in full swing. On the right of the screen is a large screen saying merely "Oscarito" (with Grande Otelo, Oscarito epitomizes the *chanchada* in Brazilian cinema). The film then re-creates the entire sequence from Adhemar Gonzaga's *Alô Alô Carnaval* (1936), in which Carmen and Aurora Miranda (in this case Nara Leão and Maria Bethânia), dressed in tuxedos and top hats, sing "Nós Somos os Cantores do Rádio." *Quando o Carnaval Chegar* is filled with references to national and international cinematic tradition: Carvana sees actress Odete Lara in the hall of an office building and says he adored her in *Antônio das Mortes*; the film almost literally re-creates the typewriter gag from Chaplin's *The Great Dictator*; Chico Buarque sings "Swanee" in the style of Al Jolson before beginning his rendition of "Just One of Those Things"; on several occasions the troupe or one of its members breaks into "No Business Like Show Business." There are songs by Ari Barroso, Lamartine Babo, and Joubert de Almeida in homage to Brazilian popular music, and the film itself is of course an homage to the cultural universe of the *chanchada*; it even uses two actors (José Lewgoy and Wilson Grey) who earned their fame in that popular genre.

But the illusionistic naturalism of the *chanchada*'s mode of representation breaks down in *Quando o Carnaval Chegar*, as the singers often perform to highly decorated empty spaces or as, through jump cuts, they begin a song in one scenario (say, a stage) and finish it in another (along a deserted highway, for example). The diegesis itself becomes highly synthetic, much like that of *The Heirs*, without, however, that film's complexity. Although it would be possible to draw allegorical conclusions from the film (e.g., the "king" as the military government, the troupe as the "people" who decide to have their own festivities and refuse to obey the "king" or his henchmen; the empty spaces representing the impossibility of discussion under the repressive regime; the "carnival" as the allegorical overthrow of the military regime), Carlos Diegues insists that his intention was simply to make an enjoyable film that reflects the spontaneity of the Brazilian people. When asked if he saw *Quando o Carnaval Chegar* as a break with Cinema Novo, Diegues responded with a certain irritation: "As far as I'm concerned Cinema Novo never existed . . . so I cannot break with something that did not exist." He continued by saying that he was tired of the "authorial imposition" of the sixties, which he saw as fascist in its insistence and that now he was interested in a certain "relaxation within the tension" of military repression.[27] Although often overlooked by critics, *Quando o Carnaval Chegar* is an important film in Carlos Diegues's career, as it reflects and foreshadows a conception of cinema and a number of themes that will be more and more predominant in his films through the 1970s and into the 1980s.

With *Joana Francesa* Carlos Diegues returns to the thematics of *The Heirs* and to his intention of "revealing the ghosts" of Brazilian society through the dialectical setting of its fantasies against history. In *Joana Francesa* Diegues returns to 1930 and the liberal revolution that led Getúlio Vargas to power. The starting point for a discussion of forty years of history in *The Heirs*, in *Joana Francesa* the crisis of 1930 and its effect on the landed aristocracy becomes the central subject, even though it is clear that Diegues intends to speak not only of 1930 but also of the conjuncture in which he made the film. It is, in Diegues's own words, a film about death, about the death of a society and a civilization for which he wants to dig the grave. It is a film about the decadence and the sins of a class near the twilight of its existence.

Joana Francesa, narrated in the first person, tells the story of Jeanne, a French madame (played by Jeanne Moreau—it is often said ironically that Brazil imports everything, even prostitutes) in a São Paulo bordello who accepts an invitation by Aureliano (played by Carlos Kroeber) to live with him on his northeastern sugarcane plantation, Santa Rita. She had said that she would go with him after the death of his fatally ill wife, Das Dores, but finds when she arrives that Das Dores is still on her deathbed. As Jeanne becomes integrated and accepted into Aureliano's family, she assumes the sins of its decadence.

The family consists of Ricardo, Aureliano's illegitimate son, who runs off and supposedly joins a group of Brazilian "Bolsheviks"; Dona Olympia, Aureliano's neurotic mother, who plans and carries out her own death; Das Dores, who, on her deathbed, pleads for the "strength of her stud" and calls herself Aureliano's "mare"; Lianinho, Aureliano's oedipally inclined son; Dorinha and Honório, Aureliano's incestuous son and daughter; Gismundo,

Plate 8. Jeanne Moreau, *Joana Francesa (Joana the Frenchwoman)*

a black servant who is twice symbolically "mounted" by Jeanne; and a boy tied up and kept in a cage, who is, according to Dona Olympia, "the son of a great sin . . . the child of a son with his mother" (i.e., he is the son of Lianinho and Das Dores).

Set in the period immediately following the Revolution of 1930, which presaged the end of the landed oligarchy's power and the rise of the industrial bourgeoisie, *Joana Francesa* reflects the political and economic decadence of the infamous rural "colonels" and the supposedly impending death of the rural oligarchy under the administration of Vargas. It was during Vargas's term that the process of industrialization began to reach the plantations themselves and modernized processing factories began to replace the old sugar mills. In short, it was a period of political and economic transition and Aureliano's family was unable to accompany the rapid changes the country was undergoing.

The immediate economic conflict outlined in *Joana Francesa* is between Aureliano's Santa Rita plantation and a neighboring plantation owned by the Lima family. In conjunction with American interests, the Limas are modernizing their sugar mill and making plans that will inevitably disrupt the antiquated business of Santa Rita: they plan to extend a line of the railroad to their plantation for easier commercialization and want to divert the course of a local river to make it run through their property. Unable or unwilling to compete with or to participate in such changes, Aureliano's family slowly dies off, either consciously (Dona Olympia) or unconsciously, by drifting into madness.

As Jeanne is absorbed into the family and begins to share its secrets, she also absorbs its sins, and her own process of decay begins. Diegues has often said that *Joana Francesa* is the "story of and an experience in cultural anthropophagy, integrated on all levels with human behavior, where the end of society foreshadows the end of a civilization."[28]

The sins of Aureliano's family symbolically devour Jeanne. At times she identifies with Das Dores, to the point that Lianinho begins to think that his mother has returned from the dead. Later she takes on the deceased Dona Olympia's task of "exposing the sins of this house." Before her self-planned death, Dona Olympia exhorts Jeanne to kill the boy who resulted from the union of Lianinho and his mother, Das Dores: "Das Dores did not die a natural death. You killed her through the hands of Aureliano. Now take advantage of Lianinho's absence and finish what you began." If Jeanne is indeed responsible for the death of Das Dores, she is more clearly responsible for Lianinho's death, as she forces him to face his "execution" by the Lima family after he had killed one of their sons. She completes the cycle, at least indirectly, by driving Aureliano to madness and apparent suicide.

A double movement governs Jeanne's cannibalistic absorption. On the one hand Joana (no longer Jeanne) assumes the conservative values of a decadent class as she takes on the leadership role that Aureliano gradually abdicates and as the family absorbs her. Her relationship to Aureliano's incestuous children, Dorinha and Honório, reveals this evolution. Early in the film she finds them amusing as they bathe and play together, even to the point of thinking that they represent a breath of life among the dead and dying. Later, when she finds them making love in the bath, she chastizes them, calls them "scum" and "filth," and has them locked up in cages. From the "enlightened" madame of a São Paulo bordello she has become a conservative matriarch, a moralizing force consistent with the values of a decadent class. Her progressive assumption of Aureliano's role indicates her rise to power, a rise that climaxes when she determines that Lianinho will be a candidate for Congress in opposition to the Limas' candidate, and shortly thereafter, when she sends him to his death at the Limas' hands.

On the other hand, she is the "colonizing" agent that leads to the family's ultimate destruction. Two sequences, one near the beginning of the film and another at the end, further emphasize her colonizing role, as she rides on the black servant Gismundo's back. In Glauber Rocha's words, these sequences symbolize "Joana/DeGaulle riding Ganga Zumba/Lumumba [in] the true History of colonization. . . . Furthermore, Joana Francesa and Scarlett O'Hara . . . are fascist matriarchs."[29]

Joana becomes, through her relationships with Aureliano's family, an element of destruction, a mythical exterminating angel. As an agent of destruction, Joana's nature is reinforced by certain mythical elements in images of fire.[30] Immediately after she is seen sitting in Das Dores's rocking chair on the porch (the rocking chair is an element of her integration into the family) there follows an insert of a cane field burning. Such images accompany Joana throughout the remainder of the film. When her close friend the French consul (played by Pierre Cardin) visits her, there are additional shots of fields afire. The final image of destruction occurs when she orders Gismundo to burn down the shack where the retarded son of Das Dores and Lianinho is kept.

In opposition to fire (still on a mythic level) is water, which supports characters such as the incestuous children (they are first seen in the pool/bath), Gismundo (he controls the water level of the bath), Aureliano, and, at a certain moment, even Joana herself as she writes her memoirs while seated beside the river. That water is an ultimately positive, constructive element can be seen above all in the fact that the film's narrative is a visualization of Joana's memoirs.

A conflict thus appears on the mythic level between water (construction, life) and fire (destruction, death). Her relationship to these two elements traces the change Joana undergoes. She first meets Dorinha and Honório, for example, when they are in the bath, and immediately joins them in their fun, clothes and all. But as she changes, her attitude toward them (and toward water) changes. After catching them once again in the bath, she orders them punished. The dialectic of construction/destruction/deconstruction is the film's underlying structure. The *destruction* of Santa Rita and Aureliano's family is evoked by the *construction* of Joana's version of these events. Through its critical vision of Joana, the film's discourse encompasses, transcends, and ultimately deconstructs Joana's self-narrated story.

After the allegorical experience of *The Heirs* and, to a lesser degree, *Quando o Carnaval Chegar*, with their breakdown of traditional modes of representation, *Joana Francesa* returns to a classical narration and a realist mode of discourse. As Diegues notes, Brazilian cinema is in a process of rebuilding its relationship with the Brazilian public. He is interested in creating a "verisimilar cinema," constructed with truth as a starting point (people in confrontation with the world around them), organized within an alternative universe on the screen. *Joana Francesa* is structured classically through a long flashback as Joana writes her memoirs. Its careful, esthetic composition is reminiscent of Leon Hirszman's *São Bernardo*, which is not surprising, since both were photographed in the Northeast by Dib Lufti, and both have similar themes. *Joana Francesa*, like *São Bernardo*, returns to the slow, reflective rhythms of first-phase Cinema Novo. But it goes far beyond the first phase of Cinema Novo in its depth of analysis. Diegues was not content merely to denounce an obviously unjust social, political, or economic situation, he was "after the national unconscious and its meaning in [their] lives, trying to materialize the sounds and images of its history through [his] own fantasies and utopias."[31]

Carlos Diegues's sixth feature, *Xica da Silva* tends toward the utopian.[32] The director refers to the film as a "multicolored glass butterfly resting on the solemn wall of a colonial church."[33] The image is appropriate, for the film, made in a political context that gave perhaps less cause for joy and commemoration, is a dynamic, colorful, noisy, playful celebration of a little-known historical figure. Like *Quando o Carnaval Chegar*, *Xica da Silva* is an ode to the creative spontaneity of the Brazilian people, a spirit that, the director suggests, transcends any specific political situation. The film reflects a renewed optimism and faith in the vitality of the Brazilian people in the process of liberation.

Its reception in Brazil was enormous: it was seen by over three million spectators in its first two and one half months of exhibition. It was equally well-received by popular critics. The film is not, however, without its detractors, who base their criticism on political problems they see as inherent to the film. Such diverse reactions derive, ultimately, from the ambivalence of the film's conception: a comedy about slavery, a defense of the irrational set in a political context, a historical reconstruction in which fantasy and myth are more important than historical accuracy.

Xica da Silva is a fictional re-creation of events that occurred in the State of Minas Gerais in eighteenth-century colonial Brazil. Like Diegues's first feature, *Ganga Zumba*, it deals with slavery and the possibility of freedom. In the second half of the eighteenth century, the Portuguese Crown inaugurated a system of contracts for the extraction of diamonds and other precious stones from the rich mineral areas of Brazil's interior. Such contracts guaranteed a monopoly for a Portuguese capitalist of the king's choosing. The most famous of the successive holders of contracts for diamond extraction was João Fernandes de Oliveira, who first obtained his contract in 1739. João Fernandes instituted modern, efficient (if corrupt) systems of extraction, discovered new beds of precious stones, and

Plate 9. Zezé Motta, *Xica da Silva*

accumulated a wealth approaching that of the Crown itself. His wealth and power were soon seen as threatening to the Crown, and he was forced to return to Lisbon in 1773. While in Brazil, João Fernandes took as his lover the slave woman Francisca (Xica) da Silva, freed her, and made her one of the most powerful persons in the State of Minas Gerais. For several years, until João Fernandes's downfall, Xica da Silva dominated the politics, economics, and fashion of the region. Her rise to power and frequently extravagant behavior (in retaliation for humiliations suffered while a slave) scandalized the bourgeoisie of the diamond-mining region as well as the Portuguese court. Very little is known about Xica da Silva, since after her fall the people of Diamantina (then Arraial de Tijuco) undertook a virtual exorcism and burned most of the documents concerning her. The myths surrounding Xica and her love of freedom are the basis of Carlos Diegues's film. If *Ganga Zumba* is a story of the love of freedom, *Xica da Silva*, observes Diegues, is about the possibility of freedom through love.

The first sequence develops the political space through which the story's major contradictions are worked out. In a rather unlikely bucolic scene shot in soft focus, João Fernandes (Walmor Chagas), traveling to Tijuco to assume his position as contractor, stops along the road and plays flute with a couple of itinerant musicians. The European music is strangely out of place in the rugged interior of Brazil, and a major opposition develops: the incongruous refinement and "solemnity" of European culture contrasted with the "primitive," yet authentic, vitality of things Brazilian.[34] The musicians comment on the economic and political situation of the region until they realize with whom they are speaking. One of them looks directly at the camera and says, excusing himself, "Artists shouldn't be involved in politics, isn't that right?" Such a statement certainly reflects the dominant ideology's position, here represented in the person of João Fernandes, but just as certainly does not reflect Carlos Diegues's viewpoint.

The director suggests that *Xica da Silva* is perhaps even more political than some of his earlier films, since it is a consideration of the nature of power and how one enters the different arenas of power. The film is political, albeit not in the traditional sense of political cinema. In it, the exuberant and quick-witted Xica upends existing political, economic, and moral hierarchies in ribald fashion. The film's politics are a festive, carnivalesque commemoration of the people's vitality.

During medieval folk festivals and carnivals, from which the carnivalesque derives, existing social hierarchies were abolished, and there was no distance between actors and spectators. Participants led, so to speak, a second life, free from the rules and restrictions of official cultural life. According to Mikhail Bakhtin, the people achieved a temporary liberation from the established order through the suspension of hierarchical rank. The carnival spirit "offers the chance to have a new outlook on the world, to realize the relative nature of all that exists, and to enter a completely new order of things."[35]

In the carnivalesque, a material bodily principle, especially of the body's "lower stratum" (including eating, drinking, copulation, defecation, and other bodily functions), prevails as a positive force. Folk humor and laughter, another important element in the carnivalesque, represent universalism (communication between all people without regard to social rank), freedom, and the people's unofficial truth (as opposed to the "official" truth of the socially dominant classes). Such laughter "presents an element of victory not only over supernatural awe, over the sacred, over death; it also means the defeat of power, of earthly kings, of the earthly upper classes, of all that oppresses and restricts."[36] In Diegues's film, Xica da Silva commands a profoundly carnivalesque attitude toward the world. One of her major features is her joy and power in copulation, which reveals the predominance of the "material bodily principle" in her.

The film deals with Xica's rise to power, her vindictiveness and extravagance while in power, and her subsequent fall from power. She is the object of desire of the most important men in the village, including the intendant (the holder of civilian power), the sergeant (the holder of military power), and, finally, the contractor himself (the holder of economic power). She first attracts João Fernandes's attention by premeditatedly exposing her body as the contractor meets with the intendant and the sergeant. He buys her from the sergeant, and soon after, his other slaves comment wryly that he has become her slave sexually. Xica's frontal, festive attack on the ruling class's solemnity thus comically overturns social hierarchies.

Diegues's apparent rationale in the characterization of Xica is that, as a slave she has no possessions except her body, and she controls it. Therefore, in addition to being the object of desire of the most powerful men in the village, she is also an acting agent in relationship to them. Indications abound that she, not her partners, controls and determines the sexual relationships she maintains. Even though she has no economic, military, or political power, she exercises the power of Eros, erotic power.

As Xica ascends, rumors of her strange behavior circulate, both in the mining district and in Lisbon. After she complains of never having seen the sea, João Fernandes builds her a private sailing ship that only blacks can use: no whites allowed except as musicians and servants, another social inversion. While she pretends to enjoy herself on the ship, we learn that the sergeant's son, José, who had earlier left for Vila Rica to participate in a revolt against colonial rule, has been accused of subversion and is now hiding in a local monastery for black monks. We also learn that a dam built by João Fernandes to aid in the extraction of diamonds has burst and killed many workers. The contractor had been warned of such danger but obviously preferred profit to safety and failed to heed the warnings. The intendant's wife, a pale, whiny, petty woman, begins to conspire against Xica out of jealousy and overt racism.

Shortly thereafter, a pompous revenue agent, with the equally pompous name of José Luis de Menezes Abrantes Castelo Branco de Noronha, the Count of Valadares, arrives from Lisbon to inspect João Fernandes's management of the diamond-extraction business and to investigate reports of Xica's behavior. He and Xica immediately dislike and mistrust each other. He makes racist jokes about her color, saying that things should be cleared up (in Portuguese, the word for "clear," *claro*, also means "light colored"). Xica reacts in high carnivalesque fashion by wearing white-face make-up to dinner and suggesting that the count not eat the chicken with "brown sauce." The count, dressed in European finery and an absurd white wig is totally out of place in tropical Brazil and constantly refers to the primitive and strange customs he witnesses.

Despite Xica's attempts to convince him to return to Europe and leave João Fernandes alone, the count publicly reads the decree of João Fernandes's recall to Lisbon. It is at this point that the true limits of Xica's erotic power are revealed. After João Fernandes rides off, the townspeople turn on her, and some of the boys begin to stone her.

Xica flees to the monastery where José is hiding. She feels that her life is over and that she is once again nobody. José tries to convince her that she herself is life and that together they will show "that this country is not made up only of weaklings. We're going to get out of this together and piss on the king and his followers." The film ends with a replay of shots of Xica going happily to the church carrying in her hand the papers granting her freedom. She has reverted to her previous carnivalesque attitude toward the world.

The importance of Xica's trajectory from slave to powerful free-woman to social outcast rests in the contrast she represents to the rigidity of the ruling class. She disrupts their corrupt political machinations and their social rituals. She parodies and ridicules their staid yet hypocritical behavior. In contrast to their formality, she is a dynamic, creative, personable, and quick-witted woman who exudes a tremendous vitality and energy. She creates an alternative "second life" for those whom the ruling classes repress. She enters the "official" stratum of power only to subvert it through what Bakhtin might call her "gay relativity." She ridicules the hypocrisy of the church and even suggests that it be painted black. She takes public and hilarious revenge on those who had earlier humiliated her.

Brazilian anthropologist Roberto da Matta suggests that relationships of power must be seen in relative terms.[37] The ruling classes attempt to control the masses and yet leave them content enough not to revolt. Several levels of power are evident in *Xica da Silva*, and Matta points out that it is precisely when the holder of economic power is asserting himself that Xica da Silva acts to change her situation in life. Through the premeditated exposure of her body (disrupting an official meeting of the holders of power), Xica manages to align herself with the most powerful man in the village. She is a slave who is aware of the value of the only thing she possesses, her body.

Matta also points out that it is precisely João Fernandes who feels most strongly the contradiction between individual rights and authoritarianism, since it is he who must reconcile his personal enrichment with that of the Crown. With his freedom of economic movement, in opposition to the desires of the Crown, João Fernandes creates an unofficial link with the bandit Teodoro. The conflict peaks when he has to decide whether or not to align with Teodoro in the formation of an army to fight the count. He of course rejects such a possibility.

Xica herself does not enter the spheres of power through political knowledge and action, as does the rebel José, but rather through the use of her body. If José has an intellectual, political knowledge of Brazil, Xica lives Brazil. Matta suggests that she is a repressed individual in political terms, but at the same time remarkably free in terms of her own carnivalesque sensuality and sexuality. He observes that Xica has "the power, in short, of giving pleasure, joy and strength" to those with whom she relates. That is her most powerful weapon. The politically powerful men she deals with exercise the power of the strong; Xica, the power of the weak.

Her power is carnivalesque, since it results in the leveling of social forces and hierarchies. By herself, however, she is unable to consolidate such an inversion and make it last. That is where José comes in. The link between José and Xica is meant to show that Xica's "magic vitality" alone is not enough; such vitality must be joined to the politics of revolution, a revolt not against people, as is Xica's, but against the oppressive and mystifying institutions of colonial rule. It is Xica who shows us the road to action; it is she who is victorious in the end as José expresses in carnivalesque terms ("piss on the king") a program of future action.

Xica da Silva often evokes political struggle by way of cultural differentiation. The director develops this struggle by opposing the stodginess of alien European culture and the vitality of Brazilian popular culture. By giving value to dance, music, and cuisine, the film reverses the existing social and economic hierarchies. Banquet images are typical of the carnivalesque, and in the tropical banquet she offers the count, Xica ridicules his greed and hypocrisy. As Xica ascends, she becomes increasingly alienated from her own culture, even to the point of ordering other slaves to desist with the "noise" of their highly rhythmic, percussion-based music. Only after her fall from grace is she restored to the fullness of her previous self. The situation is once again inverted, and Xica can begin a new life with José.

Although some critics have said that Carlos Diegues's portrayal of Xica as a sexual creature has racist overtones, there is also, to the director's credit, a criticism of racism throughout the film. Racism pervades the power structure pictured in the film, especially that of the church and the representatives of the Portuguese Crown. The intendant's lily-white wife, who feels threatened by Xica's vitality and ascent, is perhaps the most petty incarnation of racism in the film. Although Diegues's comic treatment of slavery has troubled many critics, the careful observer will note that as João Fernandes rides into town he passes a slave in chains. When he rides out at the end of the film, the slave is still chained in the same position. *That* is the reality of slavery in Brazil. Xica's link with the ruling classes has changed nothing. *One* slave (Xica) has been liberated. The film's ending, though offering no concrete solutions, opens the possibility of other forms of social and political transformation.

Perhaps the most important and salutary aspect of *Xica da Silva* is the debate that it has helped spark concerning the nature and role of the "popular" in Brazilian cinema. Not only the responsibility of filmmakers vis-à-vis popular culture has come into question, but also the role of film criticism. Diegues opposes what he calls "ideological patrols," that is, certain types of leftist criticism that reject any manifestation of artistic expression that does not follow narrow, orthodox, ideological prescriptions.

Diegues feels—and has felt since the beginning of his career—that Brazilian cinema will only be strong when filmmakers of all tendencies have the freedom to explore and develop myriad themes in a multiplicity of styles. In this sense, *Xica da Silva*, with its carnivalesque celebration of a heretofore little-known historical figure, is indeed a landmark film for Brazilian cinema.

After the carnivalesque explosion of *Xica da Silva, Summer Showers* represents a change of pace for Carlos Diegues. Described by the director as an "intimate epic," *Summer Showers* concerns five days in the life of Afonso (played by Jofre Soares) who, after forty years of faithful and punctual service, has retired from his job as a public employee. His reward on his last Friday at work is a cake, a kiss on the cheek, and a gold pen. He is now supposed to retire to a suburban world where he has to convince himself that he is important by exalting availability. "Long Live Sloth" read the banners his friends have prepared for his arrival home from his last day at work.

But such exaltation hides a profound sense of frustration and loneliness. He has worked forty years at a job that never interested him, and now that he has been forced to retire, he realizes that he never really lived, or that he lived a life that was not his own. *Summer Showers*, in Diegues's words, is "about people who live ambiguous lives . . . and proves that identification cards do not always identify a person."[38]

It is only after his retirement that Afonso begins to perceive and understand the lives, dramas, frustrations, and hopes of those who have surrounded him over the past forty years. Prior to his retirement he had never taken the time to really get to know them. In a sense, then, Afonso discovers life at the age of sixty-five by means of a series of dramas that are played out during his first week of retirement. He discovers, for example, that his maid is not the innocent, naive young woman he had thought, when he finds that she has brought her boyfriend, Lacraia ("Centipede"), to hide in his house. Lacraia is an infamous criminal fleeing from the police. Afonso is thus forced, almost in spite of himself, to become involved in their drama and to decide whether to call the police or help them escape (he chooses the latter). He discovers as well that one of his best friends, a former circus clown named Guaraná, hides something very sinister behind his love of children, when he learns that the clown had kidnapped and murdered a little girl after abusing her sexually. He discovers that a couple very close to him is happy only in appearance and that their son, an eternal student, is not engaged to a "dramatic actress," as he says, but rather to an aging performer in a burlesque theater review. He discovers, perhaps even closer to home, that his macho, womanizing son-in-law is a closet transvestite. Nobody is exactly what they seem to be. Surface appearances hide the reality of their lives.

Summer Showers is a microcosm of the suburban lower-middle class and its limited horizons. This is the same ambience described in such morbid terms by Nelson Rodrigues (in *Boca de Ouro*, for example). But *Summer Showers* is much more optimistic, and less moralistic, than any play by Nelson Rodrigues. It is the story of fourteen characters whose lives cross and intermingle in a period of five days within the closed space of Afonso's street, a story of people who have been impeded from living their own lives by the social, moral, and economic barriers of the system in which they play a minor role. It is a film about loneliness, frustration, the need for love, and the freedom to love and to create a meaningful life in the grey barrenness and limitations that society offers.

The film presents a man who has let life pass him by as he commuted to his boring job, returned home to eat, watched television, and slept, a man whose sexuality was stifled early by the death of his authoritarian wife and who is forced to live within the bounds of a morality that he really does not believe in. But perhaps more important, *Summer Showers* presents a ray of hope for these stagnant lives.

Despite all the frustrations and bitterness revealed in the relationships and daily lives of these characters, Afonso finds hope and re-encounters the possibility of love and of creating a new life when, during a summer rain shower, he invites a woman neighbor—one of three aging spinsters—into his house for shelter. They talk, drink beer, express their frustrations, and finally find love with each other. At one moment the woman, Isaura, takes a piece of paper from her purse and reads lines of her own poetry: "Life is not like the waters of a river that pass without stopping, nor like the sun that always comes and goes. Life is a summer shower, sudden and passing, which evaporates as it falls." *Summer Showers* is perhaps the first, maybe the only, Brazilian film to treat aging with the dignity and respect that the subject deserves. It is a film about the need for love, regardless of age.

Although it does not deal with epic themes, as do *Ganga Zumba, The Heirs,* and *Xica da Silva, Summer Showers* is a film about history, about the history of our times. Rather than look at the heroic adventures modern television dramas offer, Diegues's camera takes on, so to speak, television's perspective in order to reveal those who have, perhaps, no other real form of communication with the world outside, who have no perspective for the future, and who live in a world of impossible and always frustrated dreams.

Summer Showers, like *Joana Francesa* and *Xica da Silva*, prefers a classical mode of representation. Concerned, as always, with popular forms of spectacle, Diegues incorporates into the film a burlesque theater sequence in which the conflicts of some of the characters are worked out. Cinema, like the burlesque theater, creates an illusionary world in which to discuss and resolve the contradictions of the real world. Its political efficacy thus reduces, in Diegues's words, to "an antenna of the future" and to "a generous source of communication with others." Cinema, continues Diegues, is a form of affection and entertainment first of all, and is political only on a secondary level.

A far cry from the earlier phases of Cinema Novo? Perhaps, but more apparently than truly so. *Summer Showers*, a lyrical vision of the frustration of a class, does point out social contradictions in Brazil and the alienation that the social structure implies. In this sense, it is another facet of a pluralistic national cinema concerned with depicting Brazilian reality in all its aspects.

Carlos Diegues's most recent film, *Bye Bye Brasil*, the first to be a commercial success in the United States, returns to the utopian quest of *Xica da Silva*, but this time with a story set in modern-day Brazil.[39] *Bye Bye Brasil* presents a mural of Brazil that is as varied as the country itself. As Diegues has observed, his film presents a "country that is beginning to disappear, giving way to one that is just beginning to take form."[40] It is a Brazil in a process of rapid transformation. An agropastoral economy is giving way to industrialization; multinational corporations occupy the Amazon jungle while its original Indian inhabitants are on the verge of extinction. The film develops metaphors of prostitution and penetration as it reveals the pollution and destruction of the country's natural resources and the homogenization of its indigenous and folk cultures. It denounces the "decharacterization" wrought by internal and external cultural dependence. It includes contraband, Indian chants and the disco beat, rural Brazilian music and Frank Sinatra, an accordion and a rock band, snow in the *sertão*.

Bye Bye Brasil, dedicated to Brazilians of the twenty-first century, juxtaposes Brazil of the past, the present, and perhaps the future as seen through the travels of a small-time circus troupe, the Caravana Rolidei (a Brazilianization of "holiday"), composed of magician and clairvoyant Lorde Cigano (played by José Wilker), exotic dancer Salomé (Betty Faria), and the strongman Andorinha (Príncipe Nabor). In a small northeastern town accordionist Ciço (Fábio Jr.) and his pregnant wife, Dasdô (Zaira Zambelli) join them.

Like the circus performers in Xavier de Oliveira's *Gargalhada Final (Last Laugh*, 1978), the troupe represents a form of spectacle that finds itself less and less viable in an age of mass communication, as through their travels they experience what Robert Stam calls the "aftershocks of the 'multinationalization' of the Brazilian subcontinent."[41] In this film of the road the troupe goes from the *sertão* to the sea, then along the Trans-Amazonian highway to Altamira in the depths of the Amazon jungle to present their show to small towns not yet "contaminated" by television. In Altamira Lorde Cigano and Andorinha lose their truck and belongings to a local hustler in the service of a multinational corporation, and the troupe, now in dissolution, catches a boat downriver to the bordellos of Belém.

Plate 10. *Bye Bye Brasil*

There they separate, only to meet again "some time later" in Brasília.

Running throughout *Bye Bye Brasil* is a subtext that constitutes a good-humored yet critical retrospective of the development of Brazilian cinema over the last twenty years and its relationship to other consciousness-forming media, notably television. Critics have tended to see Diegues's film as a denunciation of television and its effect on Brazilian cinema. A close reading of the film, however, renders that denunciation ambiguous at best. *Bye Bye Brasil* in fact incorporates television into its diegesis. The film rests on a number of contradictions that, rather than invalidate it, make it a complex and rich discussion of contemporary Brazilian society.

The Caravana Rolidei's itinerary recalls Cinema Novo's evolution from the early sixties until today. Cinema Novo initially revealed a strong documentary tendency, so *Bye Bye Brasil* opens with a brief sequence that lends it a documentary tone: an extreme long shot of a primitive ferry boat crossing the muddy São Francisco River, followed by several shots of people and merchandise in a small northeastern river town's open market (the Northeast was one of early Cinema Novo's preferred locales). Groups of local musicians stroll through the crowds and, to one side, an accordionist (Ciço) plays regional music for handouts. After seeing the Caravana

Rolidei, and infatuated with Salomé, Ciço decides to leave the Northeast and go with them. In a sequence whose setting recalls Nelson Pereira dos Santos's *Vidas Secas*, Ciço tells his father that he can no longer live in the *sertão*. Just as *Vidas Secas*'s Fabiano and his family are forced to leave their land, Ciço must leave his, albeit for different reasons.

From the *sertão* the troupe goes to the sea, in a geographical visualization of the slogan in Glauber Rocha's *Black God, White Devil*: "The *sertão* will become the sea, the sea, *sertão*." But the mythical, utopian sea of Rocha's film has changed; it is now polluted with industrial and human wastes.

Cinema Novo arose initially as part of the cultural euphoria of the developmentalist period, the ultimate symbol of which was the ultramodern architecture of Brasília. But the Brasília seen in *Bye Bye Brasil* does not correspond to its original ideal. The democratic hopes of socialist architect Oscar Niemeyer and of the developmentalist period have been dashed, as the capital itself has become the exclusive residence of government bureaucrats while the people who built it are, like Ciço and Dasdô, shunted off to outlying satellite slums.

Cinema Novo had difficulty at first in communicating with a broad public; the public that had supported the *chanchada* in the forties and fifties now preferred to stay home and watch television. The troupe also has difficulty in finding large audiences to perform to and must also compete against television, which has become an audiovisual totem for small-town and city Brazilians. Faced with a market dominated by American films, Cinema Novo increasingly turned toward the state for protection, subsidies, and production financing; the Caravana Rolidei depends on the largesse of local mayors. Cinema Novo evolved from a stance of critical realism to the often hermetic, allegorical discourse of tropicalism. The documentary tone of *Bye Bye Brasil*'s initial sequence is disrupted as the Caravana rolls into town, loudspeakers blaring a pop song. With the entrance of the Caravana, the film moves to an allegorical register tempered by a carnivalesque atmosphere reminiscent of Joaquim Pedro de Andrade's tropicalist *Macunaíma* and Diegues's own *Quando o Carnaval Chegar*.

The relationship Lorde Cigano creates with his audience is analogous to that between cinema and its public: sometimes fascinating, sometimes tedious, sometimes participatory, sometimes passive. Lorde Cigano's encounter with Zé da Luz in a small northeastern town plagued by drought renders explicit the link between the Caravana Rolidei and the cinema. Zé da Luz ("Joe of the Light," literally) offers a form of entertainment "something like" the Caravana: cinema. He travels through the interior of Brazil showing old copies of Gilda de Abreu's 1946 classic *O Ebrio* (*The Drunkard*), starring her husband, singer Vicente Celestino. Like the Caravana, Zé da Luz (played by Jofre Soares) is marginalized by television and by the impoverished economic conditions of Brazil's interior. The situation of Lorde Cigano and Zé da Luz, two sides of the same coin, is analogous to that of Brazilian cinema as a whole, which has historically been marginalized within its own market.

The opposition between the Caravana and television, symbolized by the ubiquitous "fishbones" (antennas), would seem to suggest that television is responsible for the destruction of Brazilian indigenous and folk cultures as well as for the homogenization of cultural expression in Brazil. We see the inhabitants of a northeastern village, including the priest and the mayor, narcotized by Sônia Braga in the *novela* (soap opera) "Dancin' Days" (the original title was in English), a tale of intertwined affairs among Rio de Janeiro's disco crowd. Regional cultures lose out in the face of the massive penetration of television images, as the standards of powerful commercial television networks (especially TV Globo), geared largely toward southern urban audiences, are imposed on Brazilians throughout the country, with no reciprocity.

The process of cultural "decharacterization" and homogenization is most strikingly poignant in the sequence where Lorde Cigano and the Caravana meet a group of Cruari Indians along the Trans-Amazonian highway. This sequence calls into question highly ideological interpretations of Brazil and its culture. The Indians are no longer the "noble savages" of José de Alencar's romantic novels, nor the proud cannibals of Oswald de Andrade's "cannibalist movement" in Brazilian literary modernism (and subsequently of Nelson Pereira dos Santos's 1972 film, *How Tasty Was My Little Frenchman*). Rather, they are sickly and poverty-stricken, much like the Indians pictured in such recent Brazilian documentaries as Luis Carlos Saldanha's and Jean Pierre Dutilleaux's *Raoni* (1978) and Zelito Viana's *Terra dos Indios* (*Land of the Indians*, 1979).

The Indians' village has been destroyed and, as the chief says, they want to go to town to "pacify" the whites, an ironic remark that calls to mind the Brazilian government's genocidal pacification programs. Their society has been decimated and their culture "decharacterized." The children carry toy airplanes and television sets carved out of wood. Their grandmother listens to the Everley Brothers' version of "Bye Bye Love" on the transistor radio glued to her ear. They go to town and "discover" ice cream, Coca-Cola, and color television, which, significantly, transmits nothing but the color test pattern.

Television, however, is only part of the larger process of gradual extinction of indigenous cultures. It is only one of the more visible components of the advanced technology that has brought isolated and feudal regions of Brazil into the space age (it is significant that Brazil's final linkup to international satellite transmission systems occurred in 1969, shortly before the first moon landing). Whereas television may have had a negative effect on the Indians, so too does Lorde Cigano: he takes from the chief the only natural thing they possess, a monkey. The monkey, in Lorde Cigano's hands, becomes just another commodity, which he loses, together with the truck, to the hustler in Altamira. Although he is concerned with his own marginalization, he participates symbolically in the increased marginalization of the Indians by expropriating what is theirs.

Bye Bye Brasil's critique of television, however, is ambiguous in the diegesis and also, and perhaps more importantly, in its mode of production. If, as I have suggested, the Caravana Rolidei allegorically represents Brazilian cinema, then it is in a sense equated with television. The entertainment offered by the Caravana is neither better nor worse than that offered by television. If TV Globo offers an Americanized *novela* ("Dancin' Days"), then the Caravana offers visions of snow in the *sertão* (the "dream" of all Brazilians, says Lorde Cigano) to the sounds of Bing Crosby's "White Christmas." If television presents false or spurious values and promises a paradise of consumerism, so too does Lorde Cigano offer the credulous a vision of an earthly utopia. Like "Dancin' Days," *Bye Bye Brasil* has an English title. Its soundtrack is a veritable potpourri of national and international music, including Frank Sinatra singing the Brazilian classic "Aquarela do Brasil." The difference between the two forms of spectacle is the degree of penetration each achieves, and in this sense the Caravana—and Brazilian cinema—cannot compete.

There are some 15 million television sets in use in Brazil and some 60 million viewers.[42] The Globo organization has been the most successful of the Brazilian television networks, accounting for up to 90 percent of the viewing audience. Television's penetration on a nationwide basis is on a scale unprecedented in Brazilian cultural history: although some 30 million to 40 million persons may watch a Globo *novela* on any given weeknight, in its first year of exhibition *Bye Bye Brasil*, the fifth most popular national film exhibited in Brazil in 1980, drew only 1,335,000 viewers.[43] The total number of spectators for all of Brazilian cinema is on the order of 60 million to 70 million per year,[44] a figure easily reached by Globo's eight o'clock *novela* in less than a week.

The problem is not that television has achieved a high degree of penetration, but rather that it is controlled, through advertising and other economic imperatives, by multinational interests. Of all Brazilian television programming, 57 percent consists of foreign (read U.S.) series and films. As José Silveira Raoul notes, "Television acts as an instrument in the substitution of Brazilian cultural standards through the massive importation of canned programs."[45] *Bye Bye Brasil*, however, does not so much criticize television as it implicitly calls for its democratization and its integration with other national forms of expression, such as cinema.

Television in Brazil developed independently of cinema. When television was inaugurated in São Paulo in 1950, other entrepreneurs from this industrial city were engaged in the creation, with capital from the Matarazzo group, of the ill-fated Vera Cruz Film Studios. Since cinema had not been able to establish itself with the country's potential audience as a strong audiovisual tradition, television had to depend on its own resources and on certain forms of presentation borrowed from radio. With Cinema Novo there was no question about participating in television, since filmmakers did not take the new medium particularly seriously. The result has been a total lack of integration of cinema and television in Brazil. In 1975, of 1,329 films exhibited by Rio de Janeiro television stations, only 6 were Brazilian.[46]

Although national cinema has largely been unable to get itself shown on television (with some exceptions), in the last few years television has exerted a considerable influence on cinema. *Bye Bye Brasil* is one of a number of recent films that explicitly or implicitly discuss the role of television in modern Brazilian society (others: Arnaldo Jabor's *Eu Te Amo* [*I Love You*, 1981], and Antônio Calmon's *Novela das Oito* [*Eight O'Clock Novela*, 1981]), just as it is one of a number of films that borrow production elements from television. It is the latest in a series of films produced since the mid-1970s by producer Luis Carlos Barreto and others that takes advantage of the popularity of television stars (in this case, José Wilker, Betty Faria, and Fábio Jr.). This series began in 1974 with Bruno Barreto's *A Estrela Sobe* (*The Star Rises*), a story of a radio and television star, played by Betty Faria, and continues with the same director's *Dona Flor and Her Two Husbands* (1976). *Dona Flor*, the most successful Brazilian film in history, starred television actress Sônia Braga (fresh from the *novela* "Gabriela") and actor José Wilker, but its success was also due in part to a massive television advertising campaign.

Like these others, *Bye Bye Brasil* depends at least in part on television for its success. The film's discussion of television continues and deepens through a conflict within the Caravana Rolidei between Lorde Cigano and Ciço. The opposition between them is part of a larger opposition between "artisan" culture (Ciço's regional music) and industrialized culture (cinema and television). The Caravana Rolidei would at first glance seem to be an intermediate cultural form that attempts to incorporate elements of both popular and industrialized culture. In the film's first sequence, the Caravana rolls into town, loudspeakers blaring, and drowns out Ciço's music with a pop song. When Ciço, claiming that he can play the accordian, asks Lorde Cigano to let him join the troupe, Lorde Cigano responds condescendingly, "We have a record player."

Lorde Cigano and his Caravana, like cinema and television, represent a predominantly urban phenomenon trying to impose itself on the predominantly rural space of the small villages they visit. Ciço, on the other hand, is a rural musician. Although it never tried to attract a rural audience, Cinema Novo was an urban phenomenon that frequently took rural topics as its subject. The opposition between urban and rural, industrial and popular in *Bye Bye Brasil* is developed partially through what might be called the film's embedded detail: scenes of Rio de Janeiro and São Paulo painted on the truck's doors, continued references to the troupe's itinerary ("after an extended tour in São Paulo and the rest of the South of the country"), Lorde Cigano's "Copacabana" T-shirts.

Lorde Cigano's dream is to find a place without television, not because he is concerned about its impact on Brazilian culture, but rather because it cuts into his audience. He has a utopian vision of the world and longs for the place where "pineapples are the size of watermelons." He dreams of wealth and finally achieves it, not through his performance of magic, but rather through contraband and Salomé's prostitution. He is not afraid of change and adventure and he realizes that he must go forward at all costs: "We have to keep rolling," he says, "or we will fall off and screw ourselves." He is the eternal artistic gypsy (*cigano*, in Portuguese) in search of the perfect spectacle and the perfect audience. At the same time, he continues to be the huckster who promises his audiences the unbelievable.

Ciço, on the other hand, dreams of the sea, and he departs with the Caravana as if on a magic carpet to the land of his fantasy. He represents an essentially conservative ideology based on tradition and the permanence of values. His name is that of the Northeast's beloved Padre Cícero, "Ciço" for short. Although Lorde Cigano pimps for Salomé throughout, Ciço refuses to follow his example with Dasdô. At the end of the film the contrast between the two becomes even clearer when Ciço refuses to accompany the new, improved Caravana Rolidey (now with a "y," after an American told Lorde Cigano the word was misspelled) to the territory of Rondônia in search of new audiences. Rather, he decides to stay in Brasília with his wife and daughter and play a local dance hall as the "accordianist of the plateau."

Both Lorde Cigano and Ciço have incorporated television into their acts. Lorde Cigano's truck has two screens on one side, and Ciço and his band play on a stage behind six television sets that transmit their image to the immediate public. The Caravana Rolidey, advertising itself with neon lights and sexual imagery (perhaps reflective of the current "luxury and sex" phase of Brazilian cinema), has also incorporated a troupe of go-go girls and become a rolling bordello. Ciço, in contrast, has incorporated his wife and child into his band. His advertising, unlike the gaudy neon lights of the Caravana, is drawn from the traditional wood carvings of the Brazilian interior. Ciço's use of television, in sharp contrast to the earlier "Dancin' Days" segment, seems to exemplify a democratization of television. Despite the fact that Ciço, like Lorde Cigano, has transformed his appearance, he remains closer, so to speak, to the "roots." His music, seen in the different dancing styles (not disco) revealed in the music hall, is for a melting pot of workers from all over Brazil.

If Ciço represents popular culture (i.e., "of the people"), then what does the film say about him and popular culture in general? First of all, *Bye Bye Brasil* rejects the notion that there exists somehow a pure, untainted "Brazilian" culture. Ciço is not without his own elements of hucksterism: the "show business" clothes he wears in Brasília, his stage makeup, his use of television, even his use of an accordian, which is in itself an industrial product. Brazilian culture, rather, is a mixture of elements from diverse sources, both foreign and domestic. The cultural formation of Brazilians includes Bing Crosby, Frank Sinatra, disco, and the Everly Brothers, to mention only those in the film. It also includes strong Indian and black contributions. It is urban and rural, national and international, positive and negative. *Bye Bye Brasil* thus rightly proposes a salutary form of cultural anthropophagy in which the origin of cultural elements is less important than the way they are assimilated and re-elaborated.

It would be erroneous to say that the director's sympathies lie exclusively with Ciço and his traditional values. Such a position would contradict the very nature of filmmaking in Brazil. Lorde Cigano *is* Carlos Diegues, or at least his alter ego: an urban artist who has traveled the long roads of Brazil in search of the perfect audience and the optimum form of spectacle. He knows the frustration of empty theaters, the difficulty of economic survival based on his art alone, the contradictions of his art. His cinema has evolved from the relative "poverty" of *Ganga Zumba* to the relative "luxury" of *Bye Bye Brasil*, from the "esthetic of hunger" to a more commercially oriented and more communicative esthetic of artistic pluralism. Like Lorde Cigano, Carlos Diegues has been (figuratively) run out of town by critics, but more important, like Lorde Cigano, Diegues knows that the only choice is to go forward in search of the artist's utopia.

3. Ruy Guerra: Radical Critique

Pour qu'un art soit valable, it faut qu'il puisse transformer l'individu.

For art to be valid, it must be able to transform the individual.

—Ruy Guerra (1971)

A Brazilian news weekly introduced an interview with Ruy Guerra by saying that, "in contrast to his generation, Ruy Guerra has not given up." Although it is debatable that the other members of the Cinema Novo generation have "given up" their initial critical vision of society, there can be no doubt that Ruy Guerra still preserves an uncompromisingly coherent political and esthetic ideology. One result of his uncompromising nature has been his difficulty in finding production financing in Brazil. Of all the directors studied here, he is the least prolific: he has directed (in Brazil) only four feature films in the last twenty years. He has supported himself by working as a lyricist with such composers as Milton Nascimento, Francis Hime, Chico Buarque, and Marcos Valle. He is to a great degree isolated from the Cinema Novo group, but he accepts his marginalization without bitterness. "Throughout my life," he says, "I have made definitive choices, I have constructed my work starting from choices that are neither occasional nor arbitrary. I have chosen certain values, a way of looking at reality, and I pay the price."[1]

Born in 1931 in Mozambique, then a Portuguese colony. Ruy Guerra went to Europe in 1950. Arrested by Portugal's infamous police apparatus, PIDE, for his activity in proindependence movements in his native country, Guerra soon left Portugal for Paris, where from 1952 to 1954 he studied at IDHEC. For his IDHEC diploma he filmed a short adaptation of Elio Vittorini's *Les Hommes et les Autres* called "Quand le soleil dort." In Paris he worked as assistant director with Rouquier and Dellanoy. Before going to Brazil in 1958, he attempted to film *Os Fuzis* in Greece but was barred by Greek censors. In Brazil he filmed, but did not complete, a short film titled *O Cavalo de Oxumaré* (*Oxumaré's Horse*). In 1962 he helped initiate the Cinema Novo movement with his controversial *Os Cafajestes* (*The*

Guerra's distance from the "mainstream" of Cinema Novo began as early as 1964 after discussions as to the position that filmmakers should take vis-à-vis a program of financing developed by governor of Rio de Janeiro, Carlos Lacerda. Guerra saw such financing as a form of co-optation; most of the others disagreed, and Guerra found himself distanced from the movement as a whole.

This 1964 debate is echoed in the current conjuncture of Brazilian cinema. Whereas other Cinema Novo participants have rushed to support Embrafilme and its policy of coproduction, Guerra has warned of the dangers and limitations of too close a relationship with the state. He opposes those who he feels have adopted a "public at all cost" philosophy and have abandoned a critical vision of society for commercial success. He has been critical as well of Nelson Pereira dos Santos's campaign for a "popular cinema," saying instead that Brazilian cinema will be popular ony when there is a radical transformation of the economic structures of Brazilian society.

Guerra's cinema is profoundly dialectical. It focuses on individuals or groups in what might be called extreme situations and examines their relationship to the social, economic, and political structures of society. The situations of Guerra's characters vary—marginalization and crime (*Os Cafajestes*), violent confrontation in a period of drought (*The Guns*), isolation (*Sweet Hunters*), a struggle for power (*The Gods and the Dead*), the marginalization of workers (*A Queda*)—but he creates all of them in an attempt to elucidate forms of behavior and forms of consciousness in relation to historical, cultural, and social process and change.

Critic Michel Ciment writes that Guerra's films are "very classical in form, [showing] none of the external signs of modernity, such as non-chronological time sequence, manipulation of the sound track or recherché framing."[2] But Guerra's films can be considered "classical" only to the

---

Hustlers), and in 1964 he completed *Os Fuzis* (*The Guns*) by adapting the earlier story to the Brazilian Northeast. It won the Silver Bear award in the 1964 Berlin Film Festival. Back in Europe in 1967, he made a short film entitled *Chanson pour Traverser la Rivière* (*Song for Crossing the River*), which was originally to have been included in Chris Marker's *Loin du Vietnam*. He made *Sweet Hunters* with an international cast in Brittany in 1969 before returning to Brazil to shoot *Os Deuses e os Mortos* (*The Gods and the Dead*) in 1971. He returned to Mozambique in 1975 for independence commemorations before shooting *A Queda* (*The Fall*; Silver Bear, Berlin, 1978) in Brazil in 1977. He returned to Mozambique to help organize that country's National Film Institute and to make a film about the process of national liberation, *Mueda Memória Massacre* (*Mueda Memory Massacre*). In Brazil, where he currently resides, he has been active as a lyricist and playwright. He collaborated with Chico Buarque on *Calabar* (1973), which was recently liberated by censors after years of interdiction. He has directed numerous plays in Brazil and has acted in several films, including Werner Herzog's *Aguirre, The Wrath of God*.

extent that Godard's *Breathless* or Resnais's *Hiroshima Mon Amour*—two influences Guerra cites with reference to *Os Cafajestes*—are classical. Guerra's cinema consistently breaks with the illusionism of classical cinema. It is constructed through the use of discontinuity, through the stretching of conventions of time and space, and through a deliberate breakdown of genre, modes of representation, and modes of discourse. He rejects the dramatic efficiency of classical cinema and often includes in his films extended shots or sequences that do little or nothing to move the action forward. They exist rather as information contributing to the total effect of the film. From the very beginning his films reveal a hybrid character: they mix documentary and fiction as two different but related ways of apprehending reality. "All film is documentary," says Guerra, "if only the documentary of fiction."

Guerra often juxtaposes documentary and fiction dialectically to reveal a third reality that is larger than either the immediate documentary or fictional reality. The screenplay of the unfinished *O Cavalo de Oxumaré* provides an example of Guerra's dialectical mode of filmmaking. *O Cavalo de Oxumaré*, planned as a thirty- to forty-minute film, concerns a white woman who, because of her love for a black man, undergoes the rites of initiation into *candomblé*. The rites themselves are re-created using professional actors (Irma Alvarez in the role of the white woman), but a voice-over narration (a documentary technique) describes and explains the significance of the various stages of the rites. At one point in the initiation, the film begins crosscutting to a Rio de Janeiro museum and a collection of ivory statues of Christ, thus contrasting *candomblé* and Christianity. The crosscutting continues with documentary footage of several other museums, showing silver hand fans, formal gowns, jewels, and even the chairs of the aristocracy. As if she herself is seeing the museum footage, the white woman, still in her rites of initiation, observes, "This dead world now lives only in museums and in my painful fright. . . . My blood comes from these clothes that covered the shame of my ancestors." The remnants of the rituals of a world that no longer exists contrast with the live ritual of *candomblé*, the past with the present, the white with the black, the oppressors with the oppressed. All of Guerra's films are constructed through the dialectical use of such oppositions. It is difficult if not impossible to know exactly what Guerra intended with *O Cavalo de Oxumaré*, but the important thing is his dialectical usage of different modes of cinematic discourse. Another Guerra characteristic, present in this screenplay and throughout his films, is a concern with the rituals of human beings in a given society, rituals that externalize the deepest roots of culture and that help to elucidate human behavior and consciousness.

If, as Glauber Rocha has said, *Os Cafajestes* inaugurated Brazilian Cinema Novo in Rio de Janeiro, Ruy Guerra's first feature was also Cinema

Plate 11. *Os Cafajestes (The Hustlers)*

Novo's first scandal. Released in early 1962, it was banned ten days later as "immoral, nauseating, and repugnant." The police chief responsible for its prohibition referred to the film as "an apology for crimes of rape, kidnapping, licentiousness, drug usage and other crimes against Christian morality and behavior." Some critics recognized the film's value, calling it "the most important film since *Ganga Bruta* [by Humberto Mauro, 1933]," but others, surprisingly, defended its prohibition. The church, the army, and the local government (led by Carlos Lacerda) attacked it viciously. Its prohibition, which lasted only a short time, became a rallying point for intellectuals and artists, and especially for those interested in creating a "new" cinema in Brazil.

The controversy it sparked went beyond the boundaries of Brazilian cinema. *Os Cafajestes* was exhibited in Paris in a theater specializing in erotic films, and it was denied entrance to the United States due to its "pornographic" nature. Among many other innovations, *Os Cafajestes*, included the first frontal nudity in Brazilian cinema.

Made at a time when other filmmakers were turning their attention toward Brazil's economic underdevelopment and pointing their cameras toward the misery of the Northeast or of urban slums, Guerra's film attacks the country's moral underdevelopment and points an accusing finger not at the marginalized elements of Brazilian society, nor at foreign imperialists, but rather at the middle and upper-middle class (the "film-going" class, so to speak). Underlying the film's drama is a criticism of capitalism and the reification of human beings inserted in it.

Guerra does not draw a pretty picture, which perhaps accounts for the violent controversy the film provoked. Like many other of his films, *Os Cafajestes* incorporates what Noel Burch (who studied at IDHEC with Guerra) has since called "structures of aggression" toward the spectator. It is a film about lives with no meaning, no purpose, and no hope for the future, and is thus very different from other films of Cinema Novo's first phase, such as *Barravento* and *Porto das Caixas*, which are open toward the future.

Like the planned *O Cavalo de Oxumaré*, Guerra's *Os Cafajestes* is constructed through a juxtaposition of fictional and documentary modes. But the documentary, which perhaps contains a key to the full understanding of the film, is the part most frequently forgotten or overlooked by critics. The film opens with a documentary brilliance typical of the director, as the camera, rolling with apparent instability, tracks through a tunnel. All that is seen at first are the lights on the tunnel roof, first out of focus, then in focus. Out of the tunnel and once again out of focus, the camera tracks down a street, lit only by street lamps and the lights from store windows. As the image comes back into focus, showing anonymous faces in the Copacabana night, a jazz sax begins to accompany the image. The hand-held camera focuses on faces in the crowded street, some aware that they are being filmed. Suddenly a car comes into view, and the fiction invades the documentary as two of the film's characters, Jandir (Jece Valadão) and a prostitute (Glauce Rocha), come into play. After they make a deal and drive off, the camera, once again in a documentary mode, focuses on mannequins in a store window. The mannequins are much like the fictional characters in relation to the documentary reality: they imitate human beings. The characters and the film create an illusion that imitates, contrasts, and interacts with reality.

The precredits sequence between Jandir and the prostitute is very short. After Jandir picks her up, the film cuts to a bedroom and Jandir setting the clock up several hours. He wakes the prostitute and tells her it is time for her to leave. Through a subjective camera we look through Jandir's eyes out of the window as she waits on the streets below for transportation. A passing policeman tells her the real time, and she turns, looks up and curses Jandir, who, in a shot-counter-shot, laughs cynically through the venetian blinds. The film's title is superimposed over the fragmented image of his face.

The documentary, however, once again forces the fiction from the screen, as the hand-held camera goes back out onto the street, to the world of the prostitute and of anonymous faces, and witnesses, out of focus, a struggle and chase between several men. The chase results in the arrest of two men, who are placed in the back of a police van. A flashlight shining into their eyes (into the camera) is transformed through montage into the sun, and the film's central story begins the following day.

These first three sequences—two documentary, one fictional—place Jandir in a specific social context. Underground filmmaker Rogério Sganzerla is correct when he notes that the film's first shot (careening through a tunnel) is polyvalent: although denotatively the tunnel is a means of passage, it represents a passage into a subworld, a world of empty people (the anonymous faces in the urban night), violence (the struggle, chase, and arrest), and prostitution.[3] The shot also carries the sexual connotation of penetration, as the camera itself penetrates to the other side. The sexual violence of Jandir and his friend Vavá (Daniel Filho) correlates to the social violence of the urban subworld, and the film's dramatic action is thus put into context by contemporary (capitalist) society.

The story of *Os Cafajestes* articulates a series of exchanges, plots, and counterplots. Jandir is the hardened hustler who has had to rise from his early poverty by whatever means possible. Vavá, on the other hand, is the playboy son of a wealthy banker. His father, however, is on the verge of bankruptcy, and Vavá's livestyle is threatened, so he enlists Jandir in a blackmail plot against his wealthy uncle, who is also the largest depositor in his father's bank. They trick Leda, the uncle's lover, into being photographed nude on a deserted beach. They intend to sell the photos to her lover, but do not realize that he has abandoned her. The scheme fails. Leda herself suggests that they repeat the scheme using her former lover's daughter, Wilma, as a victim. During a Machiavellian night, once again on a deserted beach, the four characters play a complex, ambiguous game in which expectations and desires are frustrated. Vavá, for example, reveals a long infatuation with Wilma and backs out of his own plan. But in retaliation for the plot against her, Wilma makes love with Jandir. Vavá threatens to kill himself, but has the courage only to shoot into the sand. He is finally left alone with Wilma, to whom he proposes marriage, as Leda and Jandir drive off in his car.

The characters of *Os Cafajestes* are on the margin of capitalism yet integrated into its system in one form or another. A series of exchanges that, in the end, lead to nothing at all structures the film. The characters, in a sense, go around in circles in search of some kind of satisfaction, but their desires are consistently frustrated and they look toward the future without hope. It is not coincidental that one of the film's central images is the long take in which Jandir and Vavá, in the car, circle the nude Leda on the beach, taking pictures. The car makes ever smaller circles around her as she herself turns in circles to follow the car's movement. The circular motion ends suddenly with a freeze-frame of Leda that reveals not only her immobility and impossibility of action but also that of Jandir and Vavá: they are trapped in a circle from which they cannot escape. The film's final shot, a freeze-frame of Jandir looking backwards as he walks alone down a highway (toward the camera) reinforces the idea of immobility, inverts the usual connotation of the image of a road (the "road of life" opening to new possibilities).

Guerra's indirect criticism of capitalism in *Os Cafajestes* is thus not unlike the more direct critique made some ten years later by Leon Hirszman in *São Bernardo*. As one critic puts it, Guerra's film is a "brutal, pathetic, desperate picture of a humanity concerned with immediate pleasure and with the title of nobility established by society: money."[4] The film's characters will do anything to reach their final goal, although that quest is consistently frustrated, which indicates not only their failures but also the ultimate failure of the system of which they are a part.

The series of exchanges installed by the film leads, in the end, to nothing but the reification of human beings. The initial exchange in *Os Cafajestes* typifies such reification of human beings in a capitalist society, as Jandir picks up, uses, and discards a prostitute—sexual relations at their most mercantile; woman as commodity. This initial exchange sets the tone and the theme for the subsequent exchanges and for the film as a whole. Vavá, shortly thereafter, proposes to exchange his car for Jandir's help in the blackmail scheme. They plan to exchange the nude photos of Leda, who then proposes to exchange her help for revenge against her former lover. Similar relationships occur throughout, but inevitably fail. Leda is left alone in a Narcissus-like image in a fountain in her front yard; Jandir walks alone down a highway looking *backwards* and not forward, as might be expected; Vavá and Wilma are left alone on the beach after humiliating each other. Roads—to the beach, through the tunnel—lead nowhere.

The despair of *Os Cafajestes*'s personages is frequently played off against barren backgrounds reminiscent of Antonioni's *L'Avventura*. Much of the film is shot on deserted beaches with high contrast between the white sand and the dark sky and water. One remarkable sequence takes place in an abandoned fort overlooking the sea. As Jandir and Vavá smoke marijuana and talk about their plans, the fort's whiteness symbolizes the barrenness of their lives. At one point Vavá enters a circular turret, thereby preserving the circular image developed in the earlier beach/blackmail scene. As Vavá walks about the fort, a free jazz bass accompanies him on the soundtrack and accentuates his disorientation.

Guerra's cinematography is based on the use of complex camera movements (e.g., the rolling camera in the tunnel), unconventional yet strangely beautiful composition and framing, and discontinuity. In *Os Cafajestes* discontinuity takes various forms. At times there is a lack of continuity between sound and image, as a conversation between two or more characters accompanies images of a third. For example, as Jandir, Vavá, and Leda talk about their scheme to blackmail Wilma, the camera shows not the three of them but Wilma climbing on rocks near the sea. On another occasion their conversation is set against a documentary sequence of workers having lunch in a park. The camera's "independence" emphasizes the great distance between the trio's destructive plot against Wilma and the lives of the productive forces of society. In the fort sequence, two teenage girls appear and begin to talk to Jandir and Vavá. Jandir talks to one of them about religion and reads from her catechism book; Vavá talks to the other about her family. The sequence is edited in such a way that the first girl's answers respond to Vavá's questions and vice-versa. Vavá's questions (about the girl's sex life) soon "contaminate" Jandir's as Vavá asks the girl if she would go away with him in exchange for an apartment and nice clothes.

Discontinuity of image also exists in *Os Cafajestes*. As the four characters ride in Vavá's car on the way to the deserted beach where the second blackmail scheme will supposedly take place, the editing establishes a system of permutations, as first Jandir and Wilma, then Vavá and Wilma, then Jandir and Leda, then Jandir and Vavá are seen in the car's front seat while the continuity of dialogue is preserved. In this way the film underlines the role of the characters as exchangeable commodities. On another occasion, near the end of the film, Vavá and Wilma, seated side-by-side, converse on the beach. The editing, however, breaks the continuity of their discussion as they repeatedly change sides without moving in the diegesis, once again equating them.

I have already referred to Guerra's important use of documentary footage in *Os Cafajestes*. After the nude scene on the beach, which ends, as I have noted, with a freeze-frame, the camera focuses, again in a freeze-frame, on a group of people carrying a child's coffin. As the group begins to move toward the camera, it crosses the street in front of Vava's car, once again emphasizing the distance between the film's protagonists and the social reality surrounding them. The film's final sequence reinforces this idea. As Jandir drives alone in his newly acquired car (given to him by Vavá), he listens to a radio broadcast about crisis in Argentina, soccer, Brigitte Bardot, U.S.–Latin American relations, Cuba's right to choose its own form of government, the Bay of Pigs, the incipient revolution in Angola, the drought in the Northeast; but Jandir is oblivious to all of this as a policeman stops him and determines that his documents are in order. Jandir then runs out of gas and begins his walk to nowhere.

Os Cafajestes stands out from the general text of first-phase Cinema Novo in a number of ways. Although it is not early Cinema Novo's only urban film (others are *Rio 40 Graus, Rio Zona Norte, Boca de Ouro*), it is the most important. Its criticism of capitalism and the social structure is

Plate 12. Nelson Xavier, *Os Fuzis (The Guns)*

more indirect and subtle than that of many other films of the period. Most of the other films reveal an influence of Italian neorealism or in some cases of Eisenstein, but *Os Cafajestes* is clearly aligned with the French *nouvelle vague*. Its editing recalls Godard's use of jump cuts in *Breathless*, its experimentation with time and space is reminiscent of Resnais's *Hiroshima Mon Amour*. *Os Cafajestes* also establishes Guerra as the most "formalist" of the Cinema Novo directors. Whereas Joaquim Pedro de Andrade, for example, has said that ideology is more important than form, Ruy Guerra's films suggest that only through the proper form can ideology be properly transmitted.

Guerra's second feature, *The Guns*, was originally to have been filmed in Greece, but prior censorship kept Guerra from making the film there. The original project was to have concerned a Greek village threatened by a pack of starving wolves that has come down from the surrounding hills in search of food. A detachment of soldiers is called in to defend the villagers. The story was to have explored the conflict between the village population and the soldiers who had supposedly come to help them. Guerra transformed this original story into one of the most powerful political films ever made, a film that has been compared to *October* and *Salvatore Giuliano*.

In the Brazilian version of *The Guns*, starving peasants during a period of drought in the Northeast have replaced the starving wolves. The soldiers are called not so much to protect the local population as to protect a wealthy landowner's food warehouse. Guerra also added an element not planned for the original version: religious mysticism.

Interestingly enough, the dramatic focus of *The Guns* is not the political and economic conflict between the peasants and the townspeople or between the peasants and the soldiers; rather, the film's central conflict is worked out within the detachment of soldiers sent to protect the owner's interests. The soldiers serve a repressive mediating function between the peasants and the powerful as the diegesis develops two antagonistic, yet always separate, blocks.

In a cogent article, Brazilian critic Roberto Schwarz notes that these two blocks seem to divide the film into two incompatible films. On the one hand there is the documentary of drought and poverty showing the fatalism, immobility, and passivity of the peasants as elements to be seen but not understood in psychological terms. On the other hand, the soldiers, in their mobility, complexity, and psychological depth, represent a more modern society. The documentary sequences concern and use as actors the local population and the drought victims; the fictional sequences use actors in assumed roles. A rupture in style thus exists between the two blocks. As Schwarz observes, "The actors are to the non-actors as the city-dwellers [the soldiers] with their technical civilization are to the evacuees, as possibility is to predetermined misery, as plot is to inertia."[5]

A virtual blockade exists between the two groups. The soldiers, who have been brought in from the coastal cities, do not understand the misery of the local population, and the local population does not understand why the soldiers have been called in. No communication can exist between them, since they come from two different worlds. In the eyes of the peasants, the soldiers must seem mythical figures; for the soldiers, the peasants are no more than an amorphous mass. The soldiers see themselves as superior, a fact their casual killing of one of the townsmen shows. Their "superiority" derives from their more advanced technology, embodied in the guns they carry. Luzia (a local woman) and the landowner (who rarely appears in the film) are the only points of contact between the soldiers and the villagers. Luzia's relationship with the soldier Mário is based on love and hate, repulsion and attraction. Although she hates him and his fellow soldiers for the role they are playing—and especially for their murder of the townsman—at the same time he fascinates her. The unrelenting tension of the love/possession scene brilliantly depicts this dialectic of repulsion and attraction. The possibility of love reduces to the act of possession.

The decentering of the dramatic focus from the peasants and their situation to the various levels of authority seems on the surface to reflect the populist vision of early Cinema Novo films, in which solutions come not from the people, but rather from enlightened sectors of the ruling classes. In truth, *The Guns* is a critical and dialectical vision, not a populist vision, of the reality it depicts. In *The Guns*, an antimilitarist film par excellence, Guerra distinguishes between the army as an institution and the individual soldiers who constitute it. No blame is laid:

> People ask me why there are no good guys and bad guys in my film. Characters are good or bad not according to a Christian morality but rather according to the role they play in society. I believe that moral values are not to be located at the narrowly individual level, but at the level of a class morality. One belongs to a given social stratum and carries with oneself all the weight of the values and judgements of this class. In *The Guns* if you belong to the class of shopkeepers whatever you do you are a bad guy for the peasant; your behavior cannot be judged outside the class to which you belong.[6]

Although the army is a repressive institution whose function is to guarantee private property and capitalism in Brazil, in this case at the expense of the starving peasants, the individual soldiers, from the urban lower classes, are little more than salaried workers. They have little or no consciousness of their true function (which does not of course excuse them) or of the people they are sent to repress. A revolutionary analysis of the situation would be beyond their ken as soldiers. From one angle, therefore, they represent authority, yet from another they are themselves representatives of the vast, marginalized masses in Brazilian society. They carry with them the contradiction of being members of an oppressed class in the service of the oppressors.

Even the truck driver Gaúcho, who at a certain point mediates between the soldiers and the peasants and who is finally killed after revolting against the soldiers, is himself a former soldier. Although he boasts of exploiting peasants, he is able to see the contradictions in the army's role. It is his awareness that leads eventually to his revolt and death at the hands of the soldiers.

Gaúcho is in Milagres (the name means, literally, "miracles," and is the scenario of other Cinema Novo films such as Glauber Rocha's *Antônio das Mortes*) because his truck, filled with onions to be hauled to the cities of the South, has broken down. His journey from the Northeast to the South not only mirrors that of the peasants, but also reflects Brazil's internal relations of dependence. Just as the interests of the metropolis to a large extent determine and control Brazil's economy, so too does the national metropolis, in this case the large cities of the South, dominate and exploit the outlying regions of the country.

It is a mere coincidence that Gaúcho encounters Mário, an old army buddy. While he waits for a helper to bring a spare part from Salvador, he spends his hours in the local bar, drinking and talking to the soldiers. At one point a peasant offers to sell Gaúcho his daughter, such is the depth of despair, but Gaúcho, responding that the price is too high, refuses. As he runs out of money and is refused credit, his own situation begins to resemble that of the peasants, although always on a much higher economic level. Only then does he begin to resent the army's role, the preservation of "order and progress" (the positivist slogan on the Brazilian flag) by keeping the starving from eating. But Gaúcho revolts only when a peasant walks into the bar carrying a dead child and refuses to react to his situation. Gaúcho tries to stop the trucks from rolling out of the village with the food stocks, but the soldiers chase him down and kill him mercilessly.

Gaúcho's presence, which functions as a mirror image of the soldiers and reveals the contradictions of their actions, becomes intolerable for them. The soldier Zé has begun to have doubts about his own courage as well as about the role he is playing in the small town. His doubts come to the fore in the form of a physical malaise as he vacillates when he and the other soldiers are protecting the trucks that will carry the food out of town. Zé's brutal killing of Gaúcho is in a sense a violent reaction to his uncertainty. As Roberto Schwarz suggests, by viciously killing Gaúcho, the soldiers, with the exception of Mário, who tries to stop the killing, are in fact exorcising their own consciousness and freedom to act.[7]

Gaúcho's revolt and the moral crisis his death causes among the soldiers, notably in Zé and Mário, do nothing, of course, to alter the basic economic and political stratification of the situation. Even the peasants' slaughter and consumption of the supposedly "sacred" ox is more a distant echo of Gaúcho's revolt than a direct result of it. And yet his actions are the spark that leads the soldiers (or at least Zé and Mário) to an awareness of their own responsibility vis-à-vis their military action and the seed of Mário's subsequent reversal (seen in *A Queda*) from oppressor to oppressed. After Gaúcho's death, Mário no longer wears a uniform, but rather a white shirt, a visual indication of his own perception of the contradiction of his role and his potential rejection of that role. But at this point his awareness is only perceptual, not critical. He perceives the contradiction, he knows something is wrong, and yet he can neither analyze nor articulate his "malaise."

The film's dialogue suggests that Gaúcho's awareness of the soldiers' contradictory role derives from a previous military action of the same sort. Earlier in the film, at the precise moment that the soldier Pedro kills a local townsman on a bet, Mário is in Luiza's house talking about his life as a soldier. He tells her about another incident in which he was called to protect private property. A gun battle broke out and Mário was wounded. He tells of a companion in that action, a companion who has now left the army and has changed (obviously Gaúcho). "We all change," observes Mário. "Funny, they really thought the property was theirs . . . . We shouldn't have done so much killing." But the important thing is that change is possible, perhaps not necessarily revolutionary transformation, but change nonetheless. Through experience Mário is slowly becoming aware of who he is in relation to the social structure.

Change is possible even among the peasants, who reveal an exasperating passivity and fatalism. Many of them are following a prophet/mystic who promises that if they worship the "sacred" ox it will rain (this aspect of the film is based on an incident in the Northeast in 1929). Although he serves as a catalyst for alienation, the prophet is aware of the limits of the people's patience. At one point he tells the ox, "If it doesn't rain soon, you will no longer be sacred, you will no longer be an ox."

The film's criticism of mysticism and of religion in general is not as heavy-handed as it may seem. Although Guerra almost certainly sees most forms of religion as alienating factors that impede peasants from taking control of their own lives, there is no "external" critique of religion in *The Guns*. No one comes from the outside to tell them that they are wrong, that they should rise up against the prophet. Rather, peasants' gestures and religious forms are merely documented, as if the documentation itself were sufficient to transmit the criticism.

Religious alienation is revealed in three distinct manners in *The Guns*: first, the prophet and the sacred ox represent mystical millenarianism; second, the procession around the village church equates mysticism and Catholicism; and third, a popular singer's version of the events of Canudos reveals how popular culture has incorporated these traditional values. But the most serious critique of religion and its forms is achieved visually. At one point the dead man's body is stretched out on a dirt floor. In the foreground, out of focus, a man's arm makes vertical gestures as if blessing the body. Rack focusing, however, shows that the vertical gestures are of a soldier taking food from his plate to his mouth. Symbolically, the soldiers anthropophagously consume the dead man and, by extension, the peasants.

Like *Os Cafajestes, The Guns* is dialectical on a formal level by means of the articulation of various modes of cinematic discourse. Documentary sequences, as I have already suggested, record the physical suffering of the drought-plagued Northeast. Particularly striking is a shot of a peasant digging an edible root from the ground to feed his family while in voice-over the prophet preaches that men and women should thank God for their hunger and thirst. This and similar sequences give *The Guns* a telluric quality absent, of course, in the urban *Os Cafajestes*. Cinema verité sequences in which aged inhabitants of the region tell of mystics such as Antônio Conselheiro, who in 1896 held off various military expeditions sent by the federal government to destroy his millennial movement, further punctuate the film. Such sequences reveal the history and pervasiveness of the region's religious mysticism.

The dominant mode of the film, however, is the realism of the sequences that deal dramatically with the soldiers. The fiction is grafted onto the documentary, which itself is encompassed within a larger universe of Brazilian social and political reality. Guerra's camera, as in *Os Cafajestes*, is never passive; it creates an unrelenting tension throughout that the use of harsh, grating sounds reinforces and exacerbates. Toward the end of the narrative, especially in the violent and erotically charged love/possession scene, in a series of advances and retreats between Mário and Luiza, and in the chase sequence, the unrelenting tension explodes with phantasmagoric effect. In the love scene the camera pushes Luiza and Mário along, precedes them, circles them until it finally loses its orientation and turns sideways and upside down, thus reflecting the characters' disorientation. In the chase sequence that leads to Gaúcho's death, Guerra substitutes the 28mm lens he had used throughout with a 150mm lens, to give an unreal, distanced tone to the action. The director prefers sequence shots over montage (also similar to *Os Cafajestes*) and also stretches time by following and extending the characters' actions in an attempt to give a feel for the real time of the northeastern *sertão*.

The rhythm of *The Guns* may appear slow to the spectator accustomed to the "efficiency" of Hollywood's cinema, since, as Guerra explains, the film is constructed in blocks and circles, some of which do not advance the action:

> They exist as information which acquires meaning at the level of the acquisition of consciousness: they have a meaning within the film considered as a totality. . . . Every level of the film has its own structure, which introduces information relative, for example, to geography, to customs, to the history, to the mentality which the characters carry within themselves. I try at every moment to inform the public of the problems confronting them. . . . I am trying to follow the spiral that leads to the individual, to within the individual himself.[8]

Guerra's style, which combines periods of stasis with moments of explosion, rejects dramatic structures in which everything contributes to moving the plot forward. The texture of his photography—of walls, of streets, of faces—is often as important as the characters themselves.

It is through this totality of information and its effect on the individual that change can come about. Although Gaúcho's revolt is an individual one, it is important for having placed doubts in Mário's consciousness. The peasants' revolt, although not an immediate result of Gaúcho's, is nevertheless equally important. The killing of the sacred ox is, in Guerra's words, "the first stage in the growth of a collective consciousness in which individual violence does not find political expression in a revolutionary reality."[9] At their current stage the peasants lack the consciousness necessary to bring about a true revolution. The killing of the ox is the only revolt that is *possible* for them at the moment, just as Mário's subdued expression of doubt is all that is possible for him. The characters and groups are thus consistent with the characteristics of their class and their circumstance.

The Guns, along with Vidas Secas and Black God, White Devil, is often considered part of Cinema Novo's most important "trilogy." All three of the films take the Northeast as their setting, and all of them deal with problems resulting from drought and poverty. Only two, The Guns and Black God, White Devil, deal with religious mysticism, although Vidas Secas contains an understated critique of religion. Rocha's film is the only one of the three to use the legendary figure of the cangaceiro.

Of the three protagonists, only Mário (The Guns) evolves or changes through the course of the film. Fabiano, the humble cowherd in Vidas Secas, ends the film much as he began it: homeless yet hopeful that he and his family would find a better life. Nothing changed, either socially, economically, culturally, or psychologically. The film's implicit optimism rests in the diegesis itself—in Nelson Pereira dos Santos's perspective—and not necessarily with Fabiano.

Despite his temporary alliances with "god" and the "devil," Black God, White Devil's Manuel is also a monolithic character. Although he runs across the sertão in a burst of freedom at the film's end, there is no indication that his own consciousness has been transformed. His freedom results from a mythic struggle between Good and Evil, or, as Ismail Xavier puts it, between History and Myth. He has little to do with his own (possible) transformation. Mário, as I have said, does evolve. At the beginning of The Guns he, like the other soldiers, possesses no more than a naive awareness of his role. Because of his experience he evolves toward a critical awareness. Guerra seems to be saying that change is possible, but that it must come on the individual level and through practice rather than theory, an idea that approaches Paulo Freire's concept of conscientização ("consciousness-raising"). This is not intended to belittle either Vidas Secas or Black God, White Devil—both are masterpieces in their own right—but merely to say that there are deep and fundamental differences between the cinematic and political approaches of the three directors.

After the release of The Guns, Ruy Guerra returned to Europe, where he made two films, Chanson pour Traverser la Rivière and Sweet Hunters, neither of which has been publicly exhibited in Brazil. Very little information is available about the first film, other than the fact that it was originally intended for inclusion in Chris Marker's Loin du Vietnam but, according to Guerra, was excluded because of its length. Sweet Hunters is a French production with an American cast (Sterling Hayden, Susan Strasberg). It was filmed in Brittany and presented in the 1969 Venice Film Festival (where it won a gold medal) as a Panamanian film. Sweet Hunters focuses on a number of characters isolated on an island. They all wait for something that never arrives: Allan is an ornithologist waiting for migratory birds that never arrive; his wife, Clea, awaits an escaped prisoner, who arrives only to die; Allan, Clea, their son, Bob, and Clea's sister, Lis, leave on the boat for a party, but never arrive. In Guerra's words, *Sweet Hunters* is a film about noncompletion. Michel Ciment suggests that "Guerra's characters have always been hunters: *cafajestes* laying in wait to profit from their prey, soldiers tracking down a man like a game animal. The four heroes of *Sweet Hunters* are all seeking something: freedom, money, love."[10] But, like the characters of *Os Cafajestes*, they never achieve their desires and goals.

More importantly, the film, shot on the grey, misty coast of Brittany, "exudes magic and contact with dark forces. Guerra has always been a lover of ritual, incantations and spells."[11] Blood is the film's underlying theme. Linked to blood is the symbol of the vampire, which surfaces as Clea and Lis recall their childhood games. "The myth of the vampire," suggests Guerra, "linked to blood, is truly the genesis of love. Vampirism . . . is the necessity of the total possession of the object that one loves."[12] Vampirism is the most complete and total image of love. In it violence and blood mix with the possession of the Other. Clea possesses the escaped prisoner only after his death; she possesses him in death, because in life she could possess him only through her imagination. *Sweet Hunters*, according to Guerra, "deals with the encounter between a personage's imagination and reality, with the discovery of an ignored cultural atavism, which is also a kind of subconscious and collective form of knowledge."[13]

With *The Gods and the Dead*, Ruy Guerra attempts a synthesis of the political-economic analysis of *The Guns* and the psychological-magical exploration of *Sweet Hunters* to attain a deeper, more complete level of analysis corresponding to what Guerra calls a "historical discourse." Economic and political analysis alone cannot explain history. Although individuals reflect the class and historical circumstance to which they belong, these factors are not sufficient for a full understanding of how society and its power mechanisms function. Culture, in the sense of the reservoir of knowledge of a given society, its myths, its values, must be equally understood to avoid the schematicism of much economic analysis.

The Gods and the Dead, like *The Guns*, is set in a specific historical, geographical, and economic context, in this case, the cacao plantations of southern Bahia in the 1920s, a violent period during which landholding families warred over the control of rich cacao properties. The film is based loosely on the same historical events that inspired Jorge Amado's *Terras do Sem-Fim (The Violent Land)*. But, interestingly, the film's initial sequences take place on a modern highway filled with trucks and lined with gas stations, the same locale where both Guerra's *The Guns* and Rocha's *Antônio das Mortes* ended.

Plate 13. Othon Bastos, *Os Deuses e os Mortos (The Gods and the Dead)*

This reference, in a modern time frame, to both films serves a double function: first, it indicates that the situation depicted in the film is not confined to the past only but continues in the present; second, it points toward a certain universe already well-known and codified within Brazilian cinema, that is, the political conflict in *The Guns* and *Antônio das Mortes*. The highway also represents on a functional level the roads to the south along which migrant workers have historically been forced to flee in times of economic hardship (e.g., the peasant evacuees of *The Guns*). The cacao region was one of many that absorbed this extra work force.

The passage from the highway to the cacao forests is also the passage from the present to the past, as if the change in scenario were also a change in historical time frame. This transformation of the present into the past places the action not only historically, but also mythically. The film thus deals with history and with myth, or to put it differently, with the ghosts of that history, with the mythical/historical cultural reservoir that informs the region and its inhabitants.

The Gods and the Dead concerns the struggle for control of the cacao region between two families: that led by Santana da Terra and that led by Urbano Agua-Limpa. Santana da Terra (Santana "of the earth") is concerned primarily with ownership of the land and cacao production and thus represents a certain declining if not decadent landed oligarchy. Urbano ("urban") Agua-Limpa, on the other hand, is at a more advanced, mercantilist phase of capitalist development, involved not only with production, as is Santana, but also with the commercialization of cacao. Neither of them, however, has ultimate control over the product, since its prices are determined in London. Their struggle, therefore, is ultimately destined to fail at the hands of foreign capital. As election time nears, rivers of blood begin to flow between the two families, and the government cancels elections.

If a third force (foreign capital) holds ultimate power, another outside force intervenes between Santana and Agua-Limpa. He is known simply as "The Man," or "Sete" ("Seven"), a reference to his having survived seven gunshots early in the film. Sete (Othon Bastos) is an enigmatic figure with an unknown but violent past (the first time he appears, walking along a railroad track, his arms are bound by ropes). After being shot, he is taken in at a local bordello (representative of a cultural subworld). As he begins to understand the situation he also begins to intervene violently, killing off the members of the two warring families one by one.

Sete thus enters a struggle for power, rises by means of violence, and leaves a bloody trail behind him. He repeats time and time again words from a Brazilian folksong: "I am the king, I am the palace, I want the kingdom, I want the father, I want the mother, I want the son." His trajectory is Machiavellian as he struggles for personal power like his newfound enemies, Santana and Agua-Limpa. At no time do they propose a structural change of power. But as he gains power, Sete also begins to assume the external characteristics of the Santanas and the Agua-Limpas. He takes Santana's lover, Sol (Norma Benguell), and marries his daughter, Jura. But he too is defeated in the end by a force more powerful than he: foreign capital. His empire, like that of his predecessors, is no more than a mirage.

Through Sete's path of violence and death, *The Gods and the Dead* traces a process of capital formation within a specific social structure at a specific historical moment: during the transition from a phase of primitive production to a mercantilist phase. Sete, in a sense, represents capitalism itself in its struggle for control of the means of production. But he represents capitalism in a context of peripheral development, since the true power does not rest with the local antagonists.

The Gods and the Dead is highly allegorical in its modes of representation and cinematic discourse. It comprises some fifty-four sequence shots, all but three of which are filmed by Dib Lufti's hand-held camera. Lufti's camera work, which has been variously referred to as vertiginous, serpentine, baroque, and tortuous, calls attention once again to the film's form. Each sequence carries a large amount of information, and most of them are highly allegorical, allowing for the transmission of a maximum of information and a maximum of spectator participation.

Color, for example, is used allegorically in *The Gods and the Dead*. To the extent that each group is treated collectively, it assumes a given color. The Agua-Limpas are associated with blue, the Santanas with green, the masses with white. But yellow and red are the film's dominant colors. The background of the credits sequence is a yellow liquid—oozing like petroleum out of the ground—that turns red before the first true sequence. Yellow is of course the color of gold, but takes on other meanings through the diegesis, such as betrayal, fever, and power itself. One of the most remarkable scenes in the film is the one in which Sete ritually kills a piglet, lets the blood drip on his face and body, then immerses the animal in a hole filled with yellow water. In a repeat of the chromatic image of the credits, the red blood mixes with the yellow water. This moment is a key in Sete's evolution, for it represents his decision to struggle for power against the Santanas and the Agua-Limpas: on a symbolic level, through the development of a chromatic code, power (yellow) is linked indissolubly with violence and death (red).

The Gods and the Dead is intended to break through the spectator's complacency. As critic Harold Thompson writes, "Your stomach may turn, but you will never forget" Guerra's film.[14] The film is drenched in blood and magic rituals. Its violence has often been criticized, but Guerra himself explains that the violence is shocking not because of its quantity but rather because of its *quality*. It is the violence of the underdeveloped, using knives, razors, and the like, and not the "hygienic" violence of more advanced industrial societies. It is a violence to which the First World viewer is unaccustomed.

In his struggle for power, Sete joins initially with Sereno (Itala Nandi), a former prostitute whose husband the Agua-Limpa brothers have killed. Women characters are often stronger than men in Guerra's film, and Sereno typifies this greater strength and lucidity. After her husband's death, for example, she does not want Santana's protection, but rather the deed to her husband's property. She has an acute awareness of her own needs and the economic side of power. In her own struggle for power, she sides with the one person who can be of most help to her, Sete. In a strangely beautiful sequence-shot in a cacao plantation, she runs nude through the trees, drawing Aurélio Agua-Limpa ever deeper into the woods to kill him.

Guerra was admittedly influenced by Shakespeare in the construction of *The Gods and the Dead*, especially by Shakespeare's "refusal to reject violence" as part of dramatic spectacle. But more importantly, *The Gods and the Dead* is reminiscent of the endless power struggles of Shakespeare's histories. Sete is the Machiavellian palace prince conspiring against the king. But as he gains power, other princes conspire against him in what Jan Kott has called the "Grand Mechanism": when he begins to make history, he becomes no more than its object, no more than a cog in an ever-turning wheel. The mechanism of power is stronger than those individuals who may hold it at a given moment. The influence of *Richard III* is explicit in the film as Guerra reenacts with Sete and Sol a portion of the scene between Richard and the widow Lady Anne. But one also sees traces of other Shakespearean dramas in *The Gods and the Dead*. Like *Macbeth*, Guerra's film is stained with blood and murder; like *Hamlet* and other plays, the spectres of the past are forever present. Much of the action of Guerra's film, furthermore, takes place in an oneiric atmosphere reminiscent of the Elizabethan playwright.

Guerra has demonstrated an interest in magic and ritual since his first film projects. *O Cavalo de Oxumaré* is a documentary-fictional re-creation of *candomblé* initiation rites, which include a double sacrifice of chickens. As the narrator explains in the screenplay of that proposed film, "sacrifice is an ancestral custom. In African tribes the holocaust to the gods at times even includes the sacrifice of human beings. The gods accept only the blood of animals of their preference." In *The Guns* the peasants sacrifice, albeit for more immediate reasons, the once-sacred ox. The soldiers have their own rituals imposed by caste and circumstance. *Sweet Hunters* also includes scenes of sacrifice and ritual. In *The Gods and the Dead* Sete's sacrifice of a piglet is part of a rite of passage as he bathes himself in blood to participate in the struggle for power. The ritual provides him with "magical" powers that permit him to defeat his numerous enemies. At the same time it is a recognition of his own consciousness and decision to join the struggle.

The mystical/magical context of the film approaches the magic of African mysticism and preserves the syncretism of Afro-Brazilian religious cults. Magic is used in the film as a way of approaching the real. Sete, for example, arrives with no past, and it is through some unexplained magical power that he is able to survive the seven gunshots. The ritual bloodbath provides him with further power to defeat his enemies. But his magic lucidity, as Guerra calls it, is limited because used only for personal profit.

Magic also takes the form of madness in *The Gods and the Dead*, the principal example being the pregnant woman (played by Dina Sfat) who wanders through the forest with her apocalyptic message. Her madness results from her lack of arms for the struggle, but it brings with it a form of lucidity. Hers is a madness of lucidity and powerlessness. As Guerra describes her,

Elle est la seule que garde un hargne, une violence. Dans son ventre il y a du pus, toute la pourriture, des couteaux, pour detruire tout ce monde qu'elle hait. D'autre part, elle est assez lucide pour voir les morts représentés aussi, comme les dieux, d'un façon présente, par des personnages que entourent la fille d'un des grands colonels, tradition du passé, présence des ancetres, fin de race, elle peut les regarder avec un regard critique que n'a pas la fille . . . comme elle regarde aussi ceux que ne son pas encore morts mais que vent mourir: c'est la lucidité de l'avenir.[15]

The gods and the dead of the title assume physical form in the film. The dead, which surround Colonel Santana, are in a sense the living dead, representing the end of a civilization, the end of a race and a class. They are ancestors in the present. Like the gods, they do not interfere in the action. They represent a form of thought and an economic structure that are being called into question. They, like the things they represent, are passive and static. The gods, on the other hand, are dynamic. They accompany and are visually similar to the masses in their misery. They represent the vast repertoire of knowledge of the people (culture) and, at times, of the holders of power themselves. The gods are a "representation of the primary idea inculcated in the masses through tradition," explains Guerra. They symbolize a certain biblical-Afro-Brazilian syncretism, and in this sense are an impediment to future progress and the creation of new ideas. Like the dead, they are invisible except to the pregnant madwoman (and the audience). Both historical and ahistorical, the gods and the dead are a sort of Greek chorus that, by its mere presence, comments silently on the action. They are the primary example of the magic that is installed on the concrete level of the film's story (*récit*), a magic that rejects realism as sufficient to explain the meaning of historical process.

All of these elements—from economic data to ritual, from a struggle for political power to magic, from capitalism to madness—are combined in *The Gods and the Dead* in an attempt to deepen Guerra's analysis of the forces at work in the organization of society. "The magical or irreal aspect," says Guerra, "is not a way of contradicting the historical material with which the film begins, but rather a way of explaining it in all of its levels and of exploring in all directions the complex of ideas, relationships, and characters" of the film.[16] *The Gods and the Dead* thus takes cinema to a level of complexity rarely seen in any political cinema.

After seven years of "magnificent silence," during which he acted in a number of European films, coauthored the play *Calabar* (1973) with Chico Buarque de Hollanda, directed several plays (including Nelson Xavier's *Trivial Simples*, 1977), and returned to his native Mozambique to participate in independence celebrations, Ruy Guerra completed his long-awaited sequel to *The Guns* in 1977. Codirected by actor Nelson Xavier (Mário in *The Guns*), *A Queda*, which deals with "social conflicts that the time between the two films has not been able to resolve," was awarded the Silver Bear at the 1978 Berlin Film Festival, the same award that *The Guns* won in 1964. *A Queda* is perhaps the first Brazilian fiction film to deal seriously with the urban proletariat as an oppressed class, a class conspicuously absent from most Cinema Novo films. It is thus one of the first films to recognize the growing strength of the Brazilian working class, a strength forcefully demonstrated in the metalworkers' strikes in 1979 and 1980, which mobilized hundreds of thousands of workers.

Plate 14. Nelson Xavier, *A Queda (The Fall)*

Besides reflecting a growing political and economic reality, the film grows out of an internal debate within Brazilian cinema concerning the nature of "popular cinema" and the role of cinema in the current national conjuncture. In the early 1960s Glauber Rocha launched Cinema Novo with the slogan "a camera in hand and an idea in mind." Nelson Pereira dos Santos has recently amended Rocha's slogan to "a camera in hand, an idea in mind, and the people in the forefront." This modification reflects dos Santos's idea that filmmakers should strive toward the affirmation and defense of popular culture and political ideas, popular culture being defined here as the spontaneous cultural expression of the vast, marginalized majority of the Brazilian population. Rather than impose elitist preconceptions on popular culture, dos Santos seeks to adopt the perspective of the people. But his view comes close to suggesting that the popular vision is always right. This vision is echoed by the protagonist of his *Tent of Miracles* (1977), which deals with Afro-Brazilian religion as a form of resistance against oppression.

Ruy Guerra, calling for a more critical vision than that offered by dos Santos, has further amended Rocha's slogan, in a tone laced with irony: "The people in the forefront, certainly, but not only in their festivities." Guerra thus responds to what he sees as the danger in Nelson

Pereira dos Santos's position of seeing the people only in their festive and folkloric aspects, which are perhaps the most accessible aspects for the middle-class audience toward which most films are aimed. "The people that this type of cinema shows don't work, they are not seen in their daily struggle, they do not struggle against the established social structures."[17] Guerra sees this type of cinema as paternalistic, a result of the petit bourgeois artist's feelings of guilt for not participating actively in the political struggle. Guerra feels, furthermore, that Brazilian cinema will only be truly "popular" when it effectively communicates with the potentially revolutionary classes. The structure of the domestic film market has and continues to impede such communication. The domestic market's structure in turn reflects the economic power structure of Brazilian society. Structural changes must occur before Brazilian cinema can even begin to consider itself "popular."

The Fall is Guerra and Xavier's cinematic manifesto in favor of a straightforward, direct discussion of the Brazilian proletariat as a dominated class. It is concerned with presenting the workers as they are, without idealization. *The Fall* sets out to discover what has happened to the soldiers in *The Guns* who were sent during a drought to a small northeastern town to protect the local food warehouse from starving peasants. (Guerra had originally planned a trilogy concerning the soldiers, but was unable to complete the second part, which was to show Mário's decision to leave the army, because of financial difficulties.)

The two completed films can in fact be read as a single text. The director attains continuity by using the same actors in the same roles, albeit in a different setting, and through the inclusion of entire sequences from *The Guns* in the later film. Mário, played by Nelson Xavier, *The Fall*'s codirector, is the central figure of both films. Both follow his movement toward conceptual knowledge that will lead him, potentially, to concrete political action. They follow his movement from the false consciousness of the soldier employed at the service of the oppressors to the critical consciousness, at the end of *The Fall*, of the worker who has come to consider his own history and present condition and begins to understand the relationship between his individual life and the larger historical, social, and economic process in which he lives. Neither film provides concrete solutions, but rather leave Mário at a new stage of awareness open to possibilities of putting his newly gained conceptual knowledge into political practice. Guerra has said in interviews that he plans to take up Mário again in a later film, as he encounters new situations.

The Fall deals with Mário, Zé, and Pedro some fifteen years after their military service in the Northeast. Like many northeasterners, they have migrated to the urban centers of the South. Mário and Zé are construction workers on Rio de Janeiro's subway system, and Pedro is still in the army because, as he puts it, "these days a man without a uniform is not worth anything." Guerra and Xavier also use *The Guns'* sergeant, played by Leonides Bayer, as a police detective in *The Fall*, but his role is small and there is no specific indication that it is a continuation of his role in *The Guns* (although parallels can be drawn between his exercise of power in the two films). The story is simple. Zé falls to his death on the construction site (whence the title), and Mário attempts to obtain proper compensation for his widow. It so happens that Zé was not a registered worker, and this causes potential problems for the construction firm. The company offers the widow limited financial compensation in exchange for her signature releasing it from responsibility in her husband's death (the company is competing with another construction firm for a major contract, and reports of unsafe working conditions would damage its position in the bidding). Mário defends her and thus assumes a position of leadership in dealing with problems that affect all workers. The job foreman, Salatiel (Lima Duarte), who is Mário's father-in-law, tries to convince Mário to desist from his attempts to protect the widow and promises financial rewards if he will play by the company's rules. Mário goes to the press for aid in his struggle, but soon learns that special interests control the newspapers. Finally, the company bribes the widow's lawyer, she signs the desired document, Zé's death is recorded as an automobile accident, and Mário loses his job. He quarrels with and separates from his wife, Laura (Isabel Ribeiro), but toward the end they reconcile in an attempt to rebuild their lives.

As in *The Guns*, Mário is confronted in *The Fall* with an anonymous mass of northeasterners—the workers—toward whom he feels a certain sense of superiority. As assistant job foreman, he is their boss, and yet his situation reveals his ultimate powerlessness.

The Fall evolves from *The Guns* not only thematically, but also formally, however. The sequel is even more formally innovative than the first film. It alternates between past and present, between the black and white image of the past and the color of the present, between the slow, heavy, reflexive rhythm of *The Guns* and the fluid, hand-held mobility of the urban setting. *The Fall* was filmed in 16mm and later enlarged to 35mm, thus giving the directors a freedom of movement impossible in the earlier film. The camera follows the workers into their jobs and homes, probes and examines various aspects of their lives. It often appears to have a life of its own, to participate actively in the events before us. Like the workers, the camera slithers through the muddy work site, it ducks under beams, and struggles to get the best possible angle on the events depicted. As Robert Stam has observed, the use of entire sequences from the earlier film serves both to enhance and to subvert the realism of *The Fall*: enhance, since it shows that the characters have a history, that they did not come into being only with the present film; subvert, since the change in pace, rhythm, and color undercuts the illusion of reality developed by traditional cinematic codes.[18]

As Mário struggles against the construction firm, and by extension against capitalism, he remembers scenes from his days as a soldier in the Northeast. The oppressor in the earlier film has become the oppressed in Rio de Janeiro. Through flashbacks, we see the soldiers arriving in the small town, Pedro killing the local man, and the soldiers guarding the warehouse. Immediately after the police go to Mário's house to arrest him for threatening the construction firm's president with a gun, a sequence shows the soldiers and their rifles.

Parallels are thus drawn between the past actions and current situation of the soldiers/workers of the two films. Elements of the first film become their opposites in the second. The most important flashback is one in which Mário and Gaúcho have an argument in the bar after the death of the townsman. Mário tries to rationalize by saying that people die all the time and no one says anything. Besides, he continues, "it was an accident." The very next sequence in *The Fall* is a freeze-frame of the construction company's owners talking of Zé's death. One of them remarks that "people dying on construction sites is nothing new." The meaning of this syntagmatic juxtaposition needs no further explanation.

The film precisely and lucidly narrates the problems construction workers face in their everyday lives, their daily struggle for survival, and their physical marginalization when they begin to be aware, as does Mário, of the contradictions of class structure. It, as did *The Guns*, incorporates cinema verité sequences of workers talking about their own lives and the economic difficulties they face as marginalized elements of Brazilian society. They are ignorant of their own rights; they are brutally oppressed by a system interested in deadlines, profits, and productivity rather than in human dignity. One of the workers remarks that "the only thing I can say is that it is cloudy and cold."

The company owners are seen only in grainy freeze-frame accompanied by a voice-over postsynchronized with an echo-chamber effect. On a formal level, this technique contrasts the workers and owners in at least three ways: the owners are seen only in grainy images, but the workers appear only in sharply focused, clear images; the owners are seen in freeze-frame, the workers, the dynamic class, are constantly in motion, as is the camera that films them; finally, the echo-chamber effect contrasts with the roar of the work place as workers have to yell to be heard and understood. The contrastive technique underscores the stagnation and irreality of the owners as human beings, their distance from the reality of their workers, and finally the closed nature of their discourse. By showing them in this way, Guerra also avoids vacuous psychological speculation and concentrates on the power they hold in society and the mechanisms they use to serve it.

The Fall begins with four seemingly unrelated shots before the credits: (1) a building imploding, evidently to make way for the subway construction; (2) poverty-stricken urban dwellers picking through a trash heap; (3) cattle being slaughtered; and (4) the owners drinking blood in a meat-packing firm. The full significance of these four shots becomes abundantly clear toward the end of the film in the sequence where Mário and Laura attempt reconciliation to build a new life together. Their dialogue takes place in Mário's unfinished house, a symbol of Brazil's unfinished development, and is intercut with hand-held traveling shots moving through an urban shopping center filled with electrical appliances and other trappings of consumer society. As Mário remembers Gaúcho and his death at Zé's hands, the camera slinks up an escalator in the glittering shopping mall. The futility of both deaths is brought out when Mário observes that, if he were to die, "everything would still be the same; a person cannot die like Zé did; it's just not fair." At that moment, the roving camera focuses on a color television whose screen fills with the Brazilian government's propaganda symbol for national integration. The meaning is clear: just as the benefits of the developmentalist policies of Kubitschek, Quadros, and Goulart had earlier (at the time of *The Guns*) passed northeastern peasants by, so also has the so-called economic miracle passed by the urban proletariat. The economic miracle, achieved by brutally repressing both peasants *and* workers and putting one class against the other, was, in fact, no more than a violent redistribution of wealth upward, taking what little the lower classes had. The economic miracle has in fact imploded on itself, since it has left only the scrap (the trash heap) of development for the majority of the population while the rich have accumulated unprecedented wealth at the poor's expense (metaphorically, have drunk their blood).

The film also deals with the marginalization and violence faced by women in phallocentric Brazilian society. A sequence in which Mário arrives home drunk and almost rapes his wife underscores the violence of their lives. Laura responds not with coy resistance followed by acquiescence, but with bitterness and resentment toward her husband. Mário's brutality shows that Guerra and Xavier do not idealize the working class in *The Fall*. Although they may struggle on one level against oppression, on another, more personal level many workers continue to be oppressors as well.

Laura's own revolt against marginalization erupts in one of the film's most powerful scenes. One afternoon the family and some friends go to the house Mário is building. Her father, Salatiel, mentions Mário's "problem" in vague terms, then refuses to explain the problem to her. She explodes in a raging argument (improvised by the actors) about the fact that she is not considered important enough to be told the truth about her husband's dilemma. The whole argument is recorded in a single take of considerable duration as Laura expresses her rage at being thought inferior.

The Fall thus works dialectically with conflicts first developed in *The*

Guns. That the film puts a realistic view of urban workers on the screen is enough to make it a landmark film in Brazilian cinema, and yet Guerra and Xavier went far beyond their initial proposition. Implicit throughout is a critique of other filmmakers who maintain an idealistic, festive, populist view of the Brazilian people. Guerra and Xavier offer no solutions, but they do offer the optimism that solidarity brings, solidarity not only among workers, but also between men and women for the building of a new society. The final sequence, in which Mário walks out of his unfinished house in the early morning and over to a worker who has just made coffee leaves him at a new stage of theoretical development. Through his experience, his practice, he no longer has a merely perceptual understanding, but rather a conceptual knowledge of his relationship to the larger historical, social, and economic process of Brazilian society.

Of all the Cinema Novo directors, Ruy Guerra remains the most faithful to the initial tenets of the movement. Like the movement's early films, *The Fall* attempts to document a reality that has long been absent from national cinema, and it does so without embellishing that reality. It accepts as part of its discourse the intrinsic conditions of Brazilian cinematic reality: filmed in 16mm, it was blown up to 35mm on inadequate equipment, which resulted in a scratched final copy, thereby incorporating the continued underdevelopment of much of the film industry in Brazil. Guerra has said that *The Fall* shows that in modern Brazilian society one either adheres to the dominant ideology and plays the game by its rules (as Salatiel wants Mário to do) or one is marginalized. Guerra's own cinematic proposals throughout his career have led to his marginalization from the mainstream of cinematic production in Brazil. "Mine is a critical, hard, analytical, and corrosive art," says the director. And it is an art that is difficult for Brazilian cinema to assimilate.

4. Glauber Rocha: Apocalypse and Resurrection

> *Glauber was Protestant and Protestants had the mania of speaking in tongues.*
> —Márcio Souza, *Operação Silêncio*
>
> *Death is a festive theme for Mexicans, and an essentialist Protestant like me does not consider it a tragedy.*
> —Glauber Rocha

The epigraphs to this chapter—the first from a recent cinematographic novel and the second from the press book of Glauber Rocha's short documentary *Di*—are not as facetious as they may at first seem. Indeed, taken figuratively they synthesize Rocha's cinematic concerns throughout his career. Rocha's "Protestantism" informs his choice of themes in a number of ways, although by no means in orthodox terms. His work presents a double movement that is profoundly religious in its formal and structural conception.

Death and rebirth are essential symbols in many religions: life arises from death; a new world from the old. This basic structure pervades all of Rocha's films, albeit frequently deprived of its immediate religious significance. Rocha has taken the *form* of the myth and used it in endless variations in his films until finally, in *Di* and *A Idade da Terra*, the form reassumes the original content, and resurrection becomes the theme of his work. The underlying religious form is often expressed in terms of revolutionary politics: a new political order arising from the destruction of

Born in 1938 in Vitória da Conquista in the State of Bahia. In Salvador and later Rio de Janeiro he was active in student groups and worked as a journalist and with diverse theater groups and film societies. He began writing film criticism in Salvador before moving to Rio, where he wrote numerous seminal articles on the development of a new Brazilian cinema for the *Jornal do Brasil* and *O Metropolitano*. His *Revisão Crítica do Cinema Brasileiro* was published in 1963, and *Revolução do Cinema Novo* appeared in 1981.

the old or from the ruins of mysticism, alienation, and archaic ideologies. His films are a protest ("protest-ant") against mystification, capitalism, and imperialism at the same time that they are a prophecy of revolution. The prophetic and the messianic are profoundly rooted in Rocha's Protestant ethos and are present throughout his work.

The apocalypse takes many forms in Rocha's films: the violent transformation of the turning wind in *Barravento*; the destruction of mysticism and alienation in *Black God, White Devil*; the ruin of populism in and the agonizing delirium of *Land in Anguish*; the death of Coirana, the peasants, and later Mata Vaca and his henchmen in *Antônio das Mortes*; the end of colonialism in *Der Leone Have Sept Cabeças*; the requiem of Ibero-American dictatorships in *Cabezas Cortadas*. But it also takes on more personal forms, as one character dies, figuratively or literally within the diegesis, only to be transformed and reborn as another.

Resurrection is part of the same movement: the demystification of Aruan (in *Barravento*), which contains both poles of the movement within a single action; Manuel's burst of freedom (in *Black God, White Devil*); the prophecy of revolution (*Land in Anguish*); Lampião redux (*Antônio das Mortes*); the cinematic bringing to life of Di Cavalcânti during his wake and burial (*Di*); the second and revolutionary coming of Christ in the Third World in Rocha's last film, *A Idade da Terra*.

The structuring element of Rocha's films is not only Protestant, however; it is, rather, syncretic, like Brazil itself, and mixes a baroque, Catholic *mise-en-scène* with Afro-Brazilian rituals and saints. Rocha's films are replete with religious imagery. René Gardies has perceptively suggested that his

While still in Salvador he made two short experimental films, *O Pátio* (*The Patio*, 1959) and *A Cruz na Praça* (*The Cross in the Plaza*, 1960). His feature films include *Barravento* (*The Turning Wind*, 1962), which won top honors at the 1962 Karlovy Vary Festival, *Deus e o Diabo na Terra do Sol* (*Black God, White Devil*, 1964; exhibited in Cannes, first prize in Porretta Terme), *Terra em Transe* (*Land in Anguish*, 1967; Luis Buñuel Prize at Cannes, Critics Prize at Locarno), *O Dragão da Maldade Contra o Santo Guerreiro* (*Antônio das Mortes*, 1969; Best Director, Luis Buñuel Prize, plus other awards at Cannes), *Der Leone Have Sept Cabeças* (*The Lion Has Seven Heads*, 1970), *Cabezas Cortadas* (*Severed Heads*, 1971), *História do Brasil* (*History of Brazil*, 1974), *Claro!* (1975), and *A Idade da Terra* (*The Age of the Earth*, 1980). In 1968 he shot an experimental film titled *Câncer*, but finished it only in 1974. He also directed a number of documentaries, including *Amazonas Amazonas* (1966), *Maranhão 66* (1966), and the award-winning *Di* (1978). He wrote numerous short stories and one novel, *Riverão Sussuarana*, published in 1976.

Glauber Rocha was the most vocal, visual, and polemical of all the Brazilian directors. He wrote extensively on Brazilian and international cinema, granted many interviews to Brazilian, European, and American publications. He was the undisputed leader of the Cinema Novo movement. He died after a short illness in August 1981.

films, taken as a single text, are informed by the repetition of a single, Catholic myth—Saint George slaying the dragon—that has profound resonances in *candomblé*, where St. George corresponds to Ogum.

But Gardies's analysis would seem to suggest only one side of the coin. St. George himself is often the dragon resurrected and transformed. The difficulty of many of Rocha's films is that images, people, and things are rarely what they appear to be, or, better said, rarely *only* what they appear to be. In the signs of Rocha's cinema, multiple, often contradictory signifieds inhabit a single signifier or even change signifiers midway in the discourse; signifieds are often transmuted in other signifiers. In a discussion of typage in Rocha's text, for example, William Van Wert notes that the *cangaceiro* is

an immediately fully developed character, because he embodies all the traits of a specialized dress, stylized mannerisms and social behavior that we expect of a bandit. Yet, when portrayed as a kind of messiah for the masses, he is a reversal of the societal hero that we would expect extra-cinematically. Further, he is a contradiction in himself. He is at the same time all-good and all-evil, struggling against equally contradictory forces of all-good-all-evil.[1]

Glauber Rocha's types, Van Wert continues, "are in constant and continual metamorphosis, always at contradiction with their landscape, always at contradiction within themselves."[2]

The complex, ostensibly contradictory nature of Rocha's filmic constructions leads to the second pole of Márcio Souza's epigraphic description of the filmmaker, as "speaking in tongues." "Tongue" in Portuguese is *língua*, which can be translated back into English as "language." Glauber Rocha forms part of a broad, worldwide movement that arose in the sixties to propose alternatives to what has been called the "dominant cinema," that is, Hollywood's polished, efficient, idealistic illusionism. Throughout his career Rocha was concerned with the creation of a "decolonized" cinematic language, a *new* cinematic language based on Brazilian social reality.

As early as 1959 Rocha wrote that cinema, as language, must be seen as an "esthetic fact" that can be understood only by understanding "the architecture of rhythm and plasticity, the laws of the image in motion, the meaning of the capturing of real facts in the fictitious image, or facts transubstantiated in poetry."[3] Rocha soon politicized this concern, even going so far as to say, a year later, that cinema cannot be an art, but rather must be a manifesto turned toward the social reality of the country.[4] The two poles—art and politics—were soon to be reconciled, however, as Rocha developed his own version of an "*auteur* theory," which crystallized in 1965 in the "esthetic of hunger."

In *Revisão Crítica do Cinema Brasileiro* (1963), Rocha aligns himself with the *nouvelle vague* and its struggle to free itself from the rigidity of industrial cinema and its norms. The *auteur*, according to Rocha, revolts against the mercantilist mentality of industrial cinema, which puts profitability and easy communication above art. Although he quotes Truffaut ("Il n'y a pas davantage ni bons ni mauvais films. Il y a seulement des auteurs de films et leur politique") and mentions Bazin and Godard, Rocha goes a step farther than the initial formulations of the *nouvelle vague* and proposes an opposition between "commercial cinema" (illusionistic technique and untruth) and "*auteur* cinema" (freedom of expression and "truth"). In Rocha's words, "If commercial cinema is the tradition, *auteur* cinema is the revolution. The politics of a modern *auteur* are revolutionary politics: and today it is not even necessary to qualify an *auteur* as *revolutionary*, because *auteur* is a totalizing noun. . . . The *auteur* is responsible for the truth: his esthetics are his ethics, his *mise-en-scène* his politics."[5]

Perhaps the most detailed expression of Rocha's formal and political concerns is to be found in his long article "Cinema novo y la aventura de la Creación":

> Like Lumière, Cinema Novo begins from zero in each film. When filmmakers are ready to start from zero, to create a cinema with new kinds of plots, interpretation, rhythm, and with new forms of poetry, they deliver themselves to the dangerous revolutionary adventure of *learning while they make films*, of uniting theory and practice, of changing each theory with each practice. . . .
>
> [Our films are] technically imperfect, dramatically dissonant, poetically rebellious, sociologically imprecise . . . politically aggressive and insecure . . . violent and sad. . . .
>
> For us, *new* does not mean *perfect*, because the notion of perfection is a concept inherited from colonizing cultures that have determined their own concept of perfection according to the interests of a *political ideal*.
>
> True modern art, ethically and esthetically revolutionary, is opposed, through its language, to a dominant language. . . . The only solution is to oppose through the impure aggressivity of our art the moral and esthetic hypocrisies that lead to alienation.[6]

The idea is not, therefore, to transmit revolutionary ideas through bourgeois forms, but rather to create new forms adequate for new messages: one cannot combat alienation by using alienated forms. But at the same time, the "proper" political ideology cannot justify bad art. The cinematic instrument must be known in depth and its elements articulated in such a way as to break with the old and usher in the new. As Maiacovski has said, "Without revolutionary form there can be no revolutionary art."

Barravento is perhaps typical of the seemingly contradictory nature of Rocha's discourse. Controversy and conflicting statements surround its genesis and production. The film was conceived and written by Luis Paulino dos Santos, who was to have been its director as well. Midway in the filming, dos Santos abandoned his role as director, which Rocha, at that time one of the film's associate producers, assumed. Rocha finished the shooting, but

Plate 15. *Barravento (The Turning Wind)*

was not pleased with, or perhaps lost interest in, the results. He edited it only at the insistence of Nelson Pereira dos Santos. On several occasions he has remarked that he dislikes *Barravento* and that he does not consider it his film: "*Barravento* is not really my film, because I directed it almost by chance. . . . It's virtually an unfinished film, primary in its construction. There were a number of ideas that I was unable to develop. But some elements of *Barravento* are part of my concerns: mystical fatalism, political agitation, and the relationship between poetry and lyricism, a complex relationship in a still primitive world."[7] But although Rocha has ambivalent feelings about the film and considers it no more than a "beginner's experiment," many critics feel, paradoxically, that it is his best and most balanced work.[8] Regardless of these contradictions, *Barravento* gives birth to certain structures and themes that will accompany Glauber Rocha throughout his work.

Barravento inaugurates what Ismail Xavier has called a "contradictory narration." "In its convulsive style," Xavier writes, the film "adheres to and backs away from the object of its discourse in a movement that renders ambiguous the values which, in the final analysis, orient it, just as it renders opaque certain episodes of its story."[9] Xavier argues convincingly that the articulations of the narrative work contradict what is generally assumed to be the film's "message" and that the director consciously assumes the contradiction as a means of transcending the Manichaeism inherent or too-often prevalent in films dealing with topics such as alienation and religious mysticism. According to Xavier, the film "attributes to the narrator . . . an attitude of adherence to the religious values of the personages in a reiteration of the efficacy of their 'magic' explanations."[10]

To understand Xavier's reasoning fully and to place his argument within the structure that I see as underlying Rocha's work (death/resurrection), I must first summarize the film's story. *Barravento* is set in a small fishing village, Buraquinho, near the city of Salvador, Bahia. The fishermen work with a net lent by an absentee capitalist, who demands a large percentage of the catch in return. As the fishermen are pulling in their net, Firmino (who had previously abandoned the village) returns from the city with a new mentality and determined to change the villagers' backward ways and antiquated beliefs. His struggle immediately centers on Aruan, whom the villagers esteem because of his supposed "enchantment" by the goddess of the sea, Iemanjá. As a sort of living saint, Aruan cannot have physical contact with women, although Naína, a white girl who lives in the village, is in love with him. Naína herself is linked to Iemanjá (also called "Janaína") through her very name. Firmino convinces his prostitute lover, Cota, to seduce Aruan and thus demystify him in the eyes of the villagers. At the same time Firmino cuts the fishermen's net. The fishermen must either find another net (and another "owner," so to speak), or return to their traditional, and more dangerous, methods of fishing on the high seas in their fragile wooden rafts (*jangadas*). Firmino convinces Naína's father, Vicente, that Iemanjá beckons, and the old man goes out into the rough seas alone. Aruan and Chico set out to save him, but Chico is lost at sea, and Aruan's "saintliness" is unmasked. Firmino continues his denunciation, telling the villagers that he saw Aruan sleep with Cota, who also drowns in mysterious circumstances. After a final, physical struggle with Aruan, Firmino disappears, telling the villagers to follow their new leader (Aruan). After much hesitation throughout the film, Naína begins her initiation rites into *candomblé* as a "daughter" of Iemanjá. Aruan leaves the village, promising Naína that he will return in one year to be with her. At dawn Aruan is seen walking alone down the beach past the lighthouse Firmino passed on his arrival.

Barravento's filmic system derives from the fundamental ambiguity of characters and from the film's découpage. The oppositions that develop between different characters and groups are shifting and unstable. The conflict between Firmino and Aruan, for example, is resolved dialectically as Aruan assumes and transcends Firmino's role. The same thing occurs between Cota and Naína, who, ultimately, assumes the values incarnate in

Cota.

If religion is demystified in the diegesis, its mystical nature is reassumed in the montage and the camera work. Characters are not simple configurations of opposition ideologies (religion versus progress, for example), but rather are complex and ideologically ambiguous. Van Wert is correct in observing that in *Barravento* "no single opposition is ever clear-cut or resolved. . . . Irremediable opposites search for factors (analogies) that allow of a mediating factor, which in turn becomes one of two opposing factors which will allow of another mediating factor, and so on, until finally the intellectual impulse behind the myth, not the myth itself, dies."[11]

Firmino is from the village, and yet he no longer belongs, because he had abandoned it for life in the city. His marginalization from the villagers is apparent in his clothing. In contrast to the half-nude fishermen, he wears an ill-fitting white suit, which carries a charge of ambiguity within itself. The suit connotes progress, and yet its dirtiness reveals the means of Firmino's survival: he has had to steal and pimp in the city.[12] The opposition of dressed/naked resounds in the more generalized opposition of progress/primitivism. The white suit also contrasts with Firmino's skin and emphasizes his marginalization in the city. Although he belongs neither to the city nor to the village (his language is that of the city, his culture that of the village), he is a catalyst for change. "Firmino is the *barravento*. In the abrupt happening and dissolving he is the convulsive presence, and suddenly he is nothing at all."[13]

Naína inversely shares Firmino's marginalization: although she lives in the village, her whiteness reveals that she does not belong. She struggles against initiation into *candomblé* at first, but her name identifies her with Iemanjá. She is neither woman (because the villagers see her as belonging to Iemanjá) nor saint (because she rejects initiation). She loves Aruan, but cannot love Aruan, because he too belongs to Iemanjá. Their separation reinforces their identification. As Aruan is demystified, she, conversely, undertakes initiation.

Aruan is a fisherman, but differs from the other fishermen because Iemanjá protects him. He is a man, and yet is not a man, a god, and yet not a god. After his struggle with Firmino, he assumes Firmino's position as an outsider. After his struggle, he, like Firmino before him, is isolated from other characters in the *mise-en-scène*. He has lost his position in the village and leaves for the city, where, like Firmino, he will be marginalized, until the day he returns, perhaps to continue or repeat Firmino's action. The final image of the film—Aruan and the lighthouse—repeats the first image, when Firmino arrived. Whereas on one level the lighthouse represents hope for the future brought about by a revolutionary change, it also closes the film with a circular structure.[14]

Cota, the fourth major personage of the film, is in an equally ambiguous position. Like Firmino, she is an outcast of sorts. She is a prostitute in the village and longs for the city. She believes in *candomblé*, but aids Firmino in his plot against Aruan. Although she violates the wishes of Iemanjá, she does so by assuming the *form* of the sea goddess. In the seduction sequence, the camera focuses on her *coming out of the sea*: she becomes Iemanjá even as she betrays Iemanjá.

The *barravento* is the moment of violent transformation, "the moment when the sea and the earth become changed, the moment of storm and metamorphosis, the moment of complete eclipse and apocalypse."[15] It is also the moment of resurrection, the moment when the tensions and conflicts reach their breaking point and are transformed into a new reality. It is the moment of Aruan's demystification, of his death as a demiurge and his resurrection as a man, of Firmino's disappearance and resurrection in Aruan, of Cota's death and resurrection in Naína, and of Naína's resurrection in Iemanjá.

The *barravento* occurs after Aruan's profanation, after Cota seduces him as part of Firmino's attempt to discredit him. If on one level Firmino's actions are directed against the alienation implied in religious mysticism, on another they serve to reinforce the mythic value of *candomblé*. Firmino uses *candomblé* in his struggle against Aruan. He goes through the (also marginalized) *pai de santo* Pai Tião (a *candomblé* priest) to cast a negative spell on Aruan. The offering appears on the ground at the end of a vertical pan that begins with the camera focused on the top of a palm tree.[16] The camera pans rapidly down the trunk, as if to suggest the offering's divine provenance.

A similar shot follows Aruan's sexual profanation. The sequence opens with an extreme long shot of Aruan lying alone on the beach. A series of intermediate shots show him getting up and walking. As the camera finally closes in on his body, the film cuts to the trunk of a palm tree. A rapid tilt upward shows the length of the palm and, finally, focuses on its leaves outlined against the sky. The storm, the *barravento*, begins in the next shot, as if to suggest that its cause rests in Aruan's "sexualized" body.

Aruan has violated the unwritten, mythical law of Iemanjá. To remain her "favored son," he must remain virgin. His sexual profanation provokes Iemanjá's wrath, manifested in the *barravento*. Furthermore, Aruan is punished for his violation by demystification, ostracism, and exile.

But Aruan is not the only one to be punished. Cota, who, because of her belief in the divine power of Iemanjá, only hesitantly joined Firmino in his plot against Aruan and who visually assumed Iemanjá's image in her seduction of Aruan, mysteriously drowns shortly thereafter. She drowns, of course, in the sea, which is the realm of Iemanjá. Naína, at the end of the film, begins initiation rites into the cult of Iemanjá after being convinced that such an action could help save Aruan. Naína's integration thus compensates for Aruan's exile.

If, then, on one level *Barravento* denounces religious mysticism and the alienation it causes, on another and perhaps deeper level, the film's discourse reinforces Afro-Brazilian religion as a collective and mythic force. The conflict between Firmino and Aruan is at the same time a mythic conflict between Pai Tião and Iemanjá. Statements by Glauber Rocha at the time of the film's release tend to support the contention that his view of *candomblé* is not exclusively negative:

> *Barravento* .... believes in possibilities that do not belong to it [the film] but rather solely to the people on the march, in this case black people. It is the affirmation of a race that has been enslaved and victimized by racists, anthropologists, sociologists, and artists; the black sentiment is the greatest in the world; it is the black who makes Brazilians rejoice during Carnival and in soccer, two dangerous manifestations for the industrialists of hunger, because the same fury can explode in the streets. And we are doubtless marching toward this explosion.[17]

He thus empties *candomblé* of its expression and collective significance on one level, yet retains and reinforces that significance on another.

Economically, the fishermen, although free men, are slaves of an absent owner: the proprietor of the net. Although fishing with the net is more efficient than their traditional methods of fishing on their *jangadas*, it is also more costly. As one of the elders says, "When we began using the net, it got less dangerous, but then the fish weren't ours anymore." As payment for the use of the net, they are forced to give the owner a large share of the catch. They sacrifice their freedom for the guaranteed catch that the net offers. Firmino's major thrust is an attack, through Aruan, against the economic subjugation of the fishermen. Aruan plays a part in that subjugation, to be sure, but he is not its central element.

Van Wert suggests that the net is a polyvalent symbol in *Barravento*:

> The net, while necessary for their survival, suggests a barrier between them and their native Africa; the net, thus, suggests enslavement; the net becomes the symbol of their isolation from the world of whites in the cities; at the same time, the net is a symbol of their spiritual communion as a community functioning as an individual; in this respect, at least for American audiences, the net is also an obvious Christian symbol.[18]

Although the net does of course symbolize the fishermen's enslavement and their isolation from the world of whites, it also suggests their integration in that world on a dominated, inferior level. But it is perhaps less a symbol of their spiritual communion than is *candomblé*. The central struggle, therefore, is not as much between religious alienation and progress as it is between two classes in conflict, between the masters and the slaves, between the dominant and the dominated. When Firmino cuts the net, he does not, as Van Wert suggests, symbolically cut the fishermen's umbilical cord to the past (because the past is Africa, is pre-enslavement, "pre-net"), but rather to the present. By doing so, he opens the doors to the future. The fishermen are forced to return to their *old ways* (the *jangada*), to their roots, so to speak, in order to create a new future. The *jangada* ("anti-net") thus becomes the synthesis of the past and the present dialectically; it becomes the future. In this sense, *Barravento* points to the Third-Worldism of Rocha's later films, one of which (*Der Leone Have Sept Cabeças*) was made in Africa.

Barravento's mythic and economic conflicts evolve in a *mise-en-scène* that combines, as one critic has said, Eisenstein and Rossellini. The natural sounds (of the sea, the storm, the wind) and natural lighting contrast with a sometimes theatrical and didactic (à la Brecht) mode of representation. Gardies has observed a high percentage of diegetic inserts in the film's discourse, reflecting an Eisensteinian concern with detail. Such inserts provide the film with an extradiegetic temporal frame that points toward the mythic.[19] The choreographic nature of some sequences (e.g., the *samba de roda* and *capoeira* sequences) tends to reinforce such an interpretation by installing a symbolic, theatrical universe on a "natural" stage.

Filmed largely in open spaces, *Barravento* tends, paradoxically, toward the theatrical. The "stage" is delimited by the lighthouse at its lateral extreme and by the sea, the sky, and the beach at its other extremes. Firmino's mode of representation takes on a theatrical-didactic posture, as he is often isolated from the collectivity in the *mise-en-scène* (reflective of his marginalization from the group) and frequently addresses the camera as he "preaches" to the fishermen about their antiquated ways.[20]

As Glauber Rocha has often said of Cinema Novo as a whole, *Barravento* is not concerned with cinematic "perfection." The director himself describes its photography as a "photography of misery." The frequent jumps in narration indicate a rejection of classical modes of narration in favor of the revolutionary discourse of Godard. The camera, although neutral or objective in many sequences, shifts perspectives as it assumes that of the gods themselves or of one or another of the film's personages. The contradictory pervades all of the film's structures. To quote Ismail Xavier once more, "The entire film contorts so that though it may appear the oscillation between the values of cultural identity [*candomblé*, and the like]—the traditional site of reconciliation, permanence, cohesion—and the values of class consciousness—the site of conflict, transformation, political struggle against the exploitation of work."[21] By means of the contradictory nature of *Barravento*, Glauber Rocha denies and transcends Manichaean categories such as good and evil. This denial and transcendence continue in his next film, *Black God, White Devil*.

Plate 16. *Deus e o Diabo na Terra do Sol (Black God, White Devil)*

Rocha's second film, although seemingly much different from *Barravento*, continues the first's basic concern with alienation and the need for change and takes the ambivalent narrative of the first film a step farther. That the film is once again concerned with religion is evident in its title. The original title, however, is perhaps more suggestive than its English title: *Deus e o Diabo na Terra do Sol* (translated literally: *God and the Devil in the Land of the Sun*). Although the title finds resonances in *Antônio das Mortes* (translated literally: *The Dragon of Evil against the Holy Warrior*), it is interesting to note that the original title of *Black God, White Devil* does not imply a struggle *between* God and the Devil as much as it does a struggle *against* both God and the Devil, both of which, while in opposition, are together in the land of the sun. In the title they are connected by the conjunction "and" rather than by the preposition "against" as in the later film. It is only when both God and the Devil are defeated that the resurrection of humanity as the master of its destiny can occur.

Black God, White Devil plays on various levels of cinematic and cultural representation in the construction of an essentially ambiguous narrative. Much has been made of the fact that the film borrows its structure from the oral, folk tradition, more specifically from *cordel* literature, embodied in the film by the blind singer Júlio. Júlio does indeed introduce the characters and comment on the action while at the same time lending the film a legendary or even mythical quality; but even Júlio is a mere construction, a representation. The song he sings is based on the *cordel* tradition, but, like the film itself, it is no more than a stylized imitation of that tradition (imitation used here with no negative connotation). The music was composed by Sérgio Ricardo and the lyrics by Rocha himself. The use of oral ballads moves the narrative to the level of parable, where the real and the fantastic fuse and become inseparable. The *cordel* also lends the film a historical dimension, linking it to the *traditions* of the Northeast and the heroic deeds normally transmitted through such epic forms.[22]

A "superior" narrator frames Júlio's tale within a broader filmic universe. The first and last shots (aerial views, first of the *sertão*, then, at the end, of the sea) are indicative of this larger vision, which transcends that of the blind singer and the characters. As Rocha said in a discussion shortly after the film's release, "The character [Manuel] does not reach the sea—I'm the one who reaches the sea with the camera, showing the sea as an opening of everything that [the fable] can mean, including revolutionary explosion as such."[23] The vision from the outside, so to speak, often contradicts what appears on other levels of the film's discourse, much as the work of découpage in *Barravento* contradicts its narrative "message." The transcendent narrator functions as a mediator between the diegesis and the spectator, reveals what the characters themselves cannot possibly know, and concludes what is beyond their ken.

The film centers on the trajectory of the cowherd Manuel and his involvement with God (Sebastião) and the Devil (Corisco), and with messianic mysticism and the *cangaço* (social banditry). But even this trajectory is soon dislocated as the narrative passes to a higher plane, where a struggle between metaphysical forces forms a matrix for the human struggle of the diegesis. The shift of the narrative from the denotative to the connotative occurs as various functions of the discourse enter into conflict and are resolved on a higher level.

The ultimate conflict of *Black God, White Devil* is not between peasants and landowners, nor, in a broader sense, between the oppressed and the oppressors. Nor is it a Manichaean struggle between Good and Evil, for Glauber Rocha's categories negate and transcend such a dichotomy. The central conflict of the film is rather between History and Destiny.[24] Rocha's "contradictory" narrative affirms the principle of human self-determination while suggesting that a greater "Destiny" transcends human struggle.

The film's first sequence, on which the credits are superimposed, emblematically sets the stage for the folk epic to follow. Aerial views of the vast, arid *sertão* are accompanied by Heitor Villa-Lobos's "Song of the *Sertão*" (the "aria" movement from Bachianas Brasileiras no. 2) and are followed by two rapid, close shots of the decomposing head of a dead ox, thereby providing further "shorthand" information concerning the drought afflicting the region.[25] The synthetic quality of this introduction can perhaps best be appreciated when contrasted to Nelson Pereira dos Santos's *Vidas Secas*, which opens with a seven-minute static take of his characters traversing the dry desert (*caatinga*) under a blazing sun. Whereas dos Santos's film forms part of the neorealist tradition, Rocha tends toward the Eisensteinian and the Brechtian. *Black God, White Devil* deals with the *real* while denying realism as a mode of representation. Its narrative plays on contrast, juxtaposing sometimes agonizing temporal dilations with frenetic camera movements and rapid montage. The tension that builds up in the drawn-out, dilated sequences is violently released in the synthetic ones, thereby reflecting, metaphorically, the very lives of the protagonists. "The exasperating passivity, the verbal awkwardness, the atmosphere of hesitant rumination, alternating with sudden explosions of violence, characteristic of peasant life, thus find resonances within the narrative style."[26]

The appearance of a new element that alters the "peaceful" order disrupts the initial situation of *Black God, White Devil* (the daily life and work of Manuel and Rosa). This element is Sebastião, the black "god" whose procession Manuel encounters along the road to Monte Santo. The *mise-en-scène* of the procession suggests Sebastião's divine provenance. The low-angle camera frames the waving banners against the sky. A rapid tilt downward then focuses on Sebastião as the *cordel* ballad introduces the film's characters: "Manuel and Rosa lived in the *sertão* / Working the earth with their own hands / Until one day, as fate would have it / Saint Sebastião entered their lives. / He had goodness in his eyes / And Jesus Christ in his heart." Yet the image of Sebastião contradicts the narrator's description: the "goodness" appears only in song and not in the saint's eyes, which are more diabolic than saintly.[27] The "god" thus contains his opposite, the "devil"; he carries his own contradiction.

Although obviously impressed by his encounter with Sebastião (he enthusiastically tells Rosa that "he said that a miracle will come and save us all"), Manuel, confronted with his wife's skepticism, does not decide to join the saint until a series of circumstances deriving from an economic conflict forces him to do so. Manuel works for Colonel Morais and receives a certain number of all calves born. After seeing Sebastião near Monte Santo,

Manuel goes to the market to collect from the colonel, who refuses to pay him, saying instead that the dead cows belong to Manuel and those that are still alive to himself. Manuel kills the colonel. A rapid montage sequence shows the colonel's revenge, as his men invade Manuel's house, kill his mother, and force Manuel and Rosa to flee into Sebastião's fold. The rest of the film concerns Manuel's involvement first with Sebastião then with the *cangaceiro* Corisco, until he is at last freed from both God and the Devil by the action of Antônio das Mortes.

Sebastião is the "Black God" of the English title. He is a syncretic figure combining Antônio Conselheiro, Beato Lourençó do Caldeirão (from Ceará), the Beato Sebastião (from Pernambuco), and other historical, messianic figures of the Brazilian Northeast. At the same time he recalls the millenarian Luso-Brazilian myth of Sebastião, the Portuguese king who disappeared in Africa in 1578. The film's Sebastião is the self-proclaimed disciple of Saint George, who promises the faithful a utopia where everything is green, where horses feed on flowers, where children drink milk from rivers, where stones become bread, and where the dust of the land becomes flour. Sebastião promises, recalling a prophecy of Antônio Conselheiro, that "the *sertão* will become the sea, the sea, *sertão*." In short, he promises an apocalyptic transformation in which evil will be swept away and replaced by goodness. And yet his praxis is violence, as he promises to slay the "dragon." This fundamental contradiction—the god who seems more like a devil—is apparent in the film's *mise-en-scène* and montage.

I have already mentioned Sebastião's divine provenance, suggested by a vertical pan from the sky downward to frame Sebastião on the occasion of Manuel's initial encounter with him. Manuel and Rosa's slow ascension of Monte Santo to join the saint (*beato*) is accompanied by Villa-Lobos's *Magnificat Alleluia*:

> Manuel's "surrender" to Sebastião is constructed so as to celebrate a religious force capable of uniting the peasant mass. The camera anticipates Manuel and Rosa by climbing the mountain up to Sebastião's domain, thus providing a rare moment of apotheosis. Processions of banners and symbols outlined against the sky and agitated by the wind find an echo in the symphonic music of Villa-Lobos. The solemn grandiosity of the scene comes, interestingly, not from the *cordel*-singer's voice but rather from the music of a non-regional "universal" composer. Even here, however, the figure of Sebastião is treated with great subtlety, since the camera emphasizes the pomp and circumstance surrounding him, ignoring his "good eyes" in order to emphasize the collective force of religious ecstasy.[28]

Whereas the *mise-en-scène* tends to reinforce Sebastião's "saintliness," the diegesis demystifies it by showing the awe-stricken, blind, and ultimately repressive hysteria of his followers, who engage in ritual humiliations and flagellations as well as in violent raids and attacks on nearby communities.

The sequence that immediately precedes the appearance of Antônio das Mortes shows Sebastião's followers, Manuel among them, beating prostitutes, killing a priest, shooting and yelling, climbing Monte Santo in a mystical, hysterical procession as Manuel fires wildly into the air. It then focuses on the ever-skeptical Rosa, isolated by the camera while she looks at a single flower among the stones of the mountain. She sees her husband surrender to Sebastião and tries to pull him away. As the sequence reaches a climax, the film cuts to Antônio das Mortes, who is introduced through a *cordel* ballad: "Praying in ten churches / With no patron saint, Antônio das Mortes / Killer of *cangaceiros*."

Antônio das Mortes (Maurício do Valle), based loosely on the historical figure José Rufino, is an essentially enigmatic and ambiguous figure who is yet central to *Black God, White Devil*. Rufino did in fact kill the *cangaceiro* Corisco, and Antônio has been hired by local landowners and the church to eliminate Sebastião. Once again, the conflict is predominantly economic: the priest is opposed to Sebastião because he takes baptisms, funerals, and weddings away from the church; the landowner, because he takes peasants away from the work on his farm. In short, Sebastião removes peasants from the process of production and alienates them from "official" religion. Instead, he proposes only passivity in relation to their self-determination and anarchic violence against evil.

In a certain sense, Antônio das Mortes recalls the role of Cota in *Barravento*. Like Cota, he acts against religious mysticism, but, worried that Sebastião might truly be a saint, only after expressing doubts. He says that he does not kill for money (although he eventually does so), and that he wants to "right what is wrong." Yet he does not truly understand the implications of his role, but acts as an agent of destiny. As he tells blind Júlio in reference to his massacre of the *beatos*, "It was against my will, but it had to be." He has an intuition of what needs to be done, but can never successfully explain his actions. At the same time that he is an agent of a larger destiny, he is also an agent of history and frees Manuel and Rosa from one form of alienation to let them live "so that they can tell the story."

Rosa's slaying of Sebastião at the church altar shortly after he had sacrificed a child to "purify" Rosa cinematically triggers the massacre of the *beatos*.[29] The massacre itself recalls images from the Odessa-steps sequence of Eisenstein's *Potemkin* and recalls in its composition sequences from *October*. But since the camera focuses primarily on Antônio das Mortes and his rapidly firing rifle in a frenetic montage sequence, the composition stresses the idea rather than the fact of violence. The massacre is the film's second apocalyptic moment (the first being Manuel's slaying of Colonel Morais). Manuel and Rosa, moreover, are saved—resurrected, so to speak—to live again under the influence of Corisco.

The pattern of death and resurrection in *Black God, White Devil* has thus begun to develop, and its central manifestation revolves around the myth of Saint George and the dragon. Both Sebastião and Manuel refer to and figuratively become Saint George. Sebastião says, "Blessed be our Lord Jesus, who sent the sword of Saint George. . . . The lance of courage has arrived and with it he [Manuel] will slay the dragon." The dragon, in this case, is the powerful, the evildoers, the church, the army. And yet, if we look at the other side of the coin, the contradiction, and see Sebastião in his essentially negative aspects, he himself becomes the dragon and Antônio das Mortes, Saint George. Transformations of this sort ("migrating signifieds") continue throughout the film and recur especially in the sequences dealing with Corisco.

After the Monte Santo massacre, Manuel and Rosa wander about the *sertão* and serve as blind Júlio's guides until they meet Corisco. When the cowherd encounters Corisco, he asks, "Aren't you Saint George of my father Sebastião?" Manuel enters Corisco's sphere of influence as blindly as he had earlier entered that of Sebastião. Corisco represents for him another version of Sebastião's violent mysticism, and is, in fact, an extension of Sebastião. The film's demystification of the "saint" is thus aimed at the spectator, not at Manuel.

Corisco and Sebastião are in fact similar in many ways. Good and evil, God and the Devil, are depicted in Rocha's films as identical. Their voice, delivered by Othon Bastos, who plays Corisco, is the same. Both Corisco and Sebastião prophesy that "the *sertão* will become the sea, the sea, *sertão*." Both use violence as a means of fulfilling the prophecy. The same Villa-Lobos music marks Sebastião's arrival on Monte Santo and Manuel's initiation into Corisco's band.

But differences also exist between them. Whereas Sebastião is introduced at the end of a vertical pan from the sky down, the camera movement associated with Corisco is a horizontal pan of the *sertão*. In opposition to Sebastião's elevated space, Monte Santo, Corisco inhabits the "lower world" of the *sertão*. His erratic, back-and-forth movements also contrast with the straight trajectory of the *beatos* to Monte Santo.[30]

Corisco is the "White Devil" who promises a reign of terror until his prophecy is fulfilled. He slays the poor because he took a vow not to let them die of hunger. At the same time he claims to be the messenger of St. George. At one point he says, "It is the dragon of misery eating the people in order to make the government of the Republic fat . . . but St. George gave me his lance to kill the dragon of evil." Blind Júlio also says that Corisco is a warrior of St. George. Roles have once again been reversed, and St. George, slain on Monte Santo in the figure of Sebastião, is resurrected in Corisco. But once again the signified will migrate with the appearance of Antônio das Mortes.

Corisco is more than just the "White Devil" who sows violence. He is also the reincarnation of Lampião, the *cangaceiro* leader who had been killed three days earlier. In Corisco's own words, "Maria [Lampião's companion] died but Lampião did not. Virgolino's [Lampião's] body died, but his spirit is alive, his spirit is here in my body, which has joined the two. . . . [I am] a *cangaceiro* with two heads, one inside, the other out, one killing, the other thinking." Dadá (Corisco's companion) later makes a similar comparison: "I became two, I liked Corisco and Lampião, because Corisco was a strong man on the outside and Virgolino was strong on the inside." Lampião has thus been resurrected in Corisco, who promises to avenge his death. Like many other of Rocha's characters, Corisco is a complex bundle of accumulated signifieds that defies simple description. Corisco's duality as Lampião is portrayed brilliantly by Othon Bastos, who, in Brechtian fashion, plays both roles at the same time, turning to face the camera as he assumes the role of Lampião.

Manuel the *beato* is inversely resurrected (i.e., in hell) by Corisco and baptized with the name Satanás (Satan), another sign that Corisco inhabits the underworld. Manuel's initiation into Corisco's band is violent, as he is forced to castrate a young *fazendeiro* (rancher) while the victim's bride looks on. Manuel sees his involvement with Corisco as being equal to that with Sebastião. When the band invades the *fazenda*, he carries a cross in one hand and a dagger in the other. In the film's screenplay, the expression "a cross in one hand, a dagger in the other" is repeated three times, as if a litany to reinforce the connection between religious mysticism and violence. At the same time, in this sequence Manuel is referred to as Satanás until after he kills the *fazendeiro*, when the text once again refers to him as Manuel. He has once again been resurrected as Manuel the cowherd, a fact emphasized when he asks Rosa if she wants to go back to their home.

The play of death and rebirth continues and reaches what is perhaps its most significant moment in *Black God, White Devil*. As the *cangaceiro* band pillages the *fazendeiro*'s house, Rosa takes the bride's white veil and places it on her head, in place of the black scarf she had been wearing. Back in the *sertão*, she is attracted to Corisco, who sees himself on the edge of death. She approaches him, they embrace as she says, "I want your child," and the camera begins to circle around them as Villa-Lobos music is heard on the soundtrack. In the next sequence, Corisco prays, "I, Joseph, with the sword of Abraham will be covered; I, Joseph, with the milk of the Virgin Mary will be christened; I, Joseph, with the blood of Christ will be baptized." The film thus re-creates the story of Joseph and Mary in the figures of Corisco and Rosa. Later, Manuel tells Rosa, "We are going to have a child." She repeats, "Yes, a child," but her gaze into the distance reveals that the child will not be Manuel's, but rather Corisco's, who will in this sense be resurrected to continue his struggle against the dragon of evil.

Shortly thereafter, Antônio das Mortes re-enters the scene to complete his mission. As he tells blind Júlio, "I don't want anyone to understand anything about me. . . . I was condemned to this fate and I have to fulfill it without pity or thought." Once again destiny uses Antônio as its tool. When he swears to the blind man that he will kill Corisco, Júlio questions, "If the *cangaço* ends, will misery end as well? If the drought ends, will misery end? Who is wrong, Antônio das Mortes? God or the Devil?" Antônio responds, "God is the people, the Devil is wealth. . . . But *cangaceiros* pursue the people just the same. . . . Without *cangaceiros* and without *beatos*, the people will see things more clearly. . . . It is a war between God and the Devil."

In Antônio's own words the basic struggle of *Black God, White Devil* is enunciated. It is a metaphysical, dialectical struggle between forces larger than the human race itself. But at the same time the struggle denies a Manichaean interpretation. At one moment Antônio das Mortes struggles against God, at the next, against the Devil. As Luiz Carlos Maciel perceptively observes, "*Black God, White Devil* sees Good and Evil [God and the Devil] as internally contradictory values that must be understood in the concrete perspectives of the historical process."[31] Manuel wanders erroneously between both poles—Sebastião/Corisco, God/Devil—in search of salvation. But in the end, his salvation can come only through his own struggle. "The land belongs to man / Not to God nor to the Devil." This is the meaning of the film's final sequence. As Manuel runs across the *sertão*, free from the opposing, mystifying forces of Good and Evil, the camera follows him in a long aerial track before cutting abruptly to the sea. However, it is the camera that reaches the sea, that proposes the solution to the metaphysical problem raised by the film's conflict.

We do not know if Manuel himself is conscious of his new role; based on his past actions, probably not. But it matters little. What is important is the *moment* of transformation, the explosion, the ecstasy of resurrection, and not necessarily the results of the transformation.

Glauber Rocha's third feature, *Land in Anguish* in a certain sense takes up where *Black God, White Devil* left off. Whereas the previous film ended with an aerial view of the sea, *Land in Anguish*, begins with such a view. But this time the sea becomes the land, a "land in a trance," as the Portuguese title suggests, a land immersed in a carnival of eternal crisis and political madness. *Land in Anguish* is a convulsive, apocalyptic vision of Latin American politics, which, according to Rocha, has nothing positive to offer. Implicit in Rocha's view, however, is the dialectical notion that the only positive thing in Latin America is that which is normally considered to be negative and from which a new society can arise.

Land in Anguish is a cinematic poem-meditation on the death of populist politics, on the death of populist esthetics, and on death itself. Structurally, it is the agonizing death-poem of Paulo Martins, whose life passes before him in his final moments. After a brief prologue in which the film's narration

Plate 17. *Terra em Transe (Land in Anguish)*

sets the tone and stage for the discourse to follow, the film is mediated through the subjectivity of poet Paulo Martins in a sort of delirious flashback. The events of the film take place in the imaginary country of Eldorado, a name that recalls the Spanish conquistadors' dream of the promised land filled with gold. The name places the action of the film on a mythic level, where the drama is acted out between types, not necessarily individuals, although the characters of *Land in Anguish* are certainly more developed psychologically than are those of either *Black God, White Devil* or *Barravento*.

In the prologue, Felipe Vieira, populist governor of the province of Alecrim (a name that recalls the Lusitanian roots of Brazil), is reluctant to resist a coup led by right-wing leader Porfirio Diaz. Once again, the name, in its recalling of the Mexican dictator, is no coincidence. After an angry discussion in which Vieira rejects Paulo Martins's entreaties to resist, Paulo flees the governor's palace with Sara, a Communist militant who serves as Vieira's secretary. In his car Paulo breaks through a police barricade and is mortally wounded. The core of *Land in Anguish* is composed of Paulo's agonizing recollections of the political and personal events that have led to his failure and impending death.

Through his death-poem, we learn that four years earlier Paulo Martins had been "with Porfírio Diaz, navigating in the mornings, against the sea and the city." Porfírio Diaz was the "god of his youth." Disillusioned with Diaz and interested in exploring a more political form of poetry, Paulo leaves Diaz and goes to Alecrim to join Sara in Vieira's gubernatorial campaign. Vieira wins the election, but the true nature of his populist politics is soon revealed. Paulo once again becomes disillusioned and begins a life of decadent bourgeois orgies and existential anguish in the company of Júlio Fuentes, a "progressive" industrialist and media magnate who happens to own all of Eldorado's iron, silver, and gold mines, all of its radio stations, all of its television networks, and all of its newspapers. Fuentes recalls such historical figures as Assis Chateaubriand (owner of the *Diários Associados*) and Júlio Mesquita (owner of *O Estado de São Paulo*), both of whom supported the military overthrow of João Goulart in 1964.

Sara later reappears and asks Paulo to make a television report designed to destroy Diaz, now allied with Explint, the Company of International Exploitation. The film within the film, "Biography of an Adventurer," exposes Diaz's successive political betrayals. Angrily denounced as a traitor by his former mentor, Diaz, Paulo once again joins Vieira, this time in his presidential campaign. But the Right is already preparing its coup, and although Vieira's campaign gains momentum in the carnival of national politics (ironically emphasized as such in a sequence depicting a rally in which the masses dance the samba), it is doomed to failure. The narrative returns to the film's starting point as we see Paulo offer Vieira a gun, which he of course refuses. He prefers to dictate a "noble" statement of national conciliation and unity. Paulo's dying moments and silhouetted, uplifted machine-gun alternate in the final sequence with shots of Diaz's coronation.

Like Manuel in *Black God, White Devil*, Paulo Martins oscillates between two apparently opposite extremes—the rightist Diaz and the leftist Vieira—before striking out on what is ultimately a suicidal and individualistic mission of armed struggle. *Land in Anguish* is a graph of the poet's consciousness as it vacillates between a personal desire for change and transformation and a political praxis that tends to reinforce the existing power structure, whether in the form of Diaz or of Vieira (ultimately, two sides of the same coin). Paulo lives an unresolvable contradiction, between the personal and the political, between art and politics. His trajectory is informed by the impossibility of reconciling his personal life and history, by the great distance between his desires and anxieties and the possibility of achieving them, by the absence of heroes and the seemingly eternal existence of political impasses.[32] On the personal level the options are individualistic: he either continues in his decadent, festive life of orgies, or departs on a desperate suicide mission. Politically, there are no options other than Diaz and Vieira.

In his excellent study of *Land in Anguish*, Robert Stam discusses what he calls the "apparent difference" elaborated by the film:

Vieira and Diaz appear to occupy opposite ends of the political spectrum, but the parallel montage of their electoral campaigns, superficially contrasting them, on a deeper level ironically equates them. The "nationalist" press magnate Fuentes thinks himself different from Diaz; historical forces make their roles converge. Paulo fondly thinks that he is not an oppressor, but on occasion he acts as Vieira's policeman. Sara and the militants seem farther to the left, but their actions only reinforce Vieira, and ultimately, Diaz. Linked by their common ties to the bourgeoisie, all these political figures, with the exception of Diaz, nurse the illusion of their own purity. The film's doubling procedures, however, constantly expose their subterranean affinities with their supposed enemies.[33]

In *Land in Anguish* Glauber Rocha continues to employ the complex typage that characterizes both *Barravento* and *Black God, White Devil*. There exists no simple division between good and bad, for Rocha's characters are good and bad at the same time; they carry their contradiction with them. In this sense, *Land in Anguish* is a totalizing denunciation of all the various elements that make up the political "trance" of Latin America.

Vieira is the populist leader (based, perhaps, on such figures as Goulart, Brizola, Adhemar de Barros) who gives his followers the illusion of being in power through him. His true allegiance, however, is not to the people, but rather to the established order. When forced to choose between his electoral promises and the interests of the powerful, he chooses the latter.

The camera work, the *mise-en-scène*, and the montage emphasize and demystify the hesitantly ambivalent and ultimately conservative nature of Vieira's politics. Vieira normally appears on the veranda of his palace, that is, on the periphery of the symbolic center of power. Diaz, on the other hand, normally appears inside his palace. Vieira thus never *really* exercises power, while Diaz never ceases to do so. Vieira's informal political and personal style, his unaffected manner of dress, smiles, embraces, is designed to reinforce the illusion that he is "people." The music that accompanies him—samba and *candomblé* rhythms—also emphasizes a link with the masses.

But the true nature of his politics is clarified in the only two sequences in which he actually comes face to face with the people.[34] In the first, Vieira, Paulo, other militants, and a small detachment of police, encounter a group of peasants led by Felício. The peasant leader attempts to speak to the governor, but Paulo intercepts him and knocks him down for his "lack of respect." The camera rarely moves in this sequence, except when discreetly following the characters' movements. When Paulo strikes Felício, however, the camera gains a modicum of autonomy and, instead of recording the events between Paulo and Felício, it moves toward Vieira and ends with a close shot of his face. Whereas on the one hand this camera movement indicates that Vieira is directing events, on the other, it reveals his powerlessness and immobility. In other words, Vieira *apparently* commands and conducts, but in reality he is subservient to the owners of power such as Colonel Morais, who is attempting to evict Felício and his family from their land.

The second sequence is a political rally in which Vieira appears surrounded by the people. With Vieira are his "allies" in the populist cause: a monk; a senator; a student, Jerônimo; Aldo, the killer; Paulo and Sara, all of whom are at one point or another isolated in close shots. Vieira's comportment is again ambivalent. At times he seems to participate fully in the festive activities, and at others he seems distracted, aloof. His movements also suggest his fundamental ambivalence: he advances, retreats, and moves in all directions with no apparent central purpose. The camera is constantly moving, as if to suggest that no single perspective can capture all of the contradictions of the moment. The populist "pact," indicated by the presence of its elements on the podium with Vieira, soon dissolves, as a "man of the people" pushes Jerônimo out of the way and begins to speak. The unnamed killer who accompanies Vieira silences him, and the united front fades into a series of mutual accusations, as the monk, the senator, and the killer surround the man's body.

The influence of Eisenstein pervades the film. The scene just described recalls the sequence from *Potemkin* when Doctor Smirnov uses his glasses as a sort of magnifying glass to examine maggot-covered meat. Rocha's senator uses his glasses in a similar fashion to examine the murdered man's dead body while praising the "perfect" society of Eldorado: "Hunger and illiteracy are extremist propaganda! Extremism is the virus that contaminates flowers, the air, blood, water, morality! In Eldorado there is no hunger, or unemployment, or misery, or violence, or ugliness. We are a beautiful people, strong and virile like the Indians." While recalling the rhetoric of fascist artistic movements such as Verde-Amarelo and Anta (of Brazilian modernism), his words also complete the analogy with *Potemkin*, as corrupt members of the ruling class deny the existence of even the most evident social problems.

Through Vieira, Rocha denounces not only the process of populism and the fraudulence of leadership, but also the ambivalence and indecision of a society whose development has stagnated. He denounces as well the tactics of Communist militants such as Sara and Aldo in their support of men like Vieira, support that has its historical basis in the Brazilian Communist party's support of figures such as Kubitschek, Quadros, and Goulart in the period before the coup. At the same time, Sara is the only personage given a coherent political consciousness. It is she who constantly brings Paulo back to reality from his sometimes romantic political beliefs.

The other side of the political coin, Diaz, is demystified by means of the

television documentary that Paulo makes, "Biography of an Adventurer."
Rocha's use of the film within the film recalls the "News on the March"
newsreel in Orson Welles's *Citizen Kane*. Both "News on the March" and
Paulo's documentary trace the lives of powerful, arrogant, and often
treacherous men. Diaz is a small-scale Kane. Just as "News on the March"
is intended to destroy Kane, so too does Paulo's film-within-the-film
propose to destroy Diaz. But at the same time, "Biography of an
Adventurer" encapsulates *Land in Anguish* as a whole, for Paulo, too, like
Diaz, is an "adventurer" of sorts, whose own political career is marked by
his successive betrayal of his leaders.[35]

Diaz, with his mythical-ancestral roots in Mexico's Porfírio Díaz as well
as in the Portuguese conquistadors, is the prototype Ibero-American despot;
he recalls not only dictators such as Franco and Salazar, but also the career
of right-wing zealot Carlos Lacerda. Ideologically, he is linked as well to
fascist groups such as Tradition, Family, and Property, "on the march with
God" to protect Brazil's traditional ruling-class values. Diaz personifies the
imperial origins of Brazil and imagines himself being crowned emperor. As
if to reinforce his "imperial" quality, the music that accompanies him is not
the samba of Vieira's campaigns, but, rather, operatic excerpts from Carlos
Gomes and Verdi. An excerpt from Verdi's *Otello* accompanies the
argument and fight between Diaz and Paulo after Diaz learns of Paulo's
documentary. The music's grandeur mocks the pettiness of their struggle
while it recalls Iago's victory over Othello.[36] Yet the central image of Diaz,
and the one that concentrates and encapsulates his historical and political
background, is his initial appearance in the film as he rides, framed against
the sky and carrying the cross of the Portuguese navigators and the black
flag of the Inquisition, in an open car.

Vieira and Diaz represent apparently opposite poles of Eldorado's
political conjuncture. Diaz is linked to imperialism (Explint) while Vieira
has the support of the Communists. Yet both are bourgeois politicians
who ultimately represent and support the status quo. Paulo's disen-
chantment with all bourgeois leaders—expressed at one point in his
derision of Vieira as "our great leader"—is revealed fully in his
agonizing poem-scream, which is repeated in both the prologue and the
epilogue of *Land in Anguish*:

> This fiesta of medals is no longer possible
> This felicitous apparatus of glories
> This golden hope of the highlands
> This fiesta of flags is no longer possible
> With War and Christ in the same position
> No longer possible
> Is the naïveté of faith, the impotence of faith.

The solution to Eldorado's, and Latin America's, problems, the *barravent*, the transformation of society, will not come from leaders like Vieira or Diaz, nor from bourgeois intellectuals like Paulo Martins, nor from militants like Sara and Aldo. The new world will arise, rather, from the total destruction (apocalypse) of society, the "carnival" to which Rocha so condescendingly refers, and from the "barbarity" and the "savage" forces of the people. As Barthélémy Amengual writes, "The desperate crisis of reformism gives way to a nihilism that the revolutionary context of Latin America as well as different guerrilla movements in the Third World permit to be taken as the starting point for construction." "The only hope is in the people, understood as the source, roots, origin, primordial base. The only future is in barbarian, archaic, visceral Brazil."[37] As Paulo Martins cries, "We do not assume our violence, we do not assume our ideas with the violence of the sleeping barbarians that we are!"

Once again Rocha is concerned with the resurrection of a new society from the old. What interests him is the moment of "trance," the moment of crisis, the moment of *barravento*, the moment of revolution. He does not outline political programs nor map a political future. He denies the established order and the established solutions (populism and fascism), which, like God and the Devil in his previous films, are dead ends and forms of alienation that must be destroyed for humanity to take control of its own destiny. Whereas on the one hand, *Land in Anguish* is indeed an anguished cry of political defeat—the defeat of the intellectual Left—on the other, its optimism for a society rising from the ruins is implicit.

But *Land in Anguish* is much more than a cry of defeat. It is a reflection on the relationship between art and politics. Paulo Martins is a poet. He makes a film. And it is a poem that sums up the dialectic as it comments on Paulo's death:

> He failed to sign the noble pact
> between the pure soul and the bloody cosmos,
> a gladiator defunct but still intact—
> so much violence, yet so much tenderness.
> —Mário Faustino, "Epitaph of a Poet"

Poetry and politics are in conflict. Art is out of place in a "land in a trance," in a land shaken by political convulsion. As Sara says, "Politics and poetry are too much for one man." And Paulo, recognizing the contradiction, says, "I abandon myself to the vain exercise of poetry." But ultimately, art transcends not only politics, but also death. Although Paulo Martins—one poet—may die, art, the film itself, remains. *Land in Anguish*, through frenetic camera movements and baroque *mise-en-scène* and montage, negates the static, negates a privileged, univocal vision of reality. It negates, in other words, death itself.

Paulo's poem (and the film) is obsessed with death: "We live with death / within us death is converted / into quotidian time, into defeat / of everything we have used / while we retreat." And: "The people need death / more than one might suppose / blood stimulates pain in one's brother: / the sentiment of nothing that engenders love." It is only when he accepts death that Paulo Martins begins to live. As Che Guevara once said, one begins to live only when one is prepared to die. Paulo is in this sense resurrected at the moment of death. *Land in Anguish* is thus a dark exultation. Paulo Martins gains life *in art* with his death, and the idea of life in death is profoundly Christian. The "sentiment of nothing that engenders love" is the death that engenders life.

In *Antônio das Mortes* Glauber Rocha returns to the themes and location of *Black God, White Devil*, but here his approach and conclusions differ substantially from those of the earlier film. The frenetic camera work and shorthand montage of *Black God, White Devil* give way to a more symbolic mode of representation based on sequence-shots and a discontinuous montage. Due, in part, to the technical development of Brazilian cinema in the period since the first film, the black and white photography of the earlier film has given way in *Antônio das Mortes* to the exuberant colors of the *sertão*. And yet the film makes no attempt to embellish the profilmic reality through the use of lush photography; rather, it uses the natural light of the *sertão* and films directly without filters or special lenses, as a means of capturing what Rocha calls the "plastic 'visage' of Brazil—'tropicalist' because of the color, the style, the interpretation of characters." The visage to which Rocha refers is intended to put Brazil in touch with itself on a subconscious national level.

Antônio das Mortes, like *Black God, White Devil*, is informed by the myth of Saint George. The film's initial and final credits are superimposed on a triptych of St. George's heroic actions, and late in the film Antão/Oxosse kills the colonel with a lance. By the use of montage, his action is repeated several times, thus reenacting the scene of the triptych.

Although the title recalls the Portuguese title of *Black God, White Devil*, there are important differences between the titles that reflect some of the major differences between the films themselves. Whereas the first film deals with "God" *and* the "Devil" in the land of the sun, *Antônio das Mortes* concerns "God" *against* the "Devil." Whereas the earlier film attempts to unmask the twin alienations of religious mysticism and *cangaceiro* violence and transcends a facile Manichaeism that at first glance may seem to pervade the film, in the second, Rocha reintroduces a sort of Manichaeism, albeit on a different level. Now, the "holy warrior" (the people, *cangaceiros*, *beatos*, Antônio das Mortes) struggles *against* "the dragon of evil" (capitalism, imperialism). What I have called the underlying structure of Rocha's films—death/resurrection—is beginning to reassume its original religious content.

Antônio das Mortes resurrects the mystics and *cangaceiros* of *Black God, White Devil*. Sebastião and Corisco were killed in the earlier film as representatives of the negative forces inherent in the two movements. They are resurrected in *Antônio das Mortes* as positive forces. As Glauber Rocha explains, "it cannot be forgotten that the most vital popular force in the Brazilian Northeast is mysticism. Although it is a very negative phenomenon in sociological terms, I think that it is very positive from a subjective and unconscious point of view, because it signifies a permanent rebellion of the people against the traditional oppression of that region."[38] Sebastião of the earlier film is resurrected in the *santa*, who speaks in oracles and metaphors, and in Antão, who represents African religions. Antão is also the resurrection of Ganga Zumba, from Carlos Diegues's film of the same name, a symbol of black revolt. The teacher in *Antônio das Mortes* (played by Othon Bastos, who is Corisco in *Black God, White Devil*) is also named Sebastião. Corisco is resurrected in the figure of Coirana, who speaks in verse and, like Corisco, claims to be the reincarnation of Lampião. Colonel Morais reappears in the figures of the blind (physically and morally) latifundist Horácio and his aide, Mattos, who wants to industrialize the *sertão* and attract foreign investment. The priest of *Black God, White Devil* re-emerges in *Antônio das Mortes* as well, but this time on the side of the poor. If *Land in Anguish* was a discourse on death, then *Antônio das Mortes* is just the opposite: it provides a constant play of transformations and resurrections.

The film's initial sequence "resurrects" the discourse of *Black God, White Devil*. The opening shot focuses on the arid *sertão* and recalls the stage on which Corisco/Lampião spoke his last prophetic words. Shots ring out while Marlos Nobre's electronic music plays against the virtually empty, static frame. We see no gunman. In these shots the film's "ideological stance is stated: offscreen space is where action sometimes happens and framing in all films is an ideological choice (whether conscious or unconscious) that influences the various readings of the cinematic text."[39] Rocha's choice rejects the idealistic illusionism of Hollywood in favor of an open, deconstructed plastic space that permits a multitude of readings by the participatory spectator.

The shot continues to invoke *Black God, White Devil*, as Antônio das Mortes slowly crosses the screen-*sertão*-stage firing his rifle at a still unidentified target. Cinematic realism breaks down further, as Antônio das Mortes moves offscreen to the left and a wounded *cangaceiro* moves on screen from the left to die an agonizing, exaggeratedly drawn-out death. The sequence encapsulizes in Brechtian fashion Antônio das Mortes's history as a "killer of *cangaceiros*."

But time has passed, modern technology has begun to replace the feudal economy of the *sertão*. Whereas Mattos wants to industrialize the *sertão*, Colonel Horácio blames all of his troubles on the atom bomb, perhaps the supreme symbol of technological society. Lampião has been incorporated into "official" versions of history, as Jardim das Piranhas's professor teaches his students history by rote: 1500 and the discovery of Brazil, 1822 and Independence, 1888 and abolition, 1889 and the Republic, 1938 and Lampião's death. History and myth (the myth of Lampião) converge and fuse.

Antônio das Mortes has participated in history by his killing of Lampião and Corisco, and he now lives in a situation of inactivity in the city. We first see him (after the initial sequence) among a crowd watching an independence day parade. But the parade itself calls Brazilian independence into question, as a green and yellow banner is swept off the screen by a marching band dressed in red, white, and blue uniforms. Imperialism and capitalism have become the "dragons of evil" to be destroyed, a fact emphasized in the film's final sequence: Antônio das Mortes walks down a highway spotted with modern trucks and Shell Oil signs, which suggests that new battles are to be fought on a new terrain.

When Mattos approaches Antônio with an offer of money in exchange for killing another *cangaceiro*, Antônio can hardly believe what he has heard. *Cangaceiros* no longer exist. He had killed the last one. He recalls his killings of Lampião and Corisco with pride and sadness. Lampião, he said, was his mirror: "Lampião asked me to join the *cangaceiros*. I sure as hell felt like it, but I was too proud. Lampião was my mirror. I saw myself reflected in him." Instead of joining the *cangaceiros* in their mythic time, Antônio das Mortes creates and lives with his own myth, that of the "killer of the *cangaceiros*." Mattos's request is a request to leave historical time and re-enter mythical time. He accepts the offer, but not for money: "I'll go to Jardim das Piranhas to see if it is true that *cangaceiros* still exist." Antônio wants to verify and test his own historical and mythical visions of Brazilian reality.

In Jardim das Piranhas, Colonel Horácio shares Antônio's doubts about the existence of *cangaceiros* and claims that they are "pure theater." The highly theatrical mode of representation and choreagraphed actions reinforce Horácio's statement, as does Coirana himself, who at one point looks directly into the camera to straighten his hat, as if the camera were a mirror. His action suggests at the same time that he is attempting to verify his own authenticity in this mythical and timeless epic. Much of the drama is, in fact, played out as if on a stage, either in the form of the town plaza, where Coirana and Antônio play out their initially opposing roles in a choreographed duel, or in a vast, natural amphitheater carved out of a nearby mountain. It is this highly theatrical space, as well as the film's many songs and dances, that lend *Antônio das Mortes* what has often been called its "operatic" character.

As in Rocha's previous films, the characters of *Antônio das Mortes* are formed by ambiguous, shifting signifiers and signifieds, as the role of St. George passes from personage to personage. Although he is the self-proclaimed reincarnation of Lampião, Coirana also has much in common with Corisco of *Black God, White Devil*. Coirana and Corisco are both men at the edge of death who express the tenebrous voice of the "other" that inhabits them while at the same time they preserve the internal dream that ultimately destroys them.[40]

But Coirana is given a history that Corisco lacked. During his long agony, Coirana sings a lament of his life, telling how he came to be a *cangaceiro*. His life sums up the Brazilian Northeast, and in this sense Coirana represents the masses in a way that was impossible for Corisco. His descent into town is the beginning of the people's revenge, and, more specifically, that of Lampião. But there he encounters Antônio das Mortes, who is unimpressed by the resurrection of his historical adversary.

Their initial encounter is again marked by a theatrical mode of representation. Coirana says that he has come to avenge Lampião, and Antônio das Mortes wonders if what he is seeing is the truth or a ghost. Coirana's clothes, he remarks, are not enough to convince him. Coirana in turn refers to Antônio das Mortes as being "*fantasiado*," meaning, literally, "costumed." In operatic style, Antônio and Coirana replay the death scene of Antônio and Corisco, this time moving around the town square in a choreographed knife-fight/dance. Coirana, in this struggle, is the holy warrior St. George, fighting against the representative of the dragon of evil. But even as he kills Coirana, Antônio das Mortes begins to assume his adversary's role and to take on the function of St. George in a new struggle, this time on the side of the people rather than on that of the powerful.

After Antônio das Mortes's conversion from *jagunço* (hired killer) to *cangaceiro*, from the dragon to St. George, his former self re-emerges in the figure of Mata Vaca, hired by Colonel Horácio to finish the job that Antônio had started. Mata Vaca and his ruthless henchmen slay the *beatos*, but Antônio returns and eliminates Mata Vaca and his gang. If Antônio had killed part of his former self by killing Coirana, the part that wanted to accept Lampião's offer, then by killing Mata Vaca he destroys another part of his history and cleanses himself, so to speak, of his past transgression. In a rather convoluted sense, he takes revenge for the murders of Lampião, Corisco, and Coirana, murders that he himself had committed.

The *mise-en-scène* of the final struggle between Antônio das Mortes and the teacher, on the one hand, and between Mata Vaca and his *jagunços* on the other illustrates the film's complex play of transformations and resurrections. A *cordel* ballad, which provides its structure, accompanies the sequence. The *cordel* recounts Lampião's descent into hell and his struggle against the Devil and his henchmen. The dichotomy of the film's Portuguese title—the dragon of evil against the holy warrior—is played out on the soundtrack as well as on the image track. The *cangaceiro*, the "white devil" of Rocha's second film, is now the holy warrior wreaking havoc on the domain of the "black god," the dragon of evil, just as Antônio das Mortes and the teacher defeat Mata Vaca and his men in battle. It is only after the battle that Antão kills Colonel Horácio.

But to understand how Antônio, the teacher, and Antão are actually converted from their former roles to their new "revolutionary" position, we must backtrack to the moments of conversion. It is only after killing Coirana that Antônio meets the *santa* and undergoes a mystical transformation from repressor/agent of the powerful to repressed/agent of the people. When Coirana is wounded, the unlikely combination of the teacher, Laura (Horácio's mistress), and Mattos carries him into a house. Obviously, some deeper unity deriving perhaps from their common origins unites them. As Coirana dies, he screams that piranhas are devouring him. It should be recalled that the village where the film's action takes place is Jardim das Piranhas (Garden of Piranhas) and that one of its central meeting places is the Alvorada Bar (the presidential palace in Brasília is the Palácio da Alvorada). The logo under the bar's name reproduces somewhat crudely the general motif of the palace's design. We are dealing with a multilayered process of signification. The word "piranha" in Portuguese has at least two meanings: it is at the same time the name of a particularly vicious, carnivorous fish, and, in modern slang, means a prostitute. The idea of prostitution is thus linked to the Alvorada Bar, where Coirana is carried, and, by extension, to the Alvorada Palace in Brasília and Brazil's military rulers.

The piranha motif returns later in the film as part of one of the major keys to Antônio das Mortes's transformation. After meeting the *santa*, who tells him that he had killed her parents and brothers, Antônio says that the "Holy One" reminds him of a girl he once knew in Pernambuco. The girl had been seduced by a colonel's son and expulsed from her house. She had become a prostitute, consumed by tuberculosis, had fallen into a river and was eaten by piranhas. In a triple montage sequence the *santa* tells Antônio that the masses are his brothers and that "he who kills a brother will sink to the bottom of the sea. If Coirana dies, so too will the people." At the same time she urges him to undertake an "endless war" or "walk the burning paths of the earth forever." Antônio's transformation is fundamentally personal and mystical, his salvation an eternal struggle against the forces of evil.

The death of Coirana gives birth not only to a transformed Antônio das Mortes, but also to a revolutionary transformation in both Antão and the teacher. Early in the film, a passive Antão, dressed in red, in contrast to the *santa*'s white dress of purity, appears at the *santa*'s side. At one point he talks of leaving Brazil and returning to Africa, saying that both the government and God must be respected. He warns Coirana of the dangers of revolt, but the *cangaceiro* responds that no one respects him and that now it is a question of "an eye for an eye, a tooth for a tooth." Later in the film, the teacher, for no immediately apparent reason, mounts Antão and beats him viciously, as if trying to provoke him to action. The fact that Antão assumes a position on all fours out of fear "means that he wants to disappear, incorporate himself to the earth. To die in order to be radiantly reborn. The hero does not ascend to his solar glory unless, like the sun and vegetation, he first goes through an occult period." The scene also represents the *macumba* trance "in which the possessed becomes the horse of the god that has possessed him." When the teacher mounts Antão, "he is filled with divine power, and Antão, who had been wearing the traditional red clothes of Ogum, comes to possess Ogum's virtues."[41]

But the passing of Ogum's virtues to Antão can take place only after Coirana's death, since Coirana himself is referred to several times not only as Ogum (the *candomblé* equivalent of St. George) but also as Oxosse, the equivalent of Saint Barbara. When Coirana is wounded, the *beatos* lament that "Ogum is dead," and yet the song of his life continues. Toward the end of Coirana's lament the song changes from first person (Coirana) to a third person narrator who sings of meeting Coirana and giving him his name.

The change in narrative perspective coincides with a change in scale, as the film cuts from the close of Coirana to a long shot of him, dying on the mountain. Beside him Antão continues the song, although the voice does not change, nor does the guitar accompaniment give way to Antão's drum. Just as Antão continues Coirana's song, so too does he take over his role as St. George/Ogum.[42] He fulfills this new role toward the end of the film by killing Colonel Horácio with the lance of St. George. Antão is transformed from the passive, conservative black man longing for the past to an African warrior, Ganga Zumba, who incorporates the virtues of Ogum, Oxosse, and St. George.

The sign of death comes to govern the *sertão* as Antônio tells the *santa* that he is going to bury Coirana in the desert. At the same time, the teacher drags Mattos, who had been killed by Laura for his successive betrayals, through the *sertão*. Before the priest's frantic eyes, the teacher and Laura begin to embrace and kiss on Mattos's dead body. The priest had come to warn them that Horácio had ordered the *beatos'* slaughter. This sequence, dominated by the twin signs of Eros and Thanatos, counterpoints the *beatos'* songs and the wild cheers of the *jagunços*, who are ready to kill, with the electronic music of the *sertão* death scene. As shots are heard far off, Antônio embraces Coirana's inert body before the film cuts to Mata Vaca laughing at the *santa* and Antão, the sole survivors of the massacre. The sequence ends with Mata Vaca backing away in fear from the *santa*.

The teacher, after beating Antão (after the massacre), attempts to flee by hitching a ride on the truck-filled highway. Antônio pursues him and halts his flight, but it is the music that provides the key to his resurrection: "Get up, shake off the dust, start climbing up the path . . . a strong man doesn't stay down." As Antônio and the teacher re-enter the *sertão* they are both startled by the sight of a resurrected Coirana, his vertical body "crucified" on a tree. They look at Coirana (and the camera), and it is at this moment that the *cordel* recounting Lampião's descent into hell begins. There Lampião caused a revolution, burned Satan's empire, and freed the oppressed. The teacher solemnly commits himself to Lampião's cause, takes a sword and gun from Coirana's body, and assumes his role. The *cordel*, which ceases during this ritual, resumes and illustrates on a mythic level the Peckinpah-like battle that takes place between opposing sides. As Antão/St. George/Ogum kills Horácio, the *cordel* describes Lampião's destruction of hell, presenting it in terms of a vast capitalist empire.

But the *cordel* soon gives way to Antônio's slower, sadder ballad of the man with no patron saint, condemned to walk the burning paths of the earth in search of forgiveness. The final shot shows him alone on a busy highway, going off to fight larger battles and new dragons of evil, which will certainly be resurrected throughout time.

Before leaving Brazil in 1969 for a period of self-exile that ended in 1976, Glauber Rocha shot a 16mm film called *Câncer*. He finished it in Cuba in the early 1970s. Although *Câncer* has not yet been exhibited publicly in Brazil and although it is not particularly relevant to the present study, it does present a number of formal elements that will reappear in later films, notably in *A Idade da Terra*. *Câncer*, like *Antônio das Mortes*, uses the sequence-shot as its predominant mode of discourse. It is a rather confusing story about several personages who are "marginal" to urban society. In it the actors are given complete freedom to improvise, which in part accounts for the fact that it is Rocha's first film to reveal even a modicum of humor.

The important thing about the film, however, is its self-reflexivity. Actors frequently look at the camera (at Rocha) as if to ask what to do next; on several occasions Rocha yells instructions or phrases to try to provoke them into varied responses. Rather than being printed on film, the credits are spoken by Rocha himself, and he appears in several sequences. Rocha also experiments with sound: in several sequences the sound is slowed down so that voices drag at a pitch much lower than normal. The film's production is part of its diegesis. *Câncer* thus represents a breakdown of the illusionism of traditional cinema. All of these techniques will be repeated and radicalized in later films.

While in exile Glauber Rocha made four films: *Der Leone Have Sept Cabeças* (Republic of Congo), *Cabezas Cortadas* (Spain), *Claro!* (Italy), and *História do Brasil* (Italy/Cuba). Of the four, only *Cabezas Cortadas* has been exhibited commercially in Brazil, distributed by Embrafilme in late 1979. Rocha had intended to release *Der Leone Have Sept Cabeças* as well, but was told a priori that the film would not be approved by Brazilian censors. *Der Leone*, with its multilingual title, is, in Rocha's words, a film "about the possibility of making a political cinema" based on a synthesis of the "historical myths of the Third World through the national repertory of popular drama."[43] It exacerbates the symbolic character typage of *Antônio das Mortes* as well as its explicit theatricality. The film comprises some seventy sequence-shots or blocks that provide a synthetic and allegorical rendering of the history of Third World colonialism. Rocha has described it as being "the story of Che Guevara and Zumbi dos Palmares in Africa . . . through the materialization of blacks."[44] Its extensive use of African dance and music has led one critic to call *Der Leone* a "primitive opera." Rocha himself has said that his film borrows from the character typage of the Brechtian epic, from Godardian political reflection, and from Eisenstein's concept of dialectical montage.[45]

The "story" of *Der Leone Have Sept Cabeças* rests on its personages/types: a Portuguese businessman (played by Brazilian Hugo Carvana); a German mercenary who has gone to fight in Africa because he misses war; a domineering American tourist named Marlene who also serves as one of the holders of power; a CIA agent; Doctor Xobu, who, corrupted by foreign capital, assumes power in the mythical country; a mystic priest (Jean-Pierre Leaud); and the revolutionaries Pablo and Samba Zumbi. In his excellent structural analysis of the textual system of Rocha's films, René Gardies distinguishes five different character groupings in *Der Leone*: (1) the holders of power (Marlene, Xobu); (2) the disinherited (the African dancers, Samba Zumbi); (3) the mystics (the priest); (4) the instruments of power (the German mercenary, the American agent, the Portuguese, the priest); and (5) the revolutionaries (Pablo, Samba Zumbi, demonstrators, and soldiers).[46]

The three representatives of neocolonialism (the German, the American, the Portuguese) impose the black bourgeois African Doctor Xobu as president of this mythical country, converting it into a republic. But Xobu, dressed in Louis XVI finery, including a wig, begins to dispute the country's wealth (symbolized by a bone) with Marlene. The foreign agents want their share of the wealth, but the CIA agent fends them off and keeps the bone for himself. The revolutionary heroes Samba Zumbi and Pablo, however, capture the American and the German while the priest, now converted to the revolutionary cause, crucifies Marlene. The film ends with a shot of an African army on the march, symbolizing the march of history.

The linearity of this plot description is a gross oversimplification of the true nature of Rocha's film, which is considerably more complex than the description might lead one to believe. If, in *Antônio das Mortes*, the narrative blocks are arranged in such a way that there is a consistent alternation between the different groups of characters to reveal simultaneous action in several distinct dramatic spaces, in *Der Leone* the five character groupings are organized into a "polyphonic composition."[47] The space of *Der Leone* is not only mythical, but also very theatrical. The "world" does not exist in the film except as a scenic backdrop. The film's message is transmitted through burlesque sketches, almost indecipherable symbols, complex allegories, and parables.[48] Gardies has compared portions of the film to a marionette theater in which one personage enters the filmic space, delivers his or her message, then exits, leaving the space empty for the next personage. In Rocha's words, "As *mise-en-scène Der Leone* is an extremely radical film, because I created a centralization in the sense of truly synthesizing action, that is, making each shot an act full of information. . . . Each shot can be seen alone or articulated with the others in a dialectical montage."[49]

Rocha has said that his personages are "the beasts of the Apocalypse as projected by the powerful, for whom Christianity is completely bankrupt within the nature and the mysticism of Africa."[50] Implicit in Rocha's statement is his view of Christianity as a liberating force, especially in its "liberation theology." This is seen most clearly in the figure of the priest, who represents the revolutionary work of the "new" church in Africa. The religious aspect of the film is emphasized even further, and with a good deal of humor, when Rocha declares that, "as I am Protestant by formation and African by alimentary education, I preferred to be inspired by 'The Apocalypse of St. John.'"[51]

Like Rocha's other films, *Der Leone*, with a mythic structure, reveals a concern with the inexorability of history, with the inexorability of a revolutionary destiny, with the inevitability of the resurrection of the people as a revolutionary force. As in *Antônio das Mortes*, the underlying structure of Rocha's work here continues to reassume its original content. Once again in Rocha's words, "There is the ritual of death in the beginning, where Zumbi appears; and later the ritual of the resurrection at the end where Che is resuscitated by the magic of the blacks; and there is the transformation of the religious cultists into the armed columns of Amilcar Cabral."[52]

Cabezas Cortadas resurrects *Land in Anguish*'s Porfirio Diaz in a requiem of Ibero-American dictatorships. Like the earlier film, it is governed by a tension between life and death. It is constructed through a long flashback filtered through the subconscious of a dying man, in this case the exiled dictator, Diaz II. Diaz's approaching death brings to the fore his remorse and feelings of impotence tempered by his terror of the ever-closer symbol of the unavoidable rise of the masses to power. At the same time, Diaz has delusions about the possibility of returning to power by marrying a young peasant woman. The ghosts of his past haunt him, as do those of the future. *Cabezas Cortadas* is a death ritual, a nightmare of the moribund patriarch, or, as one critic has put it, a "funeral in images and sounds."

The death of Diaz II signifies, on a mythic level, the birth of a new order. The scythe-bearing shepherd of *Cabezas Cortadas* functions as did Antônio das Mortes in *Black God, White Devil* and *Antônio das Mortes*. He is the agent of destiny. He brings knowledge, vision, and finally the crown itself to the people. Like Pablo and Samba Zumbi in *Der Leone Have Sept Cabeças*, the shepherd (played by Pierre Clementi) is the "revolutionary" who struggles against the holder of power (Diaz II).

The same character groupings of *Der Leone* can be seen in *Cabezas Cortadas*. Besides the powerful and the revolutionaries, there are the disinherited (the group of gypsies, the peasant woman Dulcinea), the mystics (the blind beggar), the instruments of power (Dona Soledad, the white man, the prostitute, the monk, the doctor).[53]

Cabezas Cortadas begins, during the credits, with a long take of an Iberian castle atop a rocky hill. Though filmed in Spain, the film takes place in an undetermined, mythical land. The arid landscape surrounding the castle recalls the arid *sertão* of *Black God, White Devil* and *Antônio das Mortes*, and the music accompanying the credits—"Rancho grande"—brings the cultural and political universe of Spanish America into the diegesis. Like Rocha's two previous films, *Cabezas Cortadas* favors the synthetic, symbolically charged sequence-shot to traditional forms of cinematic discourse. Chronology of narration here gives way, however, to an oneiric flux of images and events, to the hallucinations of a senile former dictator. Like *Câncer*, this Spanish film is highly theatrical and self-reflexive, as Diaz II frequently addresses the camera and as Glauber Rocha himself intervenes vocally—in poor Spanish—to describe the economic situation of Eldorado, from which Diaz II is exiled.

The use of myths associated with the sun and earth makes the dichotomy of death and resurrection in the film explicit.[54] Near the end of the narration, the peasant woman Dulcinea (played by Maria Rosa Pena, the *santa* of *Antônio das Mortes*) appears near a wall. She touches, then kisses a stone. The shepherd takes the stone from her and gives her sand in return. With his scythe he slashes at a blood-covered tree and kills Dulcinea symbolically. Her death is symbolized by a single drop of blood on her cheek. The shepherd is then seen working the soil. Shortly thereafter an Indian and a white man leave a corral carrying her body in a funeral procession. According to Gardies this ritual recalls precisely traditional agrarian cults and is a symbolic representation of the agrarian cycle. The peasant woman touches a stone to make herself fertile, since sacred stones have the power to overcome sterility. The figure of the agro-solar visitor (the shepherd) intervenes, substitutes the fecundity of the earth for the stone, and identifies the woman with the cosmic cycle. He kills the tree of life, which is an image of the universe and its constant regeneration, and then he kills the peasant woman, symbol of purity. Through his work the shepherd opens the earth, symbolically penetrates the woman's womb, and thereby foreshadows the marriage of the shepherd and the woman/people. When the two men carry her body, the seed has been planted inside her. The procession symbolizes the subterranean work of an apparently dead nature. A shot of Diaz's death and the appearance of his coffin follows. With his death, Dulcinea reappears, immaculate and radiant as new vegetation. The shepherd's scythe falls once more, and the hero and the people are united at their highest moment. The solar myth is the myth of a new beginning from death, a constant becoming and regeneration, an incessant resurrection.

Since neither *História do Brasil* nor *Claro!* has to this date been widely exhibited in either Brazil or the United States, very little information is available concerning them. *História do Brasil*, a two-hour and forty-five-minute documentary, was exhibited for the first time in the Pesaro Festival in 1975. According to Rocha, the film is "a material and dialectical exposition of the history of Brazil; the fixed or moving images are the historical documents, the text is the historical information and the critical commentary of the images edited chronologically and dialectically."[55]

Claro!, which has been referred to as a "delirium," concerns "the birth, in the ruins of Western Civilization, of the son of Uirapuru [a uirapuru is an Amazonian wren] and Irerê."[56] The indigenous names indicate the personages' probable allegorical nature, once again the idea of life and death, the birth of a new civilization from the ruins of the old. *Claro!*, which was screened at the 1975 Taormina Festival in Italy, has been described by one critic as "a scream that arises from the Third World, runs through the space and time of imperialist oppression and bourgeois decadence, in the exaltation of the struggle for a new world. . . . Extremely lucid in its delirium, *Claro!* gains life from a baroque expressionism with a functional use of music that is an essential part of its expressive structure."[57]

After returning to Brazil in 1976 and while awaiting possible financing for his long-planned *A Idade da Terra*, Glauber Rocha made a short documentary, titled *Di*, about famed Brazilian painter Di Cavalcânti. The occasion of the film was Cavalcânti's death, wake, and burial. Death and resurrection at last become the center of Rocha's cinema, both in content and in form. In his introductory notes to the film Rocha explains, "Filming my friend Di dead is an act of Modernist-Surrealist Humor that is permitted among *reborn* artists: Phoenix/Di never died. In this case the film is a celebration that liberates the deceased from his tragic hypocritical condition. The *Festa*, the *Quarup*—the resurrection that transcends the bureaucracy of the cemetery." And again, "In the metaphorical trans-psychoanalytical field I materialize the victory of St. George over the Dragon. . . . The Poetic discovery of the end of the century will be the

Plate 18. Glauber Rocha (right) and Mário Carneiro filming *Di*

materialization of Eternity." In the same notes Rocha asserts in somewhat delirious terms that he is St. George and Di Cavalcânti (symbolizing death) is the dragon. Life overcomes, defeats, and transcends death.

Di Glauber, as Alex Viany has baptized the film (or *Di (Das) Mortes* as Rocha refers to it), is a dialogical and intertextual film par excellence. In intertextual writing—and film is a form of "writing"—a word (a shot, an image) is not merely a fixed, static point, but rather an intersection of several different textual surfaces. The text, film or otherwise, is thus an intersection of texts where one may read or perceive the existence of other texts.[58]

The very title of Rocha's documentary is intertextual on a surface level, as the different titles Rocha and Viany have given the film enter into dialogue and point toward other contiguous universes of signification. The film's subtitle, taken from a poem by Augusto dos Anjos, participates in the dialogic play: *Nobody Witnesses the Formidable Burial of His Last Chimera, Only Ungratefulness, That Panther, Was His Inseparable Companion*. The original title, *Di*, gives way in Viany's version to a dialogue between Di Cavalcânti and Glauber Rocha: *Di Glauber*. Phonetically, this title also means "By Glauber." Rocha's own revision of the title, *Di (Das) Mortes*, remits the film and the spectator to the universe of his own films, notably *Black God, White Devil* and *Antônio das Mortes*.

But more importantly, *Di (Das Mortes) Glauber*, to take the dialogic title a step further, is intertextual in its conception and construction, as the image enters into a dialogue with the sound. As in *Câncer* and *Cabezas Cortadas*, Glauber Rocha intervenes vocally in the film, but this time to a much greater degree. He assumes an important role in the film as its narrator, and what he says becomes as important if not more so than the image of Di's wake and burial. The film therefore functions on one level as a dialogue between Rocha and Di Cavalcânti.

The director tells us at the beginning that he is a celebrity (narcissistic exhibitionism?) and so is Di Cavalcânti, so the best way to understand Di's career as a painter is through their relationship. In an ever heightening crescendo, Rocha narrates facts about, events, meetings, and phone calls with the deceased painter. From there he goes on to read critiques of the painter's art, poems, fragments of the artist's life as seen from various perspectives. His death is compared through newspaper headlines to the deaths of figures such as former presidents Juscelino Kubitschek and João Goulart, playwright Paulo Pontes, and actress Regina Rosemberg Leclery. *Di* presents fragments not only of Di Cavalcânti's life and work, but also of the universe in which he lived and worked and of the various ways in which his life and art can be interpreted. As Mário Chamie suggests, *Di Glauber* is a *"bricolage* of hypotheses and suggestions united by the incoherent coherence that supports it."[59]

The director also intervenes visually in the film. During the wake, held in Rio de Janeiro's Museum of Modern Art, a temple of Brazilian culture, Rocha is seen directing cameraman Mário Carneiro in the filming of Di's open casket. The image cuts to Carneiro's perspective as Glauber says, "One, two, three, four. Cut! Now get a close of his face!" His "disruption" of the normally solemn wake represents a fundamentally carnivalesque attitude toward the world and toward death. As Rocha himself said (in the words used as epigraph to this chapter), "Death is a festive theme for Mexicans, and an essentialist Protestant like me does not consider it a tragedy." During the filming of the burial this attitude continues as he captures actor Joel Barcellos trying to flirt with Di Cavalcânti's favorite model, Maria Montini.

The *bricolage* that is *Di (Das Mortes) Glauber* alternates relatively solemn sequences of Cavalcânti's wake and burial with shots of other elements of the artist's cultural universe, including his paintings, books about him, friends of the director flipping through books by Darcy Ribeiro and Antônio Callado, newspaper reports of the painter's life and death. These sequences are often constructed through rapid-fire, discontinuous montage and frenetic, indeed delirious, camera work, as if the camera were trying to capture something beyond the merely representational, as if it were trying to bring these "dead" cultural objects to life. Death, the director seems to be saying, is not an end but rather a beginning. It should be met not with sadness but with jubilation. Above all, death is spectacle.

A Idade da Terra is in Glauber Rocha's words the "end of the cycle of the young Glauber." It is a summation of his films up to this point, a film that re-examines, reorganizes, and recasts the concerns of his previous films in a vast (two hours and forty minutes) audiovisual, "symphonic" mosaic of the "sociomystical" reality of Brazil and the Third World. A Idade da Terra is at once the apocalypse and the resurrection. It is the apocalypse of a cinematic style based on nineteenth-century linear narrative, a style that Rocha has long denounced as "alienated" and "colonized." At the same time it represents a resurrection of cinema in its pure form. "Cinema," says Rocha, "is made with images and sound." A perhaps banal statement, but not so banal when related to A Idade da Terra, a film that proposes new ways of approaching reality and, through its dialogue with the plastic arts, new ways of making and seeing films. It has been described as a Super-8 esthetic in cinemascope. It proposes a form of emotional-sensorial-psychoanalytic-audiovisual communication in which the spectator's un-conscious is more important than the rational meaning of traditional cinema. In A Idade da Terra the fundamental structure of Rocha's filmic text surfaces, and resurrection becomes its central, explicit theme. The film revives the myths and legends of the colonized and colonizing world by mixing Shakespeare and Camões, the creation and the apocalypse, revolution and reaction. A Idade da Terra deals ultimately with the resurrection of Christ in the Third World.

The symbol of Christ that the film revives, however, is by no means an orthodox one. In fact, there are four Christs in A Idade da Terra: an Indian, inspired by José de Alencar's O Guarani, who is also a fisherman and a construction worker (carpenter?); a black modeled after Zumbi dos Palmares and Ganga Zumba; a military officer (Tarcísio Meira) based on both the Portuguese discoverers and the national hero Tiradentes; and a guerrilla (Geraldo D'El Rey). Rocha's Christ is all of these things and more, for, as in his previous films, none of the personages are only what they appear to be.

In addition to these four characters, A Idade da Terra also presents other allegorical characters: Brahms (Maurício do Valle), a blond tyrant who

Plate 19. Jece Valadão, *A Idade da Terra (The Age of the Earth)*

represents the forces of imperialism; Aurora Madalena (Ana Maria Magalhães), the indigenous nations; Norma Benguell, the strength of the Amazons; and Danuza Leão, the modern woman divided between politics and love. All of these descriptions are taken from the press notes, but in reality give no indication of the various personages' roles in the film.

The characters are both what they are in the representation (which may be several things) and actors playing characters. The film levels the two. Actors, even when being themselves, become personages when filmed and projected on a screen in a dark theater. At the same time, showing the personages as actors playing personages is to demystify the representational nature of the filmic spectacle, or to graft a second spectacle onto it. The *process* of cinematic production thus comes to the foreground as part of the diegesis.

Rocha denies the actors the illusionism behind which they hide in traditional forms of cinema. Actors are often seen receiving instructions from the director or being made up for their "fictitious" roles. Even as personages these allegorical figures are not well developed. They are what they are at the moment they appear. In the next sequence or shot they may well be something else. Brahms/Maurício do Valle, for example, is presented at one moment as a foreigner of a white, superior race, a powerful and strong industrialist whose ancestors were emperors. Later, Aurora Madalena/Ana Maria Magalhães proclaims him to be "old, ugly, and sick." But as he leaves the film's mythical Brazil, he celebrates that fact that he was able to sign many contracts. At other moments he is a devil/sorcerer, a soccer announcer, a "pharaoh" supervising the construction of his own pyramid, and also Maurício do Valle making a film about all of these other fragmentary character constructions.

A Idade da Terra works through a dialectic of denial and affirmation. It denies, first and foremost, traditional statutes of cinema. It was described in Rio de Janeiro's *Jornal do Brasil* as the film in which Rocha tells filmmakers to "throw away the Kodak tables" and discover the true light of Brazil. Its macrostructure denies and defies traditional notions about "film." It begins and ends without credits, and thus rejects the traditional notion of film-object. It has no "beginning" and no "end," as if it were an unfinished piece of work. It contains no logical, linear development, but presents, rather, fragments of possible films in what frequently seems to be a random syntagmatic ordering. There is no story line for the spectator to hang on to, although some sequences are the result of others. Just as Haroldo de Campos has described Oswald de Andrade's novel *Serafim Ponte Grande* as a "great nonbook made of fragments of books," Rocha's *A Idade da Terra* can be described as a great nonfilm made from fragments of possible films.

At the same time that it denies traditional forms of cinematic narrative and the concept of the film-object, *A Idade da Terra*, working with saturation and oversaturation of visual information, denies the efficiency of traditional cinematic discourse. Sequence shots that are held far beyond the time necessary to transmit the shot's information compose much of the film. Such temporal extensions draw attention away from the "action" and to the audiovisual configurations the film presents. It is as if the spectator were confronted with a "Guernica" in motion, where many different levels of information exist on the same plane but in which the form and composition are ultimately of most interest. The film works too with saturation in a number of other ways, notably the syntagmatic repetition of shots or lines of dialogue within the same shot.

Glauber Rocha also demystifies the director's aura or mystique in *A*

Idade da Terra. The work of direction is inscribed in the filmic discourse, the film's modes of production, in the diegesis. In traditional forms of cinema, the director and his work are effaced in the film's production, but in Rocha's film the director assumes a primary role, both visually and vocally. He is seen discussing roles with actors, resting with friends (e.g., writer João Ubaldo Ribeiro), and even directing the camera with his gestures. His voice is often heard telling the actors what to do, at one point even telling them to say their lines backwards. He tells the cameraman to close or open the diaphragm, thus directly affecting the quality of the received image. Glauber Rocha has described *A Idade da Terra* as "my portrait combined with that of Brazil." The film deals, in fact, with Glauber Rocha making a film about Glauber Rocha and the sociomystical reality of Brazil and the Third World.

A Idade da Terra brings to the foreground and unmasks other elements of the film production process. An exaggerated use of reflectors often gives a bright, flashing tone to the image. At times the reflector itself is moved during a given shot and a flash of light crosses the actor's face. On several occasions the cameraman plays with the diaphragm to increase or diminish the amount of light allowed through the aperture. The camera also calls attention to itself through frenetic, delirious movements, as if it cannot find the proper point on which to fix. In the film's initial sequence-shot, an extremely long shot records the sun rising over Brasília's Palácio da Alvorada (Palace of the Dawn). The camera is static during much of this long take, which is accompanied by a wild, unidentified chant. The long duration of the shot is an attempt to explore the modalities and tonalities of the image and of light as captured by the camera. This shot seems to synthesize the concerns of the film as a whole. On the one hand it represents a multilayered process of signification and on the other it explores the potentiality and different modalities of the use of the camera itself.

The film checks traditional narrative structures as well as the normal *perspectiva artificialis* of Renaissance anthropocentric art. It often denies the spectator a point of support, whether through rapid-fire discontinuous montage or delirious camera movements. The film explores, as I have already suggested, the use of light (over- and underexposure), focus (images are frequently out of focus during at least a portion of the shot), angle (the camera adopts unusual and disorienting angles, which destroy the traditional centrality of the subject), camera stability (or lack thereof), and possibilities of superimposition (at one point at least six different images of the same event, filmed simultaneously from different angles, are superimposed).

On one level *A Idade da Terra* may seem to be a cinematic chaos with little or no intelligible story line, experimentation with virtually all levels of cinematic discourse, an apparently random ordering of sequences, no coherent character development. But there is a certain coherence to Rocha's incoherence. As critic/filmmaker Gustavo Dahl writes, the key to all of

Rocha's work should be searched for in "this paradoxical obsession with unordering that which is ordered and finding in this unordering a new order."[60] Rocha has consistently been interested in moments of crisis, moments of "trance," the moment when the sea becomes the earth and the earth, the sea, the moment of *barravento*, the moment of death becoming life, the moment, ultimately, of resurrection.

The linguistic experimentation of *A Idade da Terra* (even though many of his "experiments" have already been done by avant-garde filmmakers the world over, which has led some critics to refer to Rocha's "vanguardist mannerisms") implies the hope that, from the ruins of cinematic tradition, from the ruins of colonized, Hollywoodian cinema, will arise a new cinema based on new uses of the cinematic instrument. Poet José Carlos Capinam writes that

Rocha's film is the revolutionary subconscious of Brazil invaded by all the universal contradictions, emerging in a direct, automatic form of writing all of its misery, chaos, an esthetic where dreams attempt to reorganize the real on a nonlinear, but rather primitive and radical poetic level. It is his film-limit, it is the age of Glauber, of his rebirth. The age in which the subconscious threatens to submerge and confront all the myths of the earth, be they the dragons of evil or the promised paradises of a future humanity.[61]

A Idade da Terra affirms, with all of the instruments that the filmmaker has at his disposal, the possibility of change, the possibility of transformation.

Early in the film, during a re-creation of the creation, the Indian Christ (at this point representing humanity in its entirety) looks at the camera and says, "Only the real is eternal." *A Idade da Terra* is in one sense a discussion of the "real" and how one approaches it, given the artificiality of the cinematic apparatus that Rocha shows by play and experimentation with its different modalities. What is, ultimately, real in *A Idade da Terra*? Is it the inscribed fiction? Is documentary more real than fiction? At one point, a ten-minute documentary sequence in which actor Antônio Pitanga (the black Christ) interviews historian Carlos Castello Branco about the military regime that took power in 1964 interrupts the fiction. With this interview the question of politics enters the film. Politics, for Glauber Rocha, is theater: *A Idade da Terra* theatricalizes and cinematizes politics, and the accompanying Villa-Lobos music renders Castello Branco's interview dramatic, indeed epic; Brasília, where the future of Brazil is being decided, is a "stage," Rocha tells us; a shot of the guerrilla being "made up" by assistants who splatter fake blood on his leg precedes his action in the film; the political slogans often spouted by different personages are highly theatrical. The Brazil that appears in the film is used as a dramatic and architectonic backdrop for the epic action taking place. Brazilian "reality" has no place in the film, except on the level of abstraction.

A Idade da Terra rejects a Manichaean view of society. It rejects categories of Left and Right, capitalism and socialism, in favor of a new order that takes advantage—anthropophagously—of all contributions. When Brahms is inspecting the construction of his cathedral (the new theater in Brasília) Rocha intervenes vocally on the soundtrack and repeats the idea that there are rich capitalist countries and poor capitalist countries, rich socialist countries and poor socialist countries. Therefore, he continues, the true conflict is not between capitalism and socialism, but rather between rich and poor. In geographical terms, the conflict is not between the East and the West, but rather between the North and the South. Such a position continues the Third Worldism that Glauber Rocha has expressed in many of his films.

The symbol of this new order is Christ. But Rocha's image of Christ (in his own words in one of his many vocal interventions in the film) is not the static one of Christ on the cross, but rather of Christ in the ecstasy and glory of the resurrection. Rocha's Christ is the Christ of the *barravento*, of the transformation, of the moment when life arises from death. Once again it is the *idea* of transformation and resurrection that matters. Rocha explains on the soundtrack that he began thinking about filming a Third World Christ when he learned of the death of Pasolini, who had filmed a people's Christ. The film itself thus gained life through death.

A brief examination of Rocha's Christ(s) might be instructive at this point. Although there are four Christs in the film, two of them appear to gain in importance through the diegesis: the Indian–fisherman–construction-worker, and the black Christ, who is a symbol of revolt. The former is played by Jece Valadão, the latter, by Antônio Pitanga. Both Christs are sensual, irreverent, ultimately carnivalesque. Jece Valadão is known in Brazil for his roles as a macho, womanizing hustler, an image crystallized in 1962 in Ruy Guerra's *Os Cafajestes*. The role he plays in Rocha's film does not differ essentially in tone from his earlier films. He remains, despite the Indian dress, Jece Valadão, playing Christ. At one point he makes love with the symbol of the Amazons, Norma Benguell. A traditional image of Christ? Hardly.

The black Christ is just as sensual as the Indian. At one point he meets a blonde outside of Brasília and wants to make love. He approaches Macunaíma in his irreverence. The sequence in which the black Christ re-enacts the dividing of the loaves and fish by distributing sandwiches and soft drinks to the people around him well exemplifies the playful tone of Rocha's Christs.

Toward the end of the film, the Indian Christ enters Salvador, where he participates in and witnesses a religious process rendered particularly dramatic, once again, by the use of Villa-Lobos music. Rocha's Christ, however, is not the center of attention, not even of the camera. If at one moment he walks through the crowd blessing the people, ultimately the camera leaves him and focuses instead on the immense crowd participating in the religious festivities. Finally the true key to Rocha's conception of this new Christ appears. The Christ of the Third World is the people themselves; their resurrection lies in their capacity for transformation. Carnival, Oswald de Andrade once wrote, is the religious rite of the race. From the people will come the creation of a new order.

The driving force of this new order is *creation*: artistic, political, social, cultural. The film begins with a re-enactment of the creation of the world. Politics is theater, thus it is an act of creation. *A Idade da Terra*, with its deconstruction of traditional cinematic structures, is itself an example of this creation. It is a moment of exultation and ecstasy, a moment of communion with the new order. *A Idade da Terra*, ultimately, is a moment of revelation, a moment of epiphany, a moment of the resurrection of the cinematic art itself based on the reinvention of its instruments. As Rocha wrote in 1970, "Cinema Novo should provoke fiery indigestion, be devoured by its own fire, and be reborn from its own ashes."

5. Nelson Pereira dos Santos: Toward a Popular Cinema

Cinema must be seen as one more instrument of struggle, just as necessary as any other, in the sense of understanding and attempting to transform Brazilian society.

—Nelson Pereira dos Santos

Nelson Pereira dos Santos is widely considered the "pope," or "conscience," in Glauber Rocha's words, of Cinema Novo. He has consistently been the gentle, presiding spirit behind this often tumultuous film movement; he has attempted to reconcile differences and lend his immense talents to filmmakers of all persuasions and generations. By means of its collective, independent production and critical stance toward established social and cinematic structures, his *Rio 40 Graus* marks a decisive step in the development of a new cinema in Brazil. Besides his direction of significant films (*Rio 40 Graus, Rio Zona Norte*), his practical contribution to the formation of Cinema Novo includes the editing of several of the movement's early films, such as Rocha's *Barravento*, Hirszman's *Pedreira de São Diogo* (*São Diogo Quarry*, 1962), and Sérgio Ricardo's *Menino da Calça Branca* (*Boy in the White Pants*, 1961).

Perhaps no other filmmaker exemplifies so well the birth and evolution of Cinema Novo. With *Rio 40 Graus* he helped introduce neorealist

Born in São Paulo in 1928. Nelson Pereira dos Santos studied law at the University of São Paulo before beginning his career in cinema as an assistant director in a number of films, including Rodolfo Nanni's *O Saci* (1951) and Alex Viany's *Agulha no Palheiro* (*Needle in the Haystack*, 1953). His directorial debut came in 1955 with *Rio 40 Graus* (*Rio 40 Degrees*), which was followed two years later by *Rio Zona Norte* (*Rio Northern Zone*). These two films, especially the former, are the immediate precursors of the Cinema Novo movement. In 1958 he produced Roberto Santos's (no relation) *O Grande Momento* (*The Great Moment*). He filmed *Mandacaru Vermelho* (*Red Cactus*) in the Northeast in 1961, using almost the entire crew, including himself, as actors. In 1962, at the invitation of producer Jarbas Barbosa, he directed a film version of Nelson Rodrigues's play *Boca de Ouro* (*Gold* techniques to Brazilian cinema, and his *Vidas Secas* is the high point of first-phase Cinema Novo. With *Hunger for Love* he participates in the anguished self-criticism of the second phase as well as in the incipient underground movement, and *Azyllo Muito Louco* represents the third or tropicalist phase. In 1974 he initiated a renewed concern with the nature of popular culture and with cinema's distance from or proximity to that culture. His entire career, with some significant exceptions, has revealed a commitment to the popular, not only in the sense of a cinema that takes as its subject the lives and problems of the marginalized segments of the Brazilian population, but also in the sense of a cinema that communicates easily with a broad public. The important thing, he once said, is to be authentic as an individual who lives in a given social context. His cinema strives consistently toward that goal.

Like Joaquim Pedro de Andrade, Nelson Pereira dos Santos has frequently turned toward literary works as the sources for his films. *Boca de Ouro, Vidas Secas, El Justicero, Hunger for Love, Azyllo Muito Louco, Quem E Beta?*, and *Tent of Miracles* are all at least partially based on literary works. Also like Joaquim Pedro de Andrade, dos Santos often reveals an attitude of "creative unfaithfulness" to the work in question, using it merely as a point of departure for his original creation. As Jorge Amado said of the filming of *Tent of Miracles*, dos Santos worked intelligently in that he would ask the author's opinion, appear to agree, then go ahead and do what he had originally intended to do.

Nelson Pereira dos Santos's trajectory toward a popular cinema traverses several not always distinct phases, which can be superficially (and

---

Mouth). He returned to the Northeast in 1963 and filmed what many consider to be Cinema Novo's masterpiece, *Vidas Secas* (*Barren Lives*), based on a novel by Graciliano Ramos. In 1967 he directed *El Justicero* (*The Enforcer*), using as a crew students from the University of Brasilia, where he was then professor of filmmaking. The following year he completed *Fome de Amor* (*Hunger for Love*) and in 1970 a cinematic version of Machado de Assis's *O Alienista* (*The Psychiatrist*) titled *Azyllo Muito Louco* (literally, *A Very Crazy Asylum*). In 1971 he directed *Como Era Gostoso o Meu Francês* (*How Tasty Was My Little Frenchman*), and in 1973 a coproduction with France, *Quem E Beta?* (*Who Is Beta?*; subtitled in the original *Pas de violence entre nous*). In 1974 he returned to the urban setting of his first films with *O Amuleto de Ogum* (*The Amulet of Ogum*) and simultaneously released "Manifesto for a Popular Cinema." He returned to a literary source in 1977, filming Jorge Amado's novel *Tenda dos Milagres* (*Tent of Miracles*). His latest film, *Estrada da Vida* (*Road of Life*), about the *sertanejo* (country) duo Milionário and José Rico, was released with tremendous popular success in early 1980. Besides these thirteen features, Nelson Pereira dos Santos has made numerous shorts and documentaries, including an adaptation of Graciliano Ramos's short story "O Ladrão" ("The Thief"). According to recent interviews he is currently working on two film projects: an adaptation of Graciliano Ramos's *Memórias do Cárcere* (*Prison Memoirs*), and a film about Brazilian abolitionist poet Castro Alves.

tentatively) outlined as follows: 1955–1967, sociological phase; 1968–1973, ideological phase; 1974–1981, popular phase. In the first phase dos Santos reveals a concern with a sociological critique of Brazilian society, although the critique does not exclude ideological analysis as well. *Rio 40 Graus, Rio Zona Norte,* and *Boca de Ouro* all concern marginal existence in Rio de Janeiro's suburbs. *Mandacaru Vermelho* and *Vidas Secas* are two different, yet similar, visions of the Brazilian Northeast, and *El Justicero* is a comedy of manners and a critique of the social and sexual mores of Rio de Janeiro's upper middle class. The films of this phase share a fairly traditional, linear narrative style and, with the exception of *Vidas Secas,* a classical mode of cinematic discourse. Although these films maintain a critical vision of Brazilian society, it is, so to speak, an external vision, the vision of an intellectual who seeks to contribute through cinema to an understanding of Brazil and its people.

The second phase, which I have termed "ideological," may also be called dos Santos's "Parati" phase, since all of its films were shot in or near Parati, the colonial coastal village south of Rio de Janeiro. It is an ideological phase in that it deals not so much with events (fictional or otherwise) or social situations and structures, as with the way in which events and society are interpreted. *Hunger for Love* calls into question traditional leftist politics in the face of the repression of the military regime, while *Azyllo Muito Louco* questions the repressive nature of *all* ideologies. *How Tasty Was My Little Frenchman* is a throwback, in some respects, to the first phase, but relates to the second in its revision of the ideological (official) interpretation of history. *Quem E Beta?,* an experimental film, denies all ideology as well as traditional forms of cinematic discourse. The films of this phase are consistently allegorical in content and discontinuous in form, breaking away from the realist discourse of the earlier phase. Cinematic forms themselves are questioned in this phase of Nelson Pereira dos Santos's work.

Dos Santos's "popular" phase follows his "Manifesto for a Popular Cinema" and the release of *O Amuleto de Ogum.* As he explains, "The idea is not merely for the film to be marketable, but rather to create a situation in which we could affirm the principles of Brazilian popular culture through cinema. My idea was also to defend popular political ideas—the legitimate claims of the people—which have been until now hidden from view and which our films should in some way reflect."[1] This phase represents an attempt to accept popular culture *as is* without the imposition of an intellectualized model of what it *should be.* In this sense it differs very much from the sociological stance of the first phase, even though in some respects the films of this phase return to a more classical mode of cinematic discourse.

Rio 40 Graus is often considered the first step in the development of Cinema Novo. Nelson Pereira dos Santos's first film grew out of a number of theoretical debates that took place in the early 1950s concerning the development of a

Plate 20. *Rio 40 Graus (Rio 40 Degrees)*

"free and independent" Brazilian cinema. In the director's words,

At two conferences which we organized in 1952 and 1953, I began to take particular interest in the cultural problems of national cinema, and I introduced several propositions related to them. Perhaps they seem obvious today [1972], but at the time there were good reasons for introducing them. We defended the idea that film as a means of artistic expression should meet Brazilian culture head-on, since the films being made at the time were always completely detached from national reality. They aspired to imitate foreign models, and were aimed at the commercial market no matter what the price. Consequently, we were confident that if our films succeeded in becoming a cultural force, they would permit an improved degree of communication and lay the foundations for a geniunely Brazilian cinema as an expression of both a particular culture and a given economy. That was our theoretical position, and *Rio 40 Graus* was a sort of "practical exercise" to illustrate what we are arguing.[2]

At a time when attempts to initiate a Hollywood-style studio-system (Vera-Cruz) were proving unworkable, dos Santos took a camera into the streets to film a simple story about the people of Rio de Janeiro. "My generation," he says, "was profoundly concerned with the problems of the country . . . and was searching for a form of political participation in the sense of transforming reality. The synthesis (between making films and discussing national reality) was found in the model of Italian neorealism."[3] *Rio 40 Graus* borrows from neorealism its penchant for independent production, location shooting, and the use of nonprofessional actors. Besides being a *political* decision, the decision to make films along neorealist lines was also a cinematic reaction against the cloistered artificiality of a cinema that, in the director's words, "did not recognize the existence of underdevelopment." It was also an attempt to project a realistic image of the Brazilian people, their dress, their language, their gestures, as a way of creating an authentic national cinematic dramaturgy.

The immediate problem, of course, was the financing of such a project. The studios, then in decay if not already in bankruptcy, could not be counted on to finance a film in which technical polish was secondary to content. Credit from financial institutions was virtually impossible, and the state had no program of financial assistance to the film industry. The solution he found (which proved to be an example for the subsequent Cinema Novo generation) was a collective form of production in which all actors and members of the crew were partners; they contributed financially and shared the risk and anticipated profits. The film was shot on a shoestring budget, and filming was interrupted on at least one occasion by the lack of raw film stock.

Problems did not cease with the film's completion. At that time censorship was regional, and the film was ordered off Rio de Janeiro screens by an appropriately named police official: Colonel Meneses Cortes ("*corte*" in Portuguese means "cut"). He had received, it seems, an anonymous tip condemning the film as offensive to Brazil's moral standards, and, besides, it "rarely reaches 40° in Rio", said the good colonel. After a campaign by artists and intellectuals led by journalist Pompeu de Souza, the film was re-released as the first *cause célèbre* of new Brazilian cinema. The film's distributor, Columbia Pictures, paradoxically, played on the film's prohibition in its distribution campaign and urged exhibitors to use the publicity slogan, "Here is the film that shocked the country!"

In reality, there is nothing shocking about the film. *Rio 40 Graus* presents a vertical slice of Rio de Janeiro society, from its poorest slum dwellers to its upper class, organized around the activities of five young peanut vendors on a single, hot, summer Sunday. Although it rejects the *chanchada*'s often idealistic vision of Brazilian society, it also incorporates many of the *chanchada*'s characteristics, notably its use of music. The film's credits are superimposed on aerial views of the city, from the picture postcard view of Sugar Loaf to the beaches of the fashionable Southern Zone, from Maracanã (the world's largest soccer stadium) to Rio's slums. Accompanying these aerial views is the samba "Voz do Morro," which was one of the most popular songs of the previous year's Carnival. The opening is typical *chanchada*, especially in its use of the samba, except that the aerial shots go *from* a touristic vision of the city *to* the reality of its slum dwellers, whereas a *chanchada* would transform the slum itself into a picturesque tourist attraction in the studio. The true focus of the film (virtually unprecedented in Brazilian cinema) is the people, the popular classes, who inhabit Rio de Janeiro's slums.

After showing the city as a whole during the credits, the film follows the "adventures" of five young peanut vendors who leave the slums and go to different points of the city to earn money. One goes to Copacabana, another to Sugar Loaf, a third to the statue of Christ the Redeemer on Corcovado Mountain, another to the Quinta da Boa Vista, and the last to the soccer stadium. In each of these locales a different story emerges, together forming a mural of Rio life.

Although effective in presenting such a mural, the narrative structure also requires that the characters remain types, with little or no psychological development or depth. Thus we have the naive maid seduced by the marine who tries to avoid marrying her until confronted by the protective and jealous brother. On the beach is the bourgeois family: the father who wants to protect his daughter from "dowry hunters" while at the same time praising the good life. He does not think twice, however, about introducing her to an influential politician in a position to do him a favor. Then there is the villain who tries to extort a commission from the boys' peanut sales; the troublemaker (played by Jece Valadão) who fights constantly; the soccer player at the end of his career, and his nervous replacement. With these types dos Santos criticizes various aspects of Rio society: the antiquated morality of the petite-bourgeoisie, the corruption of the upper class, the exploitation of the boys from the lower class, the "commercialization" of athletes, the omnipresent violence just beneath society's surface. The film even takes a jab at American tourists, who remark that Brazil is "a wonderful country, but so primitive."

But the film centers on the boys themselves and their struggle with other groups for survival. Besides being exploited by the "villain" and marginalized by the higher classes, the boys are systematically and physically excluded from participation in any meaningful way in society by its economic constraints. They cannot, for example, enter the soccer stadium because they do not have the admission price. The most poignant scene in the film, and one that anticipates Joaquim Pedro de Andrade's lyrical *Couro de Gato*, involves one of the boys and his pet lizard, Catarina. Outside of the zoo at the Quinta da Boa Vista, a bully tries to steal the boy's money, but when he pulls Catarina out of his pocket the bully is frightened and runs off. Unfortunately, Catarina also jumps out of the boy's hand and runs under the gate into the zoo. Not having the money to pay the admission price, the boy slips under the gate into a world of make-believe, filled with animals he had always heard about but never seen. A subjective camera records his wonder as he looks at the animals and trees around him. He saves Catarina from a hungry stork and is admiring a boa constrictor when a guard grabs him from behind. Startled, he lets Catarina get away. As the guard expulses the boy, the snake eats Catarina. The juxtaposition of a shot of the snake and another of the guard is a bit heavy-handed, but the sequence's poignancy remains: economic repression and marginalization render tenderness impossible.

Although *Rio 40 Graus* may at times present a romantic if not melodramatic view of Rio society, it also has to its credit a denunciation of the marginalization of subaltern classes within that society as well as a presentation, however schematic, of the class conflict that underlies it. It borrows some elements from the *chanchada*, but it rejects the *chanchada*'s artificiality. Music, for example, is of structural importance in *Rio 40 Graus*, unlike in many *chanchadas*, wherein characters may burst into song at any moment. *Rio 40 Graus*, moreover, points to new uses of music and other cinematic structures in the development of a new, independent cinema in Brazil.

Rio 40 Graus was conceived as the first part of a trilogy about Rio de Janeiro. Dos Santos filmed the second part, *Rio Zona Norte*, in 1957. The final part, to be titled *Rio Zona Sul* (*Rio Southern Zone*), was never finished because of financial difficulties. Like *Rio 40 Graus, Rio Zona Norte* takes as its subject the slums, or at least a certain segment of the slum population: the musicians and composers of Rio de Janeiro's famed samba schools. *Rio Zona Norte* is based on the life of popular composer Zé Keti, who appears in the film not as himself, but as the successful singer Alaor.

Unlike in *Rio 40 Graus*, however, in *Rio Zona Norte* dos Santos abandons neorealism for a more traditional mode of discourse. Rather than use exclusively natural settings, he often films interiors in studiolike sets, which are somewhat artificial when compared with the first film. But what it loses in neorealist authenticity, it gains in psychological complexity.

Although there is no doubt that the first film provided important insights for the creation of an independent cinema, *Rio Zona Norte*, also produced by the director, is equally important for its increased complexity and depth of analysis. It juxtaposes the social and the psychological. Some of the film's elements are in fact taken up again by dos Santos in his most recent film, *Estrada da Vida*.

The film revolves around the life and death of Espírito da Luz Cardoso (played by Grande Otelo) and his struggle for recognition as a samba composer. The character's name, "Spirit of the Light," indicates, in the sense that he represents the "people," a certain romantic notion of the popular classes and their culture, a certain acritical exaltation that will find resonances not only in early Cinema Novo films, but also in the films of what I have called Nelson Pereira dos Santos's "popular" phase. Poor and from the slums, Espírito is unprepared to deal with the unscrupulous musical "agents" who buy his songs without a contract and attribute them to better-known composers. With empty pockets Espírito goes from empty promise to empty promise until he finally stands up to his exploiters and refuses to sell them his new samba.

Like some of dos Santos's later films, notably *O Amuleto de Ogum, Rio Zona Norte* concerns popular culture and its expropriation, homogenization, and exploitation by the (capitalist) cultural industry, notably the mass media (radio) and the largely foreign-owned record industry. Espírito produces raw material (his songs) for that industry but receives none of the benefits. The parallel between his role vis-à-vis his exploiters and that of Brazil and other Third World countries vis-à-vis the industrialized world is clear and is reinforced by the lyrics of Espírito's final samba: "My samba / is Brazil's as well." His situation, in both its positive and negative aspects, is much like that of Brazil. His ultimate refusal to continue to be exploited is an artistic reflection of the developmentalist-nationalist ideology, which asserted that through steps such as the nationalization of the petroleum industry Brazil would finally stand on its own feet, independent of the capitalist exploiters.

Intertwined with the story of Espírito-the-composer is the story of Espírito-the-father and slum dweller. His psychological and existential problems counterbalance the cultural and economic sides of the protagonist. His wife has died, and he is left alone to care for Norival, his teenage son, who has become involved with the slum's criminal elements. Espírito is humiliated as he catches his son trying to rob the local bar and anguished as he later sees him gunned down. His exploitation, marginalization, and vulnerability to violence, both criminal and economic, identify Espírito with the larger community of slum dwellers.

A series of flashbacks from the point immediately preceding Espírito's death structures *Rio Zona Norte*. Like *Rio 40 Graus*, it begins with several shots of the city. This time, however, the shots are of Rio de Janeiro's downtown area and the central train station, where lower classes arrive in the city from the poor suburbs. The camera accompanies the train as it leaves the station. Espírito, we later learn, is a passenger. In an outlying area, the train rushes past the camera, a man crosses the tracks and looks down at another man fallen beside them. Espírito has fallen from the open door of the train. A small crowd gathers and first thinks that Espírito is merely drunk. When they realize that he is seriously injured, Espírito, in a close shot, opens his eyes. A slow dissolve marks the transition to the past and the film's explanation of how Espírito arrived at his present condition. From this point on, the film alternates, always using dissolves as punctuation, between past and present, as Espírito is taken to a hospital, where he eventually dies.

The film's dramatic structure plays on a contrast between popular and elite culture. Classical musician Moacyr (played by Paulo Goulart), who moonlights as a studio and radio musician for performers such as Angela Maria (played by herself), has always told Espírito to "count on him." It turns out, however, that he never has time to help. Espírito, for Moacyr, represents an "exotic" element of Brazilian society, to be exploited, but preferably at a distance. When Espírito goes to his house, he is received with a false, cold hospitality and soon feels out of place as the discussion turns toward erudite music. As in *Rio 40 Graus*, class integration is nonexistent in *Rio Zona Norte*, and class conflict underlies societal relationships.

Like *Rio 40 Graus*, *Rio Zona Norte* also plays on the *chanchada* tradition, especially by using Grande Otelo (who, together with Oscarito, virtually epitomizes the *chanchada*) and the popular singing star Angela Maria. The film is replete with musical numbers, ranging from Espírito's sambas, which he sings while tapping rhythmically on a matchbox, to the radio productions of Alaor and Angela Maria. But once again, the *chanchada* is used critically, not festively. Unlike in the *chanchada*, the musical numbers in dos Santos's film derive from the dramatic structure and are in no way extraneous to it.

Rio Zona Norte shares with the director's other films a concern with the marginalized sectors of Brazilian society, with the economic structures that determine their exploitation and marginalization, and with the nature of popular culture. Implicit in the film's treatment of Moacyr is a critique of the middle-class's distance from what the director sees to be true Brazilian culture. The film's use of the *chanchada* is a recognition of the need to communicate with a broad public—despite all that one may criticize in the *chanchada*, its popularity cannot be denied—a concern that many first-phase Cinema Novo films did not share.

Because of debts incurred with *Rio Zona Norte*, Nelson Pereira dos Santos was unable to film another feature for four years. In 1961 he and his crew traveled to Brazil's Northeast, where he had made some documentaries several years earlier, to shoot *Vidas Secas*, but, ironically, it rained in the *sertão*. Rather than lose the money invested in the project, he filmed *Mandacaru Vermelho*, using the entire crew, except the photographer, as actors. He played the male lead, and late screenwriter Miguel Torres and filmmaker Luis Paulino dos Santos played secondary roles.

As in his two previous films, in *Mandacaru Vermelho* dos Santos takes advantage of an already-codified form of cinematic expression to facilitate communication with the public: the Western. *Mandacaru Vermelho* was filmed in Brazil's Northeast (Nordeste), which in many ways resembles the American West, and is Cinema Novo's first "Nordestern." (The genre would be taken up critically by Glauber Rocha in *Black God, White Devil* in 1964.) Rocha himself has referred to *Mandacaru Vermelho* as a *"roman-*

ceiro of the *sertão*" and as a hybrid of the "rural drama and the northeastern Western."[4] The film's theme song, composed by Remo Usai and based on traditional Western motifs underlined by a distinctive Brazilian rhythm, permits us to call *Mandacaru Vermelho* the first (and perhaps only) "Bossa Nova Western" of Brazilian cinema.

But the film's link to the Western is more apparent than real. The glamour of the Western hero has been abandoned in favor of simple personages who are neither good nor bad, but rather products of their environment. Their clothes reflect the relative poverty of the region. There are no white stallions or fiery steeds; the personages ride small, slow animals when they do not ride donkeys or burros. The "hero" does not embody larger-than-life values of individuality; rather, he is simple, sometimes weak, and fragile. The characters' values do not necessarily reflect or symbolize the chauvinistic values of the nation, but rather the antiquated values of the past that infuse the region.

Called as well a "Romeo and Juliet of the *sertão*," *Mandacaru Vermelho*'s simple story of a cowherd who runs off with the niece of the powerful landowner-matriarch deals with several levels of myth and "medieval" codes of honor (which are themselves forms of social myths). The film opens with an initially unexplained ambush and gun battle that begin when an unidentified woman orders her men to fire on an unsuspecting group approaching the hill on which they are hidden. The object of the ambush is not immediately seen or known, as the camera cuts rapidly from gunman to gunman and finally frames the rifle-carrying woman in a long shot against the sky. In a closer shot she looks down, and the camera cuts to what she sees: many dead men on the ground.

A written text then explains the legend of the red cactus (the "mandacaru vermelho") which grew up on the site of the still-unexplained ambush due to the supposedly unwarranted violence of one family group against another.[5] The hill has become haunted and passage is forbidden to all who approach. The red cactus has become a symbol of the superstitious prohibition and of the blood shed on the spot. The gun battle and textual explanation serve as a prelude and background to the story to follow, providing it with a violent and mythical context.

The central drama of *Mandacaru Vermelho* concerns medieval notions of honor. Augusto (Nelson Pereira dos Santos), the cowherd, has run off with Clara, the matriarch's niece. Enraged by their temerity, the matriarch swears that the family's honor must be washed in blood. The landowner, we later discover, is the woman who commanded the ambush in the film's prelude. She organizes her men to pursue Augusto and Clara, who are soon joined by Augusto's brother, Pedro. Pedro himself attempts to maintain *his* family's honor by threatening to kill Augusto if he touches Clara before they marry.

The pursuit through the *sertão* occupies much of the film and ends, inevitably, on the forbidden hill of the red cactus. As Clara and Augusto run through the boulders up the hill, a hermit-mystic who has lived on the hill since surviving the earlier ambush grabs Clara. In physical appearance and mystical function, the hermit anticipates the mystic-prophets of later Cinema Novo films, such as Ruy Guerra's *The Guns* and Glauber Rocha's *Black God, White Devil*. The ambivalence of the mystic's role is seen in Clara's, Augusto's, and Pedro's different reactions to him: Augusto calls him a madman; Clara thinks he is a saint; Pedro, who had been pursuing the two of them after a fight with Augusto, reverently takes off his hat as he sees the hermit marry Clara and Augusto.

Essentially a romantic adventure story filmed in a classical mode of cinematic discourse—linear narrative, parallel and alternate syntagms, dissolves and fades used as temporal punctuation devices, suspenseful (nonstructural) music—*Mandacaru Vermelho* is important for anticipating and foreshadowing later Cinema Novo films. Its clear photography, use of hand-held and subjective camera as the characters traverse the *sertão* anticipate dos Santos's own *Vidas Secas*. The film's narrative structure, reminiscent of oral literature and popular ballads, anticipates Glauber Rocha's utilization of such popular forms of expression in *Black God, White Devil*.

Unlike later films, however, *Mandacaru Vermelho* does not see religion, whether in its mystical or Catholic encarnations, as the alienating force it becomes in many Cinema Novo films. *Mandacaru*'s vision is much closer to that of the northeastern people's vision, and thus links up to the films of dos Santos's later, "popular" phase.

Finally, *Mandacaru Vermelho* marks an important step in the development of Cinema Novo as it brings to the screen the violent universe of the *sertão*. It describes the *sertanejo* and his social and cultural ambience without resorting to a merely exotic perspective. As Glauber Rocha perceptively notes, in *Mandacaru Vermelho* Nelson Pereira dos Santos criticizes a romantic vision of the *sertão* by using that very vision as the film's dramatic structure.[6]

In his fourth feature, *Boca de Ouro*, dos Santos returns to the urban setting of *Rio 40 Graus* and *Rio Zona Norte*. Although a contracted film, *Boca de Ouro* is closely linked in a number of ways to dos Santos's previous films and is an important work not only in his career but also in Brazilian cinema. Sometimes the importance of works of art is seen only in retrospect, and such is the case with this film. *Boca de Ouro* is the first significant adaptation of a work by controversial playwright/novelist Nelson Rodrigues (Manuel Peluffo's earlier *Meu Destino E Pecar* [*My Destiny Is to Sin*, 1952] is inexpressive), whose work, it turns out, represents a rich vein in Brazilian cinema of the sixties, seventies, and now the eighties, with such films as Leon Hirszman's *A Falecida* (*The Deceased*, 1965), Arnaldo Jabor's *Toda Nudez Será Castigada* (*All Nudity Shall Be Punished*, 1972) and *O Casamento* (*The Wedding*, 1975), Neville d'Almeida's *Dama do Lotação* (*Lady on the Bus*, 1978) and *Os Sete Gatinhos* (*The Seven Little Kittens*, 1980), and more recently Braz Chediak's remake of *Bonitinha Mas Ordinária* (*Cute but Vulgar*, 1981; originally filmed by J. P. de Carvalho in 1963), and Bruno Barreto's remake of *O Beijo no Asfalto* (*Kiss on the Asphalt*, 1981; originally filmed by Flávio Tambellini in 1964).

But *Boca de Ouro* was harshly criticized on its release in 1963, not because of dos Santos's direction, which is consistently praised, but rather because of the source: Nelson Rodrigues, a self-proclaimed (somewhat ironically, I presume) reactionary. In an extensive article that exemplifies criticism of the period, Alex Viany, observing that the film reveals a mature cinéaste in Nelson Pereira dos Santos, devotes no more than two short paragraphs to it, and uses the rest of the article to criticize Nelson Rodrigues's vision of Brazilian society: "A danger to be avoided," Viany prescriptively determines. Viany and other commentators criticize what they feel to be Rodrigues's "degrading," "unpleasant," "venal," "abnormal," "pornographic," "sensationalist," "demeaning" texts.[7]

Nelson Rodrigues's universe is that of the Rio suburbs, the *zona norte* of Nelson Pereira dos Santos's second film, a world inhabited by a lower middle class infused with distorted, antiquated values filtered down from the upper classes. It is a world without hope for the future, stagnant and immobile; a world where the espoused values of "honor" and dignity cannot hide the fissures that allow moral putrefaction to seep from beneath. Nelson Rodrigues's is a rather morbid, if not sordid, view of the "little vices" of the inhabitants of this universe. His view is linked in spirit to the sensationalist headlines of Brazil's yellow press, exemplified in the sixties and again in the eighties by the newspaper *A Luta Democrática*. He reveals the myths of urban society in an ultimately moralistic way as he explores the limits imposed on individuals and the aberrations resulting from such limits. It is a theater concerned with the marginalization and impotence of human beings within capitalist society—without, it must be said, explicitly criticizing capitalism—their struggles that lead nowhere, their anguish. As critic Ronaldo Lima Lins observes, "Incapable of changing themselves or transforming the environment that surrounds them (and that also corrupts them in a vicious circle whose end can only be despair), Rodrigues's characters let themselves be dragged along . . . and degenerate and deteriorate like contaminated fruit."[8]

Nelson Pereira dos Santos filmed *Boca de Ouro* less than two years after its initial theatrical presentation in São Paulo on 13 October 1960. Like his first two films, this one concerns marginal(ized) sectors of Rio society. This time the protagonist is the violent head of a suburban numbers racket (*jogo do bicho*), Boca de Ouro (Gold Mouth; played by Jece Valadão), so called because he ordered his perfect set of teeth removed and replaced with solid gold dentures. Born "in the bathroom sink of a dance-hall," Boca has risen by violence and cunning to the powerful and feared position of head of criminal activities in the Rio de Janeiro suburb of Madureira. His power rests not only on his capacity for violence (he is referred to as a "woman killer") but also on his wealth, which is an obsession for this man of humble origins. He flaunts his wealth: not only does he have his mouth "paved" with gold, but he also announces that he has ordered a gold coffin and waves large-denomination bills under other personages' noses. He is in many ways the antithesis of Espírito da Luz Cardoso of *Rio Zona Norte*.

Boca de Ouro's story, in both the play and the film, is told in three flashbacks from the point of view of Guigui, his former lover. The film opens with the announcement of Boca's murder, and a sensationalist paper sends reporters to interview Guigui, whom they do not immediately tell of his death in hopes of an exclusive interview for the front page. She gives the reporters three different versions of the same event, modifying the story depending on her knowledge of the situation and her own immediate circumstance. Through these three often contradictory versions, a complex portrait of Boca de Ouro emerges.

Guigui's first version, told when she is unaware of his death and wants revenge for his rejection of her, paints Boca as a merciless urban monster, as the "Dracula of Madureira," as he is popularly called. Guigui's narration introduces us to Celeste and Leleco as examples of Boca's crimes. Celeste, according to this initial version, is an innocent young woman whose mother has just died, and she has no money to pay for the funeral. Her husband Leleco is unable to keep a job, and to raise money he asks Boca for a loan. After a series of threats and intimidations, Boca agrees to his request, but only if Celeste picks up the money, *alone*. This direct challenge to Leleco's "honor" and "manliness" goes unanswered and Celeste soon appears. As Leleco waits in the hall, Boca attempts to "take advantage" of her until her screams cause Leleco to burst into the room and threaten to kill Boca. In defiance, Boca hands Leleco a revolver and opens his shirt, exposing his chest and daring Leleco to fire. Boca recognizes that he hasn't the courage to pull the trigger and insists on Leleco's further humiliation by forcing him to order Celeste into the bedroom. After doing so and watching Boca put away the promised money, Leleco insults Boca by referring to his birth and is answered with a series of fatal blows to the head with the gun butt.

Guigui changes her story, however, when the reporter tells her that Boca has been killed. She then claims that the initial version was false and motivated by a desire for revenge. The second version of the same episode reveals a rather benevolent, Robin Hood-like Boca who is at times forced by

Plate 21. Odete Lara and Jece Valadão, *Boca de Ouro (Gold Mouth)*

circumstance to resort to violence. His image is humanized, and Celeste and Leleco are painted as the villains of the story. Leleco is the cuckolded husband who, in his desire for money, forces his unfaithful wife to search out Boca to use him financially.

It is in this second version, more than any other, that Boca's true circumstances are revealed and an element of class conflict, evident in all of dos Santos's films, enters the narrative. Three wealthy women visit Boca, ostensibly to ask for a charity donation, but in reality (and poorly disguised) to see such an infamous figure close up. For them, Boca is an exotic, exciting element of Rio de Janeiro, a symbol of the violence that class society itself determines and tries to hide. Boca attempts, but fails, to humiliate them by proposing a best-breast contest, which they willingly accept. He can humiliate people like Leleco, who comes from the same environment and knows the range of Boca's powers, but he has no power to humiliate or control classes higher than his own. The wealthy women, in fact, humiliate him with questions about his birth.[9]

Guigui's third version represents still another facet of Boca. This version is influenced by her husband's threat to leave because of her expressed love for Boca. Boca is neither the monster trying to take advantage of the innocent woman nor the innocent victim of an unfaithful woman and a scheming husband. Rather, he is involved in the drama as Celeste's lover, but not totally responsible for the tragedy that unfolds. He and Celeste kill Leleco after the extortion attempt, and, when visited by one of the wealthy women seen earlier, he kills Celeste and is in turn killed by the woman.

Like *Rio 40 Graus* and *Rio Zona Norte*, this film deals with the limitations imposed on the marginalized segments of urban Brazilian society. Although he does have relative power vis-à-vis Leleco and those like him, Boca is powerless when confronted by the upper classes. Although he aspires to wealth and recognition, he carries with him his original sin, the stigma of his birth. The only "victorious" personage in *Boca de Ouro*, if one may speak of victories in this fictional universe, is Boca's wealthy murderess. In reality antiquated values and norms and the predetermined societal rules by which they must play imprison all of the characters.

Boca de Ouro is a tragic picture of Rio de Janeiro's underside, a picture of violence against and between the city's marginal(ized) elements. The film is a relatively faithful version of the play, although to dos Santos's credit, some dialogue is eliminated and a number of scenes are set outdoors, thus giving the story a greater sense of dynamism and reducing its theatricality. It possesses obvious ties with dos Santos's first films, and its concern with the criminal side of urban society is to be taken up again as part of the director's campaign for a "popular" cinema in his 1974 *O Amuleto de Ogum*. *Boca de Ouro*, however important, is an almost forgotten film, but one that deserves, as actor-producer Jece Valadão suggests, a re-evaluation in terms of its real significance for the development of Cinema Novo and modern cinema in Brazil.[10]

In 1963, the same year in which *Boca de Ouro* was released, dos Santos returned to the Northeast to realize his long-planned project of filming Graciliano Ramos's classic novel *Vidas Secas*.[11] His cinematic reading of the Ramos novel was intended not only as an adaptation of a well-known literary masterpiece, but also as an intervention within the contemporary political conjuncture, in this case as part of the debate then raging concerning agrarian reform. As the director himself notes,

At that time, great discussions about the agrarian problem were taking place in Brazil, and all sorts of groups and sectors of the economy were taking part. I felt that the film should also participate in that national debate, and that my contribution could be that of the filmmaker who rejects a sentimentalized vision. Among all the Northeastern writers, the most representative, the one who conveys the most consistent vision of the region, is Graciliano Ramos—particularly in *Vidas Secas*. What the book says about the Northeast in 1938 is still valid.[12]

The film has been rightly praised as an early Cinema Novo masterpiece.

Plate 22. *Vidas Secas (Barren Lives)*

Dos Santos, however, did take advantage of his creative privilege in the adaptation and modified and added certain elements in the pursuance of his own critical reading of the novel.

Vidas Secas was originally published as a series of fairly autonomous short pieces whose unity derived from a common milieu and the continuity of the characters. Dos Santos's film version reorganizes its basic material into a coherent, rather more linear narrative. It groups some chapters, for example, that are separate in the novel. The events of chapter three ("Cadeia") and chapter eight ("Festa"), both set in town, are joined. A flashback in chapter ten ("Contas"), where Fabiano remembers previous difficulties with the town's tax collector, has been placed before the other events set in town. Fabiano's encounter with the "yellow soldier" (chapter eleven) has been placed before the death of the dog Baleia (chapter nine). The director has also added elements of his own, notably the *bumba-meu-boi* folk pageant and the option presented by the *jagunços* who free Fabiano's fellow prisoner from jail.

To fully understand and appreciate the differences and similarities between *Vidas Secas* novel and film, one must examine the formal aspects of the two works. An area in which the film is imaginatively faithful to the novel concerns point of view. The Ramos novel is written from what might be called a subjectivized third-person point of view. It uses an indirect free style, that is, a mode of discourse that begins in the third person ("he thought") and then modulates into a more-or-less direct, but still third person, presentation of a character's thoughts and feelings.

The discourse of *Vidas Secas* is highly subjective in that most of the verbal material is articulated via the point of view of the characters. Five chapters are named for the personage whose vision they present; four others are dominated by Fabiano. At the same time, within particular chapters a kind of subsystem organizes points of view, which passes down a hierarchy of power from Fabiano to Vitória to the two boys and, at times, to the dog Baleia.

An intense imaginative empathy, whereby the author projects himself into the minds and bodies of characters very different from himself and brings us as readers into the very physical being of his peasant subjects, characterizes the novel *Vidas Secas*. In a *tour de force*, Ramos even personifies the dog Baleia, going so far as to give her visions of a canine afterlife. At some points, obviously, it becomes clear that he does not strictly limit himself to, but rather includes and transcends, the consciousness of his characters. He makes allusions, for example, that would undoubtedly have been beyond the ken of his characters (e.g., Fabiano's comparison of himself to a "wandering Jew"), or he details their confusion (Fabiano's semicomic attempt to compose an appropriate lie for Vitória concerning his loss of money in a card game) while making it clear that he as author does not share this confusion.

Graciliano Ramos's style, a style ideally suited to the rendering of psychological states, physical sensation, and concrete experience, is transmuted successfully into film. In the film, interior monologue in the indirect free style disappears in favor of sparse direct dialogue. Fabiano's internal wrestle with language itself, for example, is dropped; all we are given is the *fact* of his inarticulateness. Fabiano and Vitória's lack of verbal communication is related by means of a "conversation": as they sit by the fire and listen to the rain outside, both talk simultaneously without hearing one another.

But dos Santos does retain what we might call the democratic distribution of subjectivity. The film plays on diverse cinematic registers to transmit the characters' and the dog's perspectives of their situations. Classically and most obviously, the film exploits point of view shots that alternate the person seeing with what the person presumably sees. Such shots are associated with each of the four human protagonists and with the dog. One sequence alternates shots of Baleia looking and panting with shots of cavies scurrying through the brush.

The film also creates subjective vision by camera movement: hand-held, traveling shots evoke the experience of traversing the *sertão*; a vertiginous camera movement suggests the younger boy's dizziness and fall. Other procedures involve exposure (an overexposed shot of the sun blinds and dizzies the character and the spectator), focus (Baleia's vision goes out of focus after Fabiano shoots her), and camera angle (the boy inclines his head to look at the house; the camera inclines as well). It is also noteworthy that the camera films the dog and children at their level, without patronizing them, so to speak, by using high angles. Luis Carlos Barreto's cinematography is dry and harsh like the *sertão*. Indeed, he has been credited with "inventing" a kind of light appropriate to Brazilian cinema.

In the film's jail sequence dos Santos introduces significant elements not in the novel. The novel's jail sequence creates a psychological space (Fabiano's rambling and anguished attempt to articulate his rage internally) that is social and political on a secondary level. The film, on the other hand, develops a predominantly social and political space (showing the *fact* of Fabiano's oppression) that is implicitly psychological. The sequence alternates subjective camera (shots and countershots between Fabiano and his fellow prisoner), objective, third-person camera (e.g., shots of Vitória on the church steps), and documentary footage (the *bumba-meu-boi* celebration) as a means of contrasting the objective (social) reality of the situation with Fabiano's personal drama. The juxtaposition of the sound of one space and the image of another (e.g., the sound of the celebration accompanying Fabiano in jail or Vitória on the church steps) makes explicit the protagonists' marginalization from the collective festivities and, by extension, from Brazilian society as a whole.

One such usage of sound is particularly significant. The ultimately repressive nature of the *bumba-meu-boi* pageant is revealed through precisely such a superimposition of image and sound, as the sequence contrasts the celebration with shots of Fabiano suffering behind bars. When the dancers finally say, "Let's cut up the ox," the camera focuses not on them, but on Fabiano. When the ox is divided and symbolically served to the ruling classes, so too is Fabiano, who represents the collectivity, served up and devoured in a ceremony of ritual anthropophagy.

The film's soundtrack is ingenious throughout. It provides, as Noel Burch points out in *Praxis du Cinéma*, an instance of the structural use of sound.[13] Rather than relieving the austerity of the images with a lush musical score, dos Santos's soundtrack offers only occasional diegetic music (the violin lessons for the landowner's daughter, the music of the *bumba-meu-boi* ceremony), along with extremely harsh sounds (the squawking of a parrot, the grating creak of the oxcart); there is no nondiegetic musical score at all. Often such scores serve to render poverty palatable, as the spectators lose themselves in the music and forget the provocative rawness of the facts depicted.

The nondiegetic sound of the creaking wheels of an oxcart accompanies the film's credits. The sound is later explained, as we see Fabiano arriving in town on the oxcart as we hear the sound. At this point, the sound forms part of an aural pun by means of which the creaking of the cart modulates into the sound (diegetic) of the scraping violin of the landowner's daughter, thus equating elite culture and oppression. The sound of the oxcart becomes, through the course of the film, a kind of auditory synecdoche that encapsulates the Northeast, both by its denotation (the oxcart represents the technical backwardness of the region) and by its connotation (the very unpleasantness of the sound constitutes a certain structure of aggression). The wheel of the oxcart also operates metaphorically, in that its circularity recalls the cyclical droughts and never-ending misery of the region.

The jail sequence and the film as a whole define the ideology implicit in the social structure by producing an opposition between elite and popular culture. Elite culture is represented by the classical violin lessons given to the landowner's daughter. In opposition to it is popular culture, represented in the jail sequence by the *bumba-meu-boi* celebration.

The ox (*boi*) pervades the entire film. The sound of the oxcart opens and closes the filmic text; midway in the film, the date 1941 is superimposed on a clay ox molded by one of the boys. When Fabiano must decide whether to join an armed gang, the sound, in the background, of a cowbell tempers his decision. He decides not to kill the "yellow soldier" partly because he hears one of the last surviving oxen in the brush. Fabiano makes the family's sandals from cowhide; the family depends on the herd for food. In short, the family's very survival depends on the ox.

The *bumba-meu-boi* celebration is a traditional folk-dance pageant in which the people symbolically divide an ox and offer it to the local dignitaries. According to Mário de Andrade, who devoted much of his life to the study of Brazilian popular culture, the cult of the ox is (1) a remnant of mythical rites concerning vegetation, which reflect the people's concern with the generosity of the earth, and (2) a moral value deriving from religious tradition and economic activity. In more modern society the cult has lost its primitive poiesis and much of its mythological significance, but the ox's social value remains.[14] The *bumba-meu-boi* celebration thus expresses a social and economic collectivity; it is a totem that reflects the socioeconomic structure and the deepest values of whose who participate in it. In *Vidas Secas*, Nelson Pereira dos Santos utilizes the ox and popular culture in a critical sense, rather than in a merely representational one.

The *bumba-meu-boi* pageant might be seen as a carnivalesque celebration, since it is probably linked through tradition to folk pageants of the Middle Ages. However, during medieval folk festivals and carnivals, from which the carnivalesque derives, existing social hierarchies were abolished; there was no distance between actors and spectators; participants led, so to speak, a second life, free from the rules and restrictions of official cultural life (i.e., the restrictions imposed, often through the church, by the dominant ideology). According to Mikhail Bakhtin, the people achieved a temporary liberation from the established order through a suspension of hierarchical rank. The carnival spirit "offers the chance to have a new outlook on the world, to realize the relative nature of all that exists, and to enter a completely new order of things."[15]

The *bumba-meu-boi* celebration is thus not carnivalesque, but rather festive, since a virtual blockade remains between the people and the figures of authority. The repressive nature of the pageant, as I have already observed, is expressed as Fabiano is symbolically sacrificed to the ruling classes. The *bumba-meu-boi* can be seen in this context as the ceremonial representation, the *mise-en-scène*, of a situation of oppression, for the dancers offer not only what is in some sense the product of their labor (the ox) to the oppressors, but also, symbolically, offer themselves. Popular culture, the director seems to be saying, is politically ambiguous: whereas it does offer a counterpole to elite culture, it can also alienate by simply representing, rather than challenging, the people's oppression.

The novel *Vidas Secas* elaborates the analogy, characteristic of naturalist fiction and rooted in nineteenth-century biologism and social Darwinism, between human beings and animals. The twist in *Vidas Secas* is that it is not in the descriptive passages that the novelist brings up the metaphor; rather, he has the characters themselves make the comparison, conversely reinforced by the author's "anthropomorphization" of animals.[16] Whereas Fabiano and Vitória constantly complain that they are forced to live like animals, the dog Baleia is given almost human qualities and is totally integrated into the family unit. The human characters are very much aware of their inability to communicate through language, but when Vitória kills the parrot to eat, she justifies her action by saying that it was worth nothing, "it didn't even talk." The importance of a leather bed for Vitória is that it represents for her the ideal of ceasing to live like animals.

In his study of *Vidas Secas* (novel), Affonso Romano de Sant' Anna examines the similarity, on metaphorical and metonymic levels, between Fabiano and Baleia and between Vitória and the parrot.[17] The same relationship holds true in the film. During the jail sequence, for example, Vitória and the boys have been left alone by both Fabiano (in jail) and Baleia (who has disappeared). Baleia returns only after Fabiano is released and reunited with his family. The dog's temporary disappearance, furthermore, foreshadows her absence (death) at the end of the narrative. Throughout the film (at least in the sequences that take place in town), Fabiano is reduced to the level of animal by the social structure, though he does resist.

The characters of *Vidas Secas* can be grouped into what might be called a hierarchy of power based on the five distinct levels of power present in different parts of the film: (1) economic power (embodied in the figure of the landowner); (2) civil power (the mayor); (3) military power (the soldiers); (4) religious power (the priest and the church); and (5) the lack of power (the masses, represented by Fabiano, Vitória, and the participants of the *bumba-meu-boi* pageant). A sixth group, composed of the other prisoner and the *jagunços*, stands outside of this hierarchy of power and represents a threat to its stability.

A blockade exists between the first four groups and the fifth. It is unidirectional, since the first four groups have access to the "space" occupied by the fifth, but the reverse is not the case. Little interchange occurs between them except when governed by signs of domination, authority, and repression. The hierarchical distinction between groups one and two is unclear, since we do not know if the mayor is himself a landowner or if the landowner holds more power than the mayor. They frequently appear together and on an equal level. It is clear, however, that the military and the church are subordinate to both the mayor and the landowner and serve a mediating function between the highest and lowest strata of the power structure.

In the novel's jail episode, Fabiano thinks to himself that, if it were not for his wife and children, he would join a band of *cangaceiros* and kill the men that command the "yellow soldier." Although in the novel Fabiano never has the opportunity to carry out his revenge, the film offers him such an option. In jail with Fabiano is an enigmatic second prisoner who soothes the cowherd's wounds and comforts him during the long night. In sharp contrast to Fabiano, who grimaces in pain and curses his jailers, the second prisoner, although wounded himself, shows no sign of pain or fear. He speaks not a word. When not helping Fabiano, he gazes calmly out of the jail window, confident that he will not be in jail long. At daybreak, the band to which he belongs rides into town and frees him, thereby also causing Fabiano's release. They later meet again on the road outside of town, and the young *jagunço* offers Fabiano his horse and invites him to join the band. The cowherd of course refuses, feeling a greater responsibility for his family.

There is nothing in the film to suggest that the members of the armed band are *cangaceiros*. They share none of the visual characteristics of *cangaceiros* (codified, for example, in Lima Barreto's *O Cangaceiro* [1953]), and are carried to a level of abstraction through silence. We are simply never told who they are, what they do, where they come from, or for whom they work. It is clear *only* that they represent a threat and an alternative to the ruling classes. Through this abstraction the director brings into the diegesis an option merely latent in the novel: armed struggle. The availability of this option is reinforced visually in a shot of Fabiano on horseback, framed against the sky with a rifle in his hands. Although the cowherd rejects the option, the image remains vivid in the film's discourse.

Both *Vidas Secas* (novel) and *Vidas Secas* (film) are masterpieces in their own right, and both share the same general political perspective. The adaptation is more a question of dialogue and admiration than of fundamental differences between the two authors. If, as Affonso Romano de Sant'Anna suggests, the novel uses language to discuss nonlanguage (i.e., Fabiano and his family's lack of language),[18] then the very lack of language is due, ultimately, to the economic, political, and social structure of Brazilian society.

In purely cinematic terms, Nelson Pereira dos Santos's film, with its soberly critical realism and its implicit optimism, represents early Cinema Novo at its best. Rarely has a subject—in this case, hunger, drought, and the exploitation of a peasant family—been so finely rendered by a style. Rarely have a thematic and an esthetic been quite so fully adequate to one another.

Vidas Secas, however, was a difficult if not impossible act to follow. Rather than continue in the same vein, therefore, dos Santos's next film, *El Justicero*, breaks completely with *Vidas Secas*. Whereas *Vidas Secas* is a somber, almost wrenching cinematic experience, *El Justicero* is a comedy. *Vidas Secas* presents an essentially rural drama; *El Justicero* has an urban setting. The first focuses on the Northeast's lumpen, the second, on the upper middle class. *Vidas Secas* discusses serious social, political, and economic problems, *El Justicero*, the "manners" of urban Brazilian society. The lower classes are as extraneous to *El Justicero* as they are central to *Vidas Secas*. *Vidas Secas*, moreover, has become an international film classic; *El Justicero* has been forgotten, even in Brazil.

There can be no doubt that *El Justicero* is a lesser film, not only in relation to *Vidas Secas*, but also within dos Santos's broader filmography. Like *Boca de Ouro*, it is a contracted film, coproduced by an international film distributor (Condor Filmes). But perhaps one reason that it is a lesser film is that its source provides weaker material than did Graciliano Ramos's novel. *El Justicero* is based on the novel *As Vidas de El Justicero: O Cafajeste sem Medo e sem Mácula (The Lives of the Enforcer: The Hustler without Fear and without Shame)* by minor Rio novelist and playwright João Bethencourt (who, by the way, rejects dos Santos's interpretation of his novel).

According to dos Santos, *El Justicero* was made in the spirit of the kind of humor then being published by Stanislaw Ponte Preta (pseudonym of Sérgio Porto) in the Rio de Janeiro newspaper *Ultima Hora*. These humorous vignettes concerning the foibles and absurdities of Rio life have since been published in several volumes under the title *FEBEAPA* (Festival of Nonsense that Plagues the Country). Bethancourt's novel also participates in this spirit, although his literary pretensions often exceed his ability as a writer.

El Justicero is the story of a "charming," picaresque playboy of Rio de Janeiro's Southern Zone who chooses the nickname "El Justicero" because of his "everlasting concern" for the downtrodden: volleyball players on the beach, people waiting in lines (any lines), anyone with skin darker than lily-white (especially after he discovers that there is no racial discrimination in Brazil), children, and prostitutes. He is always ready to enter a fight, especially when two or more policemen are involved on the other side. El Jus, as his friends call him, has hired a personal biographer—named Beethoven in the novel, Lenin in the film—who follows him and records his every gesture and word. The film follows El Jus's adventures and misadventures as he struggles through his arduous existence as a seducer of women and self-proclaimed protector of innocents.

The film is little more than a comedy of manners, although it does attempt a critical vision of the social mores of Rio's upper middle class, its moralistic sexuality and ultimately repressive values, and the great distance between ideals ("justice," for example) and society's reality. It is a critique of the lack of purpose and hypocrisy of the more fortunate sectors of Brazilian society. Because of a number of antimilitary elements, such as references to soldiers and military police as "monkeys," *El Justicero* was confiscated by federal censors shortly after its release. Surprisingly, to this date the film's producers have not requested a review of the censor's orders, and the film remains on the prohibited list. There are no copies available for viewing in Brazil.

El Justicero was somewhat less than a critical and commercial success, but it does accent some of Nelson Pereira dos Santos's talents as a filmmaker, especially with regard to what I have called his "generous presiding spirit." The film was made with a crew of students from his film class at the University of Brasília, a habit that the filmmaker still maintains. He has consistently given of his time and talent to help young filmmakers develop their cinematic talents.

In another sense, together with Domingos de Oliveira's *Todas as Mulheres do Mundo* (*All the Women in the World*, 1967) and Roberto Farias's *Toda Donzela Tem um Pai que E qma Fera* (*Every Maiden Has a Father Who Is a Beast*, 1967), *El Justicero* inaugurates the comedy as an accepted form of discourse for Cinema Novo directors and anticipates the virtual explosion of the urban comedy of manners in Brazilian cinema in the early seventies. *El Justicero*, with its traditional mode of cinematic discourse, brings the first phase of Nelson Pereira dos Santos's films to an end.

Hunger for Love represents a rupture in dos Santos's career. Admittedly influenced by the American avant-garde, in this film he rejects the cinematic "naturalism" and the neorealism of earlier films in favor of an anti-illusionistic, discontinuous form of discourse. Although certain elements of *El Justicero* (a general tone of debauchery) and *Vidas Secas* (the use of "saturation," i.e., holding a shot longer than the cinematic tradition would advise, and the structural use of sound), anticipate the rupture, it is only with *Hunger for Love* that one can speak of a new phase or a new conception of filmmaking in his work. In *Hunger for Love* the director ceases to be a critical observer of socioeconomic structures and turns his attention toward the ideological ways in which that society, that reality, is perceived. Rather than calling social structures into question, as in hi⁻ earlier films, he now questions ideology itself, especially leftist ideology, in the face of Brazil's repressive political ambience under military rule. *Hunger for Love* is thus an integral part of what has been called Cinema Novo's second phase, composed of films like Rocha's *Land in Anguish*, Saraceni's *O Desafio*, and Dahl's *O Bravo Guerreiro*, which attempt to analyze the failure of the intellectual Left in the postcoup situation. Likewise, *Hunger for Love* anticipates both the tropicalist phase of Cinema Novo, with its penchant for allegory and the "novo cinema novo" or "cinema lixo" ("garbage cinema") that arose at about the same time. Its mode of discourse rejects the earlier neorealist influences in favor of Godard, Resnais, and Fellini.

Hunger for Love is based loosely on Guilherme de Figueiredo's short novel *História para Se Ouvir de Noite*. Unimpressed, however, by Figueiredo's banality of "suspense" and infidelity, dos Santos transformed *Hunger for Love* (subtitled *Have You Ever Sunbathed Completely Naked?*) into a discourse on the state of the revolution, both political and cinematic. From the novel he kept only the basic situation—four characters, two couples, who meet on an island and become involved in a game of human chess with its moves and countermoves—and the characters' names—Mariana, a wealthy classical pianist, and her companion, Felipe, a more proletarian painter; Alfredo, who is deaf, dumb, and blind, and his wife, Ula (in the novel, Gisela Kramer).

In *Hunger for Love*, dos Santos also changes filming tactics. Although he has never adhered rigorously to prepared scripts, this film is totally improvised. As the director himself observes, he was "writing the film at the moment of filming, writing and filming, filming and writing. I was no longer subordinated to a script or even a story, but rather to a vague narrative line, and I improvised at the moment of filming. It was a great opening, at that moment, to be able to speculate freely about questions like political participation and ideology."[19] Its director thus defines *Hunger for Love* as an *opening*, a new beginning, a new form of *speculative discourse* about ideology. *Hunger for Love*'s discourse "involved questioning our whole ideological stance, excessively closed in the face of a reality that is always springing surprises on us. As soon as you think you know it well, you realize that the opposite is true, that it reveals itself to be new and different."[20]

Part of *Hunger for Love* was shot in New York, guerrilla style, in the words of the director, since he had authorization to film only tourist attractions. New York serves not only as a setting for Felipe and

Mariana's initial encounter—he is a waiter, she, a wealthy diner—but also as a counterpole to Brazil: development versus underdevelopment. New York, like the island on which much of the film's action occurs, also represents isolation and distance from political struggle. Dos Santos explains that while he was preparing the film he "realized how important the dispute was in the U.S. over the political movement then springing up in the underdeveloped countries. It was the year of the martyrdom of Che Guevara, and [he] realized how much falsity there was in the attitude of someone who lived in New York and imagined—even wished—that the revolution would happen elsewhere, but all from afar, without doing anything."[21] The film is not so much a critique of the First World's Left, however, as it is a self-criticism and a discussion of the role of the bourgeois intellectual Left in Brazil and the rest of Latin America that often assumes positions parallel to those the director witnessed in New York: a desire for revolution, but on a theoretical level and preferably at a distance.

Alfredo, the former military officer in Figueiredo's novel, is an internationally renowned scientist and former revolutionary leader in dos Santos's film. The two careers mix, at least in Ula's mind, and it is through her that we learn of his past: "By the age of thirty he had published five books about a small plant that grows in the Northeast. . . . His thesis was a true revolution . . . in botany. That's why we traveled so much. We've even passed through Viet Nam." He had been the victim of an assassination attempt, and now spends his time developing chess strategies, using different languages—Russian, Chinese, Spanish—for the opposing sides. The reference to different revolutionary lines and strategies is clear and is reinforced throughout the film by quotations from Mao (in English), Che Guevara and Régis Debray (in Spanish), Lenin and other socialist theoreticians.

But Alfredo, the "revolutionary" leader in *Hunger for Love*, is deaf, dumb, and blind. The revolutionary theories he supposedly espouses have failed in the specific context of Brazil. Alfredo is incapable of action, even of speech, and in this sense resembles other protagonists of second-phase Cinema Novo: the congressman in Gustavo Dahl's *O Bravo Guerreiro* (which ends with a shot of him looking in a mirror with a pistol in his mouth, unable even to pull the trigger), the journalist in Saraceni's *O Desafio* (who expresses total impotence vis-à-vis the political conjuncture), and even Paulo Martins in Rocha's *Land in Anguish* (who embarks on a suicidal mission of individual armed struggle). Writing of his *O Bravo Guerreiro*, Gustavo Dahl sums up their situation: "In *O Desafio*, in *Land in Anguish*, and in *O Bravo Guerreiro*, there wanders the same personage—a petit-bourgeois intellectual, tangled up in doubts, a wretch in crisis. He may be a journalist, a poet, a legislator, but in any case he is always perplexed, hesitant, a weak person who would like to tragically transcend his condition."[22]

Despite the specific circumstances of his past, Alfredo is like these other personages in his political impotence, in his inability to *act*.

The island becomes an isolated refuge serving as a microcosmic battleground (and burial ground) for ideologies and for purely personal wars between the four personages. Mariana is the only character who does not already know Alfredo, and her image of him is that which Ula and Felipe, who had apparently worked for Alfredo while in the United States, give her. Ula and Felipe share a common concern with self-indulgence and are inevitably drawn to each other. Whereas Ula has an ironic if not sarcastic attitude toward politics, Felipe at least verbalizes political concerns, saying (of Alfredo) that, "when the day of the explosion comes, no matter where, we will be with him . . . at the same place, at the same moment." Ula, on the other hand, wants to forget the past and refuses to think of the future; she accepts, in existential anguish and alienation, the meaninglessness of life on the island.

Mariana is the pivotal figure in *Hunger for Love*. More serious by nature than Ula or Felipe, she is fascinated by Alfredo and draws a mental image of him as the ideal revolutionary. Although from the upper classes, she has begun to acquire a political consciousness that, if put into practice, would lead to the extinction of her class. As she becomes more and more intellectually concerned with revolutionary politics, she becomes distanced from Ula and Felipe and drawn inevitably toward Alfredo. A solitary musical note often punctuates events concerning her, and as she is drawn to Alfredo's botanical retreat during Ula and Felipe's absence from the island, the note "represents their cryptic pattern of intellectual interaction. Subsequently they make love. The over-exposure of the shots, however, suggests two things: Mariana has become both 'illuminated' and blinded. Her idealism has weakened her grasp on reality."[23] The tape recorder she often carries with her also represents the increasing distance between Mariana and reality: at one point she records the rain so she can listen to it later with earphones. Her newfound revolutionary politics are based not on an analysis of social and economic realities, but on vacuous theorizing.

The contradictions and conflicts between the two opposing sides are worked out in a sequence that takes place after a dinner party, reminiscent of the final party in Fellini's *La Dolce Vita*. The drunken characters bring a trunk of costumes from the cellar, as latent hostilities arise in a debauched, carnivalesque atmosphere where some characters yell "Siamo tutti canni" ("We are all dogs!"). Alfredo is cruelly derided as Ula helps him into his costume as Che Guevara, "The Santa Claus of Latin America," as she brutally declares. Dos Santos's idea here is not to criticize Che Guevara, but rather to demystify the "myth" bourgeois intellectuals hold of the Argentine revolutionary. Although Felipe reacts angrily to Ula's cruelty, he himself is totally disillusioned and recognizes that, despite his past, Alfredo is now insignificant. Not even Mariana escapes the revelations of this night of debauchery, as she claims to have "crucified Marxism-Leninism" in her head.

The day breaks with Alfredo and Mariana being led around the island by Alfredo's seeing-eye dog (the "revolution" is deaf, dumb, and blind). A long reverse zoom reveals that they are now on their own island, isolated not only from Ula and Felipe, but also from political struggle, because their revolutionary theories lead nowhere. At the same time we hear Mariana's voice-over reading from Che: "The duty of revolutionaries is to make revolution." Nothing could be farther from the reality of Mariana and Alfredo. As João Luiz Vieira and Elizabeth Merena observe, Che's words are accompanied by Brazilian folk music, which for the first time in the film replaces the electronic soundtrack. Revolutions are made through action, the film seems to suggest, whereas leftist theorizing is static.

Hunger for Love's mode of discourse is discontinuous, disruptive, and fragmentary, as it attempts to understand new political realities and the failure of "ready-made" solutions and theories. It represents a return to the original Cinema Novo idea of "a camera in hand and an idea in mind" while rejecting the documentary realism of earlier Cinema Novo. Brazilian reality has become too complex to capture through a naturalistic mode of discourse, or at least the filmmakers' understanding of that reality has become more complex. The film plays with spatial and temporal discontinuity, much like the films of Alain Resnais, and juxtaposes the past and the present, New York and Brazil, fantasy and "reality." The film's complex editing emphasizes the fragmented quality of the narrative and creates thematic and intellectual association by joining disparate images. There is often a relationship of discontinuity between image and sound, as two realities are dialectically juxtaposed to develop a third idea.

Cuts from New York to Brazil, accompanied by apparently independent voice-overs, reinforce the idea of struggle between developed and underdeveloped countries. At one point Felipe invites Mariana to go for a boat ride. She had been walking along a beach reading Mao. Inserts show, in Mariana's imagination, Felipe trying to kill her and then Mariana sitting in the restaurant of New York's Museum of Modern Art. The next shot pans over the islands, with Mariana's voice (in New York) on the soundtrack: "I want to go back to my island, to my exploited, drained people." The artist discovers Brazil's underdevelopment only by being in a developed country, but when she asks, "Where are the people?" she sees them only in the distance. She conceives of the people in idealistic terms, but has no real contact with them. Such, the film seems to suggest, is the situation with many intellectuals and artists of the Left in Brazil, and such is the state of the revolution—silenced, repressed, impotent—in Nelson Pereira dos Santos's pessimistic discourse on the failure of the bourgeois intellectual Left. New ideologies must be found; the old ones have not worked. This is the beginning of a virtual exorcism in dos Santos's films, an exorcism that lasts through *Quem E Beta?* and paves the way for a new cultural and cinematic posture in what I have called the third, or "popular," phase of his work.

Dos Santos's subsequent feature, *Azyllo Muito Louco*, takes *Hunger for Love*'s critique of certain ideologies a step farther and calls into question all ideologies that set themselves up as the "truth." That, in fact, is the nature of ideology. In the director's words, *Azyllo Muito Louco* questions "*all* ideologies that confront reality with the illusion of tying it down completely in a sort of ideological 'salvation.' In this sense, *Azyllo Muito Louco* is an almost metaphysical film, an endless discussion of the problem."[24]

Azyllo Muito Louco is indeed a metaphysical film, for the questions it raises no longer concern social and economic structures as such, but rather the nature of "truth" and how one knows and defines it. Truth, the film seems to be saying, is culturally determined and therefore relative. Any ideology that claims to have the ultimate handle on truth is by nature a repressive ideology, be it political, religious, or esthetic. The truth is what authority—religious, military, political, economic, cultural—deems it to be, and should therefore be questioned and challenged by artists.

Azyllo Muito Louco, dos Santos's first color film, also continues *Hunger for Love*'s scenario (Parati and surrounding areas), its tendency toward allegory, and its discontinuous mode of cinematic discourse. *Azyllo* is highly synthetic and theatrical in form, transmitting its messages through isolated blocks and moments without a concern for continuity of narration, despite the basically linear story it relates. It is an anti-illusionistic and nonnaturalistic mode of representation enhanced by the use (as in *Hunger for Love*) of penetrating, sometimes irritating, electronic music, which lends a general tone of madness to the film as a whole. The film's use of discontinuous structures questions as well the nature of cinematic discourse and its ability to reproduce "reality" and, by extension, truth.

Azyllo Muito Louco is based on Machado de Assis's classic short narrative *O Alienista* (translated as *The Psychiatrist*). The ultimate lesson of Machado's tale, writes Afrânio Coutinho, is that "life is not absolute logicality, it does not fit in geometrical formulas, and it contains within it an immense zone of illogicality, even if it does not reach the level of madness, as Simão Bacamarte would have it."[25] Although relatively faithful to the novella's narrative structure, the film rejects the work's realism as a mode of representation and develops the tale allegorically, providing it with a political meaning merely latent in Machado's work. What Machado wrote some ninety years before dos Santos's film is particularly relevant to the Brazil of the early 1970s.

Machado's novella and dos Santos's film concern a psychiatrist who constantly changes the criteria for determining who is mad, a theme that at its most simple level has obvious implications for military-ruled Brazil. It should be remembered that the film was made in 1970 and released in 1971, the nadir of political freedom in Brazil. It was a period in which professors suspected of leftist leanings were fired en masse from the universities, in which anyone suspected of not being "ideologically pure" was subject to arrest with no habeas corpus, in which "ideological certificates" were sometimes required of candidates for posts in the bureaucracy. It was a period, in short, when the military government felt no restraints on its arbitrary powers and arrested and often tortured innocent citizens at its own "discretion."

But dos Santos's film is not merely a critique of the abuse of power or the changing ideological standards of the military regime. The director has transformed the physician-psychiatrist of Machado's novella into a priest-psychiatrist, a "worker of souls," as a means of giving him a supposed "moral" and religious authority in addition to his "scientific" authority. He thus questions the church and like institutions. The psychiatrist's wife, Dona Evarista, has been transformed into the leading lady of the local aristocracy and the holder of the town's political authority. The dramatis personae of the two works are otherwise basically the same, although for dramatic efficiency, dos Santos eliminated some characters, combined others, and added some of his own. Wherever possible he used dialogue from the novella—with the idea, as in Joaquim Pedro de Andrade's *Os Inconfidentes*, of using virtually uncensorable material—though at times he created his own in accordance with the purposes of his own filmic discourse.

The film opens with a town crier announcing the new priest's arrival. The crier, dressed in extravagant pastels and with a paper windmill twirling on his hat, introduces the film's anti-illusionistic, quasi-Brechtian discourse as he faces the camera (and the audience), describes his function, and tells of the new priest's arrival in Serafim. The town's name has been changed from the Itaguaí of the novella as a means of providing a more abstract, "heavenly" scenario. The drama thus works itself out in an imaginary, allegorical setting.

The crier's clothes, and those of other personages, also reveal a carnivalesque substratum that resounds through the film and links it to the tropicalist phase of Cinema Novo. If, as Roberto Schwarz suggests, the tropicalist strategy was to present an allegory of Brazil by juxtaposing the anachronistic and the ultramodern, *Azyllo Muito Louco* presents Brazil as a huge madhouse in which reason and logic have broken down and have been replaced with irrationality and authoritarianism.

The town crier's narration continues as a voice-over accompanies images of Padre Simão Bacamarte (the priest) arriving on a boat, then of Dona Evarista, who heads the official greeting party. The priest's last name, Bacamarte, indicates his authoritarian function. Bacamarte means "blunderbuss," an ambiguous word meaning both a kind of firearm (with all its military connotations) and a person who "blunders." His very name thus questions the priest's right to authority. Dona Evarista and Padre Simão are carried by slaves to the church, now in ruins. Dona Evarista claims responsibility for the church's condition, and Simão explains that he will start a new cult in which he will be a "worker of souls." In his first sermon, preached from a high altar distanced from a congregation composed of the local society (and from which the people, whom the decisions being made will first affect, are conspicuously and symptomatically absent), he declares that he is concerned with the soul's health and that toward that end he will study different manifestations of madness. He later asks Dona Evarista to help in the construction of the Casa Verde to house the mentally unbalanced. With incredulity Dona Evarista responds, "Putting them all in the same house is madness!" "Then God is mad," replies Simão, "since he houses them all in his heavenly home." As the Casa Verde is being constructed, she wonders if it is not too large for "our few crazies." Little does she know that, within a short period of time, most of the local townspeople, including herself, will be interned there.

The first patients are applauded as they arrive at the Casa Verde, and Simão explains some of the cases to Dona Evarista. But people are already beginning to suspect that the only crazy person in Serafim is Padre Simão himself. At the same time he makes his definition of madness more extreme, saying that normality (sanity) is the total equilibrium of all mental faculties and that outside of these strict limits everyone is mad. Such a "definition" recalls in its very "madness" the military government's Law of National Security, which neither defines national security nor specifies which crimes are covered under it. Rather, it permits the government to define national security as it sees fit, according to the circumstances at hand. Virtually any crime or "ideological deviance" is potentially in violation of the nation's "security." Of course, very few people demonstrate total equilibrium, and soon most of the town is behind bars in the Casa Verde, including Dona Evarista.

A revolt begins to take shape, as some of the townspeople ask Porfírio, a wealthy landowner and slaveholder (the representative of economic power), to lead a new government. Porfírio's revolt succeeds, but rather than releasing all the supposedly mad inmates, he wants them to work for him as slaves (a critique of populism and the nature of power).

Padre Simão manages to maintain power after Porfírio's coup. He soon realizes, however, that something must be wrong with his theory, since three-fourths of Serafim's population is in the Casa Verde. He thus concludes that the opposite theory must be the correct one: that those who appear to be perfectly normal are mad, and those in the Casa Verde are sane.

Nelson Pereira dos Santos's attack on authoritarianism and ideology is clear throughout the film, as the priest's theories rarely fit the reality of Serafim. They are, rather, imposed from above, as are the political and ideological structures of Brazil itself. Simão's ability to co-opt other sectors of the local population and maintain power criticizes the ruling classes' attempt to maintain power at whatever cost. Ideology—any ideology—is by its very nature oppressive. As the director explains, "The alienist [psychiatrist] is not only a character; he is the very idea that grasps our reality by pretending to organize it scientifically. But it is a false science, a false vision, because each time that reality changes, the words we use must also change, so it is impossible to ever find the correct interpretation that is capable of modifying reality, at least in the sense that we seek."[26]

With this statement, Nelson Pereira dos Santos is a long way from the sociological positions of his initial films. Early Cinema Novo films attempted to analyze society from a preconceived political and ideological position. But the reality they dealt with changed very quickly, and what may have been valid in 1962, before the coup d'état, or even in 1967, before the Fifth Institutional Act, is not sufficient to respond to the questions of the sociopolitical conjuncture of 1970–1971. Ideological dogmatism does not solve anything, much less the problems of Brazilian society. A disjuncture develops between ideology and society that leads (figuratively) only to madness.

Padre Simão's authoritarian nature is revealed not only through the story related, but also, and perhaps primarily, through the film's framing. His face—metaphorically, his mind, his ideology—often appears in the foreground at the edge of the screen and dominates the action that occurs in the background. At times he appears on the left, at others on the right, or at the bottom of the frame, thus giving an image of omnipresence and omnipotence. Discontinuity between sound and image and in the editing is designed to give an idea of the personages' disorientation in the face of the priest's authoritarianism, and the grating electronic music reinforces the film's persistent image of madness.

How Tasty Was My Little Frenchman may at first glance seem out of place in what I have called Nelson Pereira dos Santos's "ideological" phase, since, in a number of ways, it recalls the films of the first phase. The director observes that it is this film that is in fact closest to *Vidas Secas*: "It is almost a continuation of the earlier film, since it abandons ideology—or at least declines to discuss it—while simultaneously incorporating it into a more open vision, an anthropological one."[27] This coincidence of intention between *Vidas Secas* and *How Tasty Was My Little Frenchman* is perhaps not surprising, since dos Santos's plans to make the latter date from the period of the former. The two films share a concern with the "documentation" of a given reality through the use of hand-held camera and other documentary techniques, which lend it authenticity. They are likewise cinematic responses to debates then occurring in Brazilian society: agrarian reform, in the case of *Vidas Secas*; and, on a cultural level, "tropicalism," cultural colonization, and the cannibalistic nature of societal relations—a debate initiated cinematically by Joaquim Pedro de Andrade's *Macunaíma*—in the case of *How Tasty Was My Little Frenchman*.

But *How Tasty Was My Little Frenchman*, despite the director's disclaimer, *also* deals with ideology and thus belongs in the second phase of his work. It is in essence a historical film ("anthropological," to accept dos Santos's term) about the period of Brazil's colonization, but it also concerns the *way* in which that history has been interpreted, the highly ideological manner in which official history perceives and types the participants in the process of colonization. *How Tasty Was My Little Frenchman*'s allegorical discussion of the conflict of cultures, cultural and economic imperialism, and anthropophagy has obvious significance for today's Brazil and the way in which the cultural struggle is perceived. In this sense as well the film rightly belongs to dos Santos's "ideological" phase.

The fact that dos Santos is concerned with the present and not merely with anthropological reconstruction is apparent in the film's precredits sequence. It begins with a declaration in a radio-broadcast mode: "Latest news from Terra Firme." This statement reflects a certain "present-ness," as if what we are seeing were a documentary newsreel. It is followed immediately, in the same tone, by a portion of a letter from Villegaignon, leader of French Protestant settlers in Brazil, to John Calvin, in which he talks of a man who drowned in an escape from justice. But what we see contradicts Villegaignon's "history," as the prisoner, in ball and chain, is pushed over a cliff in an attempted execution. History, or at least the official version of history, is called into question as the director presents us with another, contradictory version.

Quotations of historical documents such as Villegaignon's letter to Calvin punctuate the film throughout (there are nine such citations) and provide the spectator with an often ironic if not contradictory commentary on the action depicted. The film itself is based on a critical reading of such documents, the most important of which is Hans Staden's *Voyage to Brazil*. Staden was a German adventurer who, while in the service of Dutch colonizers in sixteenth-century Brazil, was captured by an Indian tribe. His chronicle relates his experiences at the hands of his captors. Unlike the Frenchman in dos Santos's film, however, Staden obviously lived to tell about his adventures.

The question of the conflict of cultures pervades the film. An early quotation explains that the Portuguese have allied with the Tupiniquim Indians and the French with the Tupinambá. The Indian groups themselves are thus divided (as are the Europeans) and struggling among themselves in a sort of mutual cannibalism. The major conflict, however, is ultimately between Europeans and Amerindians. The basic goal of the French and the Portuguese is the same: the domination and economic exploitation of the New World. Temporary alliances with indigenous groups are more a question of strategy than of final goals. This fact becomes painfully clear in the film's final and self-explanatory quotation in which the Portuguese governor-general of Brazil says of their Tupiniquim allies, "We have killed so many Indians that, if we were to lay their bodies along the beach, they would cover a distance of half a league."

How Tasty Was My Little Frenchman tells the story of Jean (Arduíno Colasânti), the supposedly executed prisoner of the precredits sequence, and his brief life (and death) among the Tupinambá. The first postcredits shot shows Jean coming ashore out of the sea, still dragging his heavy ball and chain. After freeing himself, he is captured by a group of Portuguese and their Tupiniquim allies, who are in turn attacked by a group of Tupinambá warriors. Jean and several Portuguese are submitted to an impromptu language test after Jean insists that he is French. Unable to tell them apart (except for the fact that Jean is blond with blue eyes while the Portuguese have ruddy complexions), Cunhambebe, the Tupinambá chief, has the Portuguese killed. Jean is spared only because he shows them that he knows how to use the Portuguese cannons.

Jean is to be the subject of the Tupinambá ritual in which he is integrated into the tribe, made to help with the work, given a woman (Sebiopepe), and allowed to live in peace for eight months before being killed and devoured in a cannibalistic ritual. The idea of eating one's enemies, according to Montaigne, is not only the supreme act of vengeance, but is also a way of absorbing the victim's courage and bravery while simultaneously destroying him. The victim is, in this sense, absorbed into the tribal body.

The passage of time is marked not only by the diminishing beads placed around Jean's neck (one for each moon), but also by his gradual assimilation into the life of the tribe. As Richard Peña has perceptively observed, the initial scenes of Jean's life with the tribe emphasize his *difference* and separation from the Indians.[28] He is white, blond, bearded, and at least partially clothed, in contrast to the naked "redskins." He is distinguished, among these other things, by a body covered with hair. The Tupinambá engaged in the custom of depilation, since they believed that the only way to tell human beings from animals was by the human's lack of body hair. The custom also was a means of facilitating hand to hand combat in warfare. It is therefore not surprising that Jean is sent to work with the women and considered to be less than a man.

Along these same lines, in the earlier "language test," the Portuguese, when ordered to speak, repeat elements of a recipe (a joke about the Portugueses' gluttonous image) while Jean says in French, "The savages walk totally naked [*nus*], and we are unrecognized [*inconnus*]." The French and other Europeans are ultimately as savage, if not more so, than the Indian, but are not recognized as such, thereby justifying their savagery and exploitation as a "civilizing" process.[29] The true barbarians are those who dissimulate as a more advanced civilization.

As Jean becomes integrated into the tribe, he begins to lose his "European-ness." His beard comes off, then his hair; he learns to speak Tupi, and, finally, he too begins to walk naked. The arrival of a French trader (played by the actor's real-life father, Manfredo Colasânti), fully dressed in seventeenth-century style, emphasizes Jean's growing distance from the Europeans. The trader refuses to tell the Indians that Jean is indeed French and leaves him with the tribe to gather more brazilwood for export to Europe. At this point, Jean is neither French nor "American," but somewhere in between.

The French trader introduces the economics of colonization to the film. In exchange for manufactured items of little value—combs, mirrors, beads—the Indians provide such primary materials as wood and spices. The initial steps of a dependent economy based on the export of raw materials and the importation of manufactured products is established. Capitalism begins to develop in the Americas. At the same time, the trader promises the Tupinambá gunpowder in order to put their cannon to use in their struggle against the Tupiniquim: divide and conquer.

One day while swimming with Sebiopepe, Jean finds what he thinks will gain him his freedom: a gold coin Sebiopepe uses as decoration in her navel. Unaware of its value to Europeans, in the same way that the Indians fail to understand the Europeans' interest in brazilwood, Sebiopepe shows Jean that there are more coins where that one came from. Realizing that now he can get the upper hand with the trader, Jean regresses to his position as a distanced European, refuses to work, and speaks once again in French.

While staying home with Sebiopepe, Jean asks her to tell him the story of Mair, the great Tupinambá god-ancestor. The film visualizes the myth as she recounts it in Tupi in a subjective sequence in which Jean imagines himself in the role of the great white god, obviously a vision spurred by his newfound "wealth." It is in this sequence that we first see him beardless and naked. His voice suddenly takes over the narration, in French, and tells of improvements he made in the Indians' way of life. All the while, he acts out the role of Mair and imagines himself superior to the Indians. Sebiopepe, however, soon resumes the narration in Tupi, telling how the Tupinambá revolted against the god and destroyed his creations, as we see his house burning and Mair/Jean being forced to run through a fire. We subsequently see Cunhambebe reminding his tribe never to forget who their enemies are. Sebiopepe concludes the myth with a description of thunder and lightning pouring from Mair's head after his death (foreshadowing the Indians' destruction at the hands of the Europeans).

Jean, now recognizably "savage" as a result of depilation and nakedness, joins in the war against the rival tribe, even killing a Portuguese with an arrow while awaiting the trader's return. When the trader does return, Jean exchanges gold (a "raw material" of sorts, since it was found "hidden" in the ground) for manufactured gunpowder. The agent of economic exploitation is no longer the (recognizable) trader, but rather (the unrecognizable) Jean (to invert the earlier saying). As Paulo Emílio Salles Gomes has observed in another context, "The peculiarity of this process, by which the occupier created the occupied in his own image, made the occupied, to a certain point, his equal. Psychologically, the occupied and the occupier do not see themselves in these roles; in fact we ourselves are the occupier."[30] The idea, as applied to the film, is that Jean, who remains European, or at least tied to European interests, and who comes to participate in the exploitation of Brazil's raw materials, no longer appears to be foreign. In many ways he has become "Brazilian." His dissimulation has made him virtually unrecognizable as a European by making him recognizable as a "savage." Jean and the trader eventually struggle over the gold, and the trader is killed. As Richard Peña observes, the trader's death "eliminates the older kind of 'foreign agent'—the European who looks like a European who deals in manufactured commodities—and replaces him with a new kind of agent, curiously still a foreigner, yet one who looks, at least on the surface, like an American or Brazilian."[31]

Jean subsequently attempts to leave on the trader's ship, but as he begins to paddle out into the bay, he sees Sebiopepe on the shore and returns for her. She refuses to accompany him, and when he attempts to flee, she shoots him in the leg with an arrow. She has become his "wife" and companion, but maintains her ultimate rejection of the European and her fidelity to the tribe.

Jean tries to buy time by firing the cannon in a battle against the Tupiniquim, but the day of his ritualistic death approaches. He even rehearses the death ritual with Sebiopepe and appears, in an extreme close shot, with his face reddened by vegetable dye like the other Indians. His integration into the tribe is almost complete. Final assimilation, however, will occur only with his destruction and physical consumption. After the death ritual, in which Jean prophetically cries out in French that his "tribe" will return to avenge his death, a shot focuses on Sebiopepe remorselessly eating Jean's neck.

The idea (and fact) of cannibalism of course pervades the film and represents Nelson Pereira dos Santos's contribution to the never-ending Brazilian discussion of cultural colonization. The use of cannibalism as a metaphor for the cultural struggle goes back to Brazilian literary modernism and Oswald de Andrade's "movimento antropófago" (cannibalist movement, 1928–1930). Oswald's cannibalism recognizes the necessity of taking advantage of external influences and critically "digesting" and reelaborating them in terms of Brazilian reality. His "cannibalist" attitude is a way of recognizing and organizing elements already saturated with cultural meaning. Only the mixture of all cultural contributions can create an original culture. The Tupinambá, for example, devour Jean as a means of ritually incorporating his values after figuratively devouring the technology he offers (the cannon). As Nelson Pereira dos Santos puts it, "The position of outright rejection [of foreign cultures] seems mistaken to me. We are all, from a certain point of view, Europeans—in our language, in our way of life. At the same time we resent the terrible influence of American technological civilization, and our way of thinking makes that clear. All this amounts to the summation of our contradictions. On the other hand a romantic return to our origins is absurd."[32]

This statement is perfectly in line with Oswald de Andrade's original "cannibalist" propositions. In fact, one might say that *How Tasty Was My Little Frenchman* takes Andrade's movement to its ultimate conclusions (artistically, that is). Part of the "cannibalist" program included the study of indigenous cultures and languages, and Nelson Pereira dos Santos's film has dialogue almost entirely in Tupi and is based on the same kind of study that characterized Andrade's movement.

In *Quem E Beta?* (*Who Is Beta?*), the last film of dos Santos's "ideological" phase, the director returns to the more specifically ideological discourse of *Hunger for Love*. The film reverts, so to speak, to a zero degree of film writing and wipes the slate clean so as to begin anew in *O Amuleto de Ogum* with another type of cinema. Dos Santos himself anticipated this change in an interview granted at the time of the release of *How Tasty Was My Little Frenchman*:

A whole transformation of our way of seeing reality and Brazilian culture is coming about. We are on the verge of going beyond that questionable "culturist" position that led us to assume an alleged "distanciation," a facile stance regarding the reality that bothered us: misery, glaring underdevelopment. I maintain that this position was a colonial one, for we went about criticizing all that with a superior air, as if we were not Brazilians at all, drawing a certain satisfaction from our backwardness and underdevelopment that was aimed at our American and European father as if to say, "I am not that." This kind of vision is worthless today; it is indefensible.[33]

It is in this sense that the ideological phase of dos Santos's work represents a sort of exorcism—an exorcism of this distanced, superior stance, an exorcism of all ideological orthodoxy—and paves the way for the "popular" phase to follow. *Quem E Beta?* is dos Santos's tabula rasa, a film with no apparent ideology (other than the ideology of experimentation and "rebirth"), no commitment to a given program of action, and above all no commitment to cinematic traditions and structures.

Before the film per se begins, dos Santos's voice explains on the soundtrack, "Don't look for messages in this film; if there are any, they are your contribution. Don't believe what the actors do in scene. Our intention was never to give them a realistic behavior, because everything happens as in a comic book, without obligations and absolutely no commitments. So find a comfortable position in your seat, relax, and let your mind and eyes flow freely, as you should with any film." There is perhaps more truth to his explanation than one might reasonably suspect. *Quem E Beta?* is a playful story that explains absolutely nothing about its characters or their motivations. The "world" is reduced to two rival groups, the "haves" and the "have nots," who struggle for survival. As critic José Carlos Avellar puts it, "The film attempts to impede the spectator from having any information other than the external, formal characteristics of each shot. The image exists only at the moment it is projected. Or to be more precise: only the projection (of images) exists, with no posterior meaning."[34] Although Avellar's judgment may be overly harsh, it is not without some degree of truth. *Quem E Beta?* is a film from which pleasure and meaning derive from the cinematic codes themselves, from the flow of sounds and images, from the viewers' "pleasure of the text."

Quem E Beta?, a Franco-Brazilian production, is loosely based on Levi Meneses's short story "O Ultimo Artilheiro" ("The Last Artillery Gunner"). It concerns the few survivors of a nuclear blast (a rather banal science fiction situation) in an "undefined time and space" (dos Santos's verbal introduction to the film). Maurício, the film's protagonist, who was not contaminated, takes refuge in an abandoned fortress, and defends himself with a machine gun from the "contaminated," whom he mercilessly slaughters. The film's basic conflict is between the contaminated and the noncontaminated (the former wander around moaning and asking for food and water). One day Regina, also uncontaminated, appears and begins to live with Maurício. Shortly thereafter, an enigmatic woman named Beta appears and comes to exert a great influence on Maurício and Regina. Although she herself is not contaminated, she is the only one of the three to have free passage among the contaminated.

Maurício, Regina, and Beta are remnants of a "superior" culture and are the only characters with a memory. Memory is activated through the smoke screen of a "memory machine" (an old movie camera). By activating and expanding their memory, they hope to rebuild society as they once knew it. Maurício, formerly a wealthy businessman, repeatedly remembers himself playing golf. Regina, on the other hand, maintains an image of herself as a beautiful woman, concerned only with her appearance.

The image transmitted of Beta's memory, however, is composed of black and white footage from *Hunger for Love* (thus rendering explicit the link between the two films). The basic dramatic situation of the two films is, in fact, quite similar. In both films, a group of middle to upper middle class people are cloistered, so to speak, and isolated from "the people." In

Hunger for Love the discussion concerns the revolutionary transformation of society and the failure of the intellectual Left vis-à-vis Brazil's new political situation. In *Quem E Beta?* society no longer exists in any traditional sense, except, ironically, through cinema (the camera). The isolated group of personages, infused with what in *Hunger for Love* were seen to be antiquated ideas, discusses the possibility of rebuilding society, starting from nothing but what the camera offers.

In an article with the punning title "Who's Better?" Carlos Diegues suggests that Beta is similar to Antônio das Mortes. Nobody knows where she came from nor who she is, and like Antônio, she "suffers the pain of her conscience, tormented between the anarchistic violence of Corisco (Maurício and his sharp-shooters) and the immobile mysticism of Sebastião (Grande Irmão and his religious followers)."[35] Grande Irmão (Big Brother) is an enigmatic religious leader who, with his following, names plants, stones, and objects. The idea, once again, is that traditional forms of language, in this case, naming, are antiquated and inadequate in the light of a new situation. But in *Quem E Beta?* there are no solutions, even on the symbolic/mythical level, as in Rocha's *Black God, White Devil*.

The discourse of *Quem E Beta?* recalls the Godard of *Week-end*, especially the cannibal feast near the end. But dos Santos's film creates a playful atmosphere that Godard's film lacks. No logic guides the characters' actions, as if logic itself had also been destroyed. The world is reduced into the good (the contaminated), who are not really depicted as "good," and the bad (the uncontaminated), who are not really depicted as "bad." They are, however, doomed, as the contaminated hordes come ever closer to the fortress. The final sequence of *Quem E Beta?* however, calls into question the reliability of the film narrative itself, as Regina Rosemberg, the lead actress, boards an airplane and flies back to Paris with her husband, the film's producer. All that remains is the process of cinema itself, and that is in itself valid.

After the somewhat obscure experience of *Quem E Beta?* Nelson Pereira dos Santos begins a new phase of his cinematic career with *O Amuleto de Ogum*, a phase I have referred to as "popular," because it takes not only as its subject, but also as its perspective, the popular vision of Brazilian culture. *O Amuleto de Ogum* was made for a specific audience—marginalized segments of Brazilian society living in the outlying regions of major cities and in the interior—and structurally assumes that audience's vision of popular culture. Dos Santos is no longer the popular artist of the early sixties attempting to impose a specific intellectualized view of social reality on his films. Rather, he attempts to learn from the people and to transmit the image they have of themselves. "The behavior of our people is absolutely correct; it is what it is," the director has said. Gone are the sociological perspectives of the first phase (even though, as will be pointed out, specific connections

Plate 23. Ney Sant'Anna, *O Amuleto de Ogum (The Amulet of Ogum)*

can be drawn between the two phases), as are the allegorical ponderings of the second. The films of dos Santos's popular phase are open, loose, relaxed, and easily consumed by a broad public, without ceasing, however, to be culturally and intellectually complex.

Coinciding with the release of *O Amuleto de Ogum*, Rio de Janeiro's Federation of Film Societies (and perhaps it should be remembered that almost all of the Cinema Novo directors began their careers as participants of film societies) published Nelson Pereira dos Santos's "Manifesto for a Popular Cinema," a collection of interviews and critical articles concerning the director's career, the current situation of Brazilian cinema (in an interview titled "The Cinema and the State"), and most importantly *O Amuleto de Ogum* and the theory that informs the film.

Although apparently simple, Nelson Pereira dos Santos's idea of a popular cinema is radically new within Brazilian cinema and is a 180-degree reversal from earlier positions, when the dominant form of discourse was the critique and demystification of socioeconomic relationships and the beliefs and myths of the people. Films in Brazil, which, in this sense, is no different from any other capitalist country, are made by a middle-class elite (although there are some exceptions) for a middle-class public. Jean-Claude

Bernardet, a leading Brazilian critic, would say that Cinema Novo's basic problematic was a middle-class problematic.[36] The structure of the Brazilian film market, currently the battleground for national cinema, is also oriented toward the predominantly middle-class public. *O Amuleto de Ogum*, however, is not concerned with this public, although the film does contain elements, such as the struggle between criminal groups, that appeal to all publics.

In an article entitled "*O Amuleto* Changed Everything," Bernardet observes that dos Santos's film passes from the previous concept of "public" to a broader concept of "people":

Spectators are no longer considered a mass of people to be seduced into buying tickets at the box office, but rather as a segment of society for whom the production and exhibition of the film represent a social identification, a recognition of themselves, of their being, of their values, of their potential, of their limits. This cultural position assumed by the *auteur* of the film necessarily leads to the search for an original thematic and dramaturgy. The spectacle is no longer a form of oppression from above, from the film industry . . . but rather an effort toward a dramaturgy born from the bottom to the top.[37]

O Amuleto de Ogum takes as its starting point the form of Afro-Brazilian religion practiced in the slums and suburbs of Rio de Janeiro: *umbanda*. The director explains his choice of *umbanda* in *O Amuleto de Ogum*:

The deepest forms of cultural expression, those that come from the roots, such as the expansion of religious sentiment, have always been repressed and oppressed within Brazilian culture. This concept of religion has always been destroyed by a religious form at the service of the colonizer. It was what I proposed to use as a point of departure, since it gave me a global vision and a way of thinking in relation to all of Brazilian society.[38]

The idea is not to explain *umbanda* to those who are not familiar with it, especially since the film is directed precisely to those sectors of society who are not only familiar with but also practice *umbanda*, but rather to absorb the myths and rituals of *umbanda* into the film's dramatic texture. A shot of a Catholic priest administering Holy Communion would need no further explanation to a Western audience and would easily introduce a whole universe of already-codified meanings concerning a given (religious) ideology. The director's use of *umbanda* follows this same principle. Those who understand or are familiar with the religion need no further explanation, whereas those unfamiliar may miss some of the film's meaning. But that is the choice dos Santos made.

O Amuleto de Ogum, like such films as Glauber Rocha's *Black God, White Devil*, reveals a narrative structure drawn from popular ballads and *cordel* literature in which the narrator introduces, concludes, intervenes, and comments on the action. The blind singer Júlio of *Black God, White Devil* is, in a sense, incorporated into *O Amuleto de Ogum*. The first sequence shows a blind man walking down a dark alley, carrying a guitar. He is jumped by three assailants, who force him to sing. The story he tells—the film we see—"really happened, I just invented it." The singer's ambiguous, playful introduction recalls Sérgio Ricardo's theme song to *Black God, White Devil*: "So I've told my story / made of truth and imagination." Popular narratives often mix and even confuse historical and true stories with fantasy from the narrator's creative imagination. Fantasy is often more important than fact, and the film's narrator in this sense takes on extreme importance as a creative participant in the discourse.

The film recalls the earlier phases of dos Santos's career as well. At one point the samba "Voz do Morro," the theme song of *Rio 40 Graus*, is heard on the soundtrack. *O Amuleto de Ogum* returns to the urban setting of *Rio 40 Graus, Rio Zona Norte*, and to the criminality of *Boca de Ouro*. But it recalls most precisely dos Santos's classic, *Vidas Secas*. The 1963 film, it may be recalled, ends with a shot of Fabiano, Vitória, and their family *on the way to* the city. *O Amuleto* takes place among northeastern immigrants *in* the city, as if to suggest that this is the final destination of the myriad Fabianos who are forced to leave the Northeast. The blind singer of *O Amuleto de Ogum* (played by singer Jards Macalé) tells the story of Gabriel (played by dos Santos's son Ney Sant'Anna), who, in the initial "fictional" sequence, sees his father and brother massacred by an armed band in the Northeast. Maria Ribeiro, the same actress who played the role of Sinhá Vitória in *Vidas Secas*, plays Gabriel's mother. Like the family in *Vidas Secas*, Gabriel's family comprises a man (murdered in the initial sequence), his wife (Vitória), and two sons (Gabriel and the one who is murdered with his father). After the crime, Gabriel's mother leads him through the desert (in a shot reminiscent of the initial sequences of *Vidas Secas*) to a ceremony in which his body is "closed"; that is, he is provided somewhat magically with protection against physical injury and death as long as he wears the "amulet of Ogum."

Gabriel is put on a train and sent to live with an uncle, who is the head of a numbers racket (like Boca de Ouro) in Caxias, a violent suburb of Rio de Janeiro. Jofre Soares, who also played the role of *Vidas Secas*' "villain," the landowner, plays the uncle, the villain, so to speak. Thousands of northeasterners, perhaps not unlike Fabiano, Vitória, and their sons, who have migrated to the urban centers of the south, inhabit Caxias. The town has gained notoriety in recent years as the center of activities of Brazil's infamous death squads.

The narrative of *O Amuleto de Ogum* is structured, within the framework of the popular ballad, in *umbanda* cycles. The first cycle concerns the ceremony of "closing" the body and Gabriel's protection by Ogum, the divinity of warriors. Gabriel receives an amulet (whence the film's title) that protects him from physical harm. When he arrives in Caxias, his criminal uncle, Severino, takes him in and he begins to work as a gunman/assassin. Gabriel rises in prestige as members of the gang learn of his closed body. On two occasions he is shot at point-blank range and feels nothing. On another occasion he kills in cold blood the president of the Brazilian Red Cross, thereby gaining another form of notoriety.

Forced to hide out until things cool down, Gabriel takes up with Severino's lover, Eneida, and the second *umbanda* cycle begins: the cycle of the Pomba Gira, who represents evil in the form of a woman. This cycle deals with Gabriel's temptation by Eneida (Anecy Rocha). Because of his relationship with her, Gabriel breaks with Severino and joins a rival gang that organizes young toughs into robbery squads. A bloody war breaks out between the two groups. The singer-narrator intervenes explicitly in this section of the film, appearing on the streets of Caxias and later beside a statue of the Pomba Gira. The fiction is confused and intertwined with the reality of the narrator himself, the film obeying once again the nature of popular ballads. The narrator, although blind, seems to be an eyewitness to the action, thus increasing his credibility and reliability.

The cycle of Exu, messenger of the other *umbanda* saints (*orixás*) and frequently a malevolent deity, then begins as Severino himself resorts to *umbanda* in an attempt to defeat Gabriel. The film is replete with *umbanda* symbology, and Exu's food symbol is *cachaça*. Severino asks Exu to turn Gabriel into an alcoholic, and as Gabriel becomes increasingly irrational and drunken, Eneida abandons him and delivers him to Severino's gang. At one point in the Exu cycle Exu possesses Severino, who becomes a horse. Gabriel is captured and thrown into a river but is saved by the *pai-de-santo* Erlei (played by himself), and the cycle of Oxum's protection begins. Oxum, the vain and fickle divinity of the Oxum River, initiates a period of peace.

Eneida returns and takes Gabriel to São Paulo to meet her family. In a motel on the way back to Rio, Gabriel takes the amulet from his neck and is betrayed as Eneida leads Severino to him. Severino, knowing that Gabriel's Achilles' heel is his mother, orders her killed, and a sequential insert shows the assassination attempt. When Gabriel hears reports of his mother's death (in reality, her maid is killed), he becomes vulnerable. But his mother, aware of the danger to her son, is on the way to Rio to protect him. Enraged, Gabriel runs to Severino's house, and in a bloody gun battle they kill each other. Gabriel, however, falls (apparently) dead into Severino's swimming pool as his mother arrives at Rio's bus station. Water is the dominion of Iemanjá, the goddess of the sea, and Gabriel is magically resurrected, no longer in the pool, but rather on a boat on the sea, with his six-guns blazing as the fiction ends.

In the film's epilogue, the blind singer finishes his song and the toughs attack him. But the singer assumes Gabriel's powers, or perhaps reveals at last that he has told his own story, as he defeats the three thugs. The fictional fantasy thus invades the world of the narrator as the planes between the two modes of discourse—fantasy and reality—once again merge and become one.

Despite the magic ending, the discourse of *O Amuleto de Ogum* is essentially realistic, as it follows traditional forms of filmic representation. Fantasy and magic arise naturally in the diegesis in accordance with the popular vision of the power of *umbanda*. Gabriel reappears in the end (before the epilogue) as the spirit of the people, who, according to Pedro Archanjo in dos Santos's later *Tent of Miracles*, are ultimately invincible.

Although film critics and specialists in *umbanda* have criticized this resurrection, it had a tremendously favorable repercussion among practitioners who saw the film. Such is precisely the effect desired by the director: "Making a film not only based on popular values, but that also accepts and assumes them positively, the people recognize themselves in it. In this way the spectators can at the same time affirm themselves culturally."[39]

To show the differences between *O Amuleto de Ogum* and earlier Cinema Novo films, the director draws a parallel between Gabriel and Firmino in Glauber Rocha's *Barravento* (often considered the first Brazilian film to deal seriously with Afro-Brazilian religion). In *Barravento*, Firmino returns to his native fishing village *from the city*, ready-equipped with answers for the fishermen's problems. He sees *candomblé* as an element of alienation in the fishermen's lives, which impedes them from freeing themselves from the economic repression suffocating them. In *O Amuleto de Ogum*, on the other hand, no character is superior to the people themselves, and no model of proper behavior is imposed. *Umbanda* is seen in unquestioningly positive terms.

Although Nelson Pereira dos Santos's concept of popular cinema may ultimately be idealistic or naive, especially when one considers the economic structures of Brazilian cinema (*O Amuleto de Ogum* is a film aimed at a nonfilmgoing public), there can be little doubt about its importance in the development of Brazilian cinema in the 1970s. As Jean-Claude Bernardet observes,

After *O Amuleto* one can no longer discuss things [concerning cinema] as before. *O Amuleto* links cinematic production to the people. Even if one does not agree with all of Nelson's and his films' propositions, *O Amuleto* sets out the terrain on which discussions should take place as it proposes a drastic reformulation of the relations between the filmmaker (and the intellectual in general) and the people. The filmmaker's humility with respect to popular values, which we normally know theoretically rather than from experience . . . is one of the processes necessary for us to break down our pretended intellectual, scientific, or political superiority, and understand these values from within.[40]

Plate 24. *Tenda dos Milagres (Tent of Miracles)*

The powers that be in Brazilian cinema, however, considered *O Amuleto de Ogum* to be an intellectual film and exhibited it primarily in art cinemas in the large cities' fashionable districts. Despite the fact that it was very well received when shown (mostly in special sessions) to its intended audience, *O Amuleto de Ogum* by and large did not reach all of that audience.

Dos Santos's subsequent film, *Tent of Miracles,* is a hybrid in which he blends the popular concerns of *O Amuleto de Ogum*—in this case an incorporation of the rituals of Bahian *candomblé* into the narrative structure—with a critique of social structures reminiscent of his early period (an economic and cultural hierarchy based on racism). It is at the same time a discussion of ideology, of the myth of racial democracy that persists in Brazil.

Based on the homonymous novel by Jorge Amado, *Tent of Miracles* is also reminiscent of *O Amuleto de Ogum* in its construction. But now, rather than use the narrative structure of popular ballads as he does in the previous film, dos Santos uses the structures of mass communications, notably television and film. *Tent of Miracles* tells the story of Pedro Archanjo, an obscure Bahian mulatto who, while working as a janitor in the School of Medicine, doubles as a self-taught anthropologist studying black culture in

Bahia. His praise and defense of black culture conflicts with the school's dominant Aryan ideology, embodied primarily in the figure of Professor Nilo Argolo.

The story of Pedro Archanjo is relayed as a film-within-a-film. The frame film concerns poet-journalist Fausto Pena and the film he makes about Pedro Archanjo. In fact, the first scenes of *Tent of Miracles* show Pena and his editor, Dadá, discussing Archanjo at the editing table. But the structure of *Tent of Miracles* is much more complex than simply a film-within-a-film. A precredits shot of a television newswoman saying that "in Bahia the weather is good" frames Pena's story in a context of television.

The Pena-Archanjo narratives are themselves divided into four different time frames: the present (Pena and his film), the recent past (the arrival of Dr. Livingston and Pena's research into the life of Pedro Archanjo), the past (the life of Pedro Archanjo as an adult), and the distant past (Pedro Archanjo as a young man). The use of two actors in the role of Pedro Archanjo differentiates these last two temporal sequences. Composer-singer Jards Macalé (the blind singer of *O Amuleto de Ogum*) plays the young Pedro, and plastic artist Juarez Paraíso plays the adult Pedro.

After a brief sequence of Pena at the movieola, we see the arrival in Bahia of an American Nobel laureate and Columbia University professor, played by an American, nonprofessional actor. The ludicrous and embarassingly stupid Livingston, who looks more like a bench-warming Southern Cal quarterback than a Nobel laureate, parodies foreign scholars who study Brazil and often pretend to know more about the country than do Brazilians. Livingston explains to a press conference that he did not want to leave Brazil without visiting the birthplace of the great Bahian sociologist/anthropologist Pedro Archanjo, virtually unknown among Brazilians. Besides being a jab at "*Brazilianistas*," Livingston's presence also exposes and criticizes the idea that what is foreign is good and that for something to be recognized in Brazil, it is helpful to be recognized abroad first. That, in fact, was one of the major strategies of Cinema Novo: to win acceptance in international festivals in order to gain a larger foothold in the domestic film market and a broader acceptance by Brazilian audiences.

The news media consequently rush to discover exactly who Archanjo was and to glorify this unknown, but obviously important, Brazilian hero. Archanjo, it seems, not only defended Afro-Brazilian culture, but also praised miscegenation as the road to development. Livingston takes up with "the greatest living example" of Archanjo's theory, the fiery mulatta Ana Mercedes (Sônia Dias) and hires her boyfriend, Fausto Pena (Hugh Carvana), to serve as his research assistant. Pena thus begins the investigations into the life of Pedro Archanjo that eventually result in his film.

Around the turn of the century, Pedro Archanjo was employed as a beadle in Bahia's School of Medicine. Himself a mulatto, he spent his spare time investigating the customs and traditions of African culture still existent in Bahia. The results of his studies, published on a primitive press by his friend Lídio Corró in the shop and meeting place known as the Tent of Miracles, are received with great hostility by the school's professor of forensic medicine, Nilo Argolo, who espouses theories of white superiority. Both Archanjo and Nilo Argolo are synthetic personages based on several historical figures. Archanjo was possibly modeled after the Afro-Brazilian anti-illiteracy crusader Major Cosme de Faria, who printed thousands of "ABC" pamphlets for free distribution to the poor, and, even more likely, on Manoel Quirino, one of the first black scholars in Brazil.[41] Nilo Argolo, on the other hand, is based on well-known intellectuals such as Sílvio Romero, Oliveira Viana, and Nina Rodrigues, all of whom espoused theories of white superiority. Nilo Argolo in fact quotes from one of Nina Rodrigues's texts in an early sequence.

According to dos Santos, "People like Nina Rodrigues were worried about the incorporation in society of the African who had been a slave, a commodity subject to ownership, and who became by law a citizen of the country. They were also concerned with the way in which he was incorporated into society . . . in terms of the social model they wanted to impose."[42] For Nina Rodrigues and other intellectuals of the period, for Brazil to become a European society (the ideal), it would have to have a white race. The theory that Thomas Skidmore refers to as "whitening" lies behind Brazilian immigration policies in the twentieth century, policies that resulted in an increase of immigrants from white European countries. As Brazilians popularly put it, they espoused the "coffee with cream" theory: put in more cream and the coffee will become white.

Because of his countertheories, Archanjo is chastised and reprimanded for his "unscientific" attempts at the formulation of a theory of racial democracy based on miscegenation. The conflict between Archanjo and Argolo is the conflict between popular knowledge and official knowledge, between elements the people themselves have incorporated and the model that the school's professors have tried to impose on Brazilian society. Finally, it is the conflict between popular culture and official culture, in other words, between authenticity and colonization.

Archanjo's life exemplified that of a man whose thought and action strive toward a common goal. As in *Citizen Kane*, we are introduced to him at the moment of his death and slowly learn who he was. He was absolutely dedicated to the defense and affirmation of Afro-Brazilian culture and to the struggle against racism. He fought attempts by the ruling classes to ban the heavily African-influenced Carnival celebrations from the streets, as well as their attempts to use the police to suppress popular religious sentiment. Whereas for official society he was the lowly servant Pedro Archanjo, for the people he was Ojuabá, the Eyes of Xangô, the most powerful god of *candomblé*'s panoply of saints. He thus synthesized his own theories of miscegenation, the mixture of religion and science, popular and elite culture, defiance of racism and defense of his people. He was a lover of music, of women of all races, and of children. He was completely free of racial prejudice and talked proudly of his son, born of a relationship with the Scandinavian Kirsi, who he said would grow up to be a famous Norwegian poet.

Archanjo is also placed in opposition to a young, Marxist professor who espouses progressive ideas, but whose life contributes nothing to the transformation of society. As he and Archanjo converse one day in a bar, Archanjo tells him that this materialism will also lead to the repression of popular culture and that the important thing is to love the people, not the dogma. Referring to this sequence, dos Santos says that the young professor represents the orthodox Marxist who, throughout the years, has been just as colonizing as the non-Marxist, since he has simply transferred ideas, which were born in and refer to a specific situation in Europe, without questioning whether or not these same ideas may be valid for Brazil. In other words, the orthodox Marxist attempts to impose a model from without, rather than allowing the local reality to determine the model. What is necessary, says the director, is to transfer not the specific observations made concerning another society, but rather the method of dialectical thought to an analysis of Brazilian society. This idea links to his strategy, in *O Amuleto de Ogum*, of having the people serve as the model for themselves. In this sense, the director criticizes, as in *Hunger for Love*, the sometimes condescending perspectives of intellectuals who deem themselves to have the answers for the problems of society but who in reality have little contact with the marginalized majority of that society.

During his investigations, Archanjo discovers that many of Bahia's leading families, including those most active in repressing Afro-Brazilian culture and espousing theories of white superiority, have black ancestors, among them, Professor Nilo Argolo. After publishing his work tracing the ancestry of these families, Archanjo is arrested and jailed for his attack on Brazilian society. He lives the rest of his life in obscurity. One of the most poignant sequences in the film shows Archanjo in jail while on the musical soundtrack is heard part of the film's theme song in which Gilberto Gil (himself a black composer and musician) sings, "The son asked the father / Where is my grandfather? / My grandfather, where is he? / The father asked the grandfather / Where is great-grandfather? / Great-grandfather, where is he?" The sequence brings to the fore the question of the roots and origins of the Brazilian people and serves to affirm the contribution of African culture to the formation of Brazilian society. Pedro Archanjo, never ceasing his studies, dies in a brothel known as the Castle shortly after participating in a demonstration against Hitler and the Axis powers.

In the frame film, while Fausto Pena undertakes his reconstruction of

Pedro Archanjo's life, the local media and the private interests that control them make plans of their own to commemorate what they have discovered to be the one-hundredth anniversary of Archanjo's birth. Backed by an advertising agency appropriately named "Doping, Inc.," ideas are discussed about how to best honor this newfound Brazilian hero. The media's first idea is to sponsor a symposium on Brazilian racial democracy to be organized by Professor Edelweiss (Anecy Rocha), an attractive bourgeois intellectual. Professor Edelweiss first appears in the film at Dr. Livingston's press conference, and like many others, she is impressed with the news of Archanjo. But the media refuse to take her seriously, and, concerned that the national political conjuncture is not propitious for such an event, especially since the symposium also proposes to discuss racism in the United States as well as South African apartheid, and concerned that radical students might take advantage of the occasion to protest everything from racism to the military regime, they finally decide on the inconsequential idea of sponsoring a civic contest for public school students. They will offer prizes for the best essay on the subject "Why Pedro Archanjo Was a Great Man."

But the marketing of Archanjo continues, as the agency comes up with all sorts of ideas to make money for itself and its clients, including naming a new shopping center and a new brand of rum for him. Dos Santos's parody of advertising (and of consumer society) reaches its most absurd with the idea of baptizing a new deodorant with the name "Fresh Black."

To meet the needs of both the agency and the media, however, Archanjo's image must be sanitized and whitened. In the commemorative ceremony, a portrait of Archanjo in which he has somehow been promoted to the rank of professor of the Medical School is unveiled. The media's purpose, of course, is to expropriate the figure of Archanjo for their own ideological ends. They ignore his ideas and the prejudice and oppression that Archanjo faced in his day-to-day life. The media thus serve the same function in modern Brazilian society as did the professors of forensic medicine at the turn of the century. The link to the present emphasizes the continuation of racism in Brazilian society today.

Fausto Pena is to Dr. Livingston and the media what Pedro Archanjo was to the School of Medicine. Livingston turns Pena into his paid flunky and Pena's girlfriend Ana Mercedes into his whore. Pena is a lowly reporter and would-be poet at a local newspaper whose consciousness is raised as the film develops. In an early sequence, he sells information about Archanjo to the media, but toward the end he is quite concerned that the truth be told about Archanjo, or at least the truth to the extent that it can be established. Just as Archanjo transcends his position at the School of Medicine through his dedication to his people, Pena transcends his own mediocrity and makes a film—the film we see—about the Bahian hero.

Tent of Miracles, although concerned primarily with denouncing, albeit with a tremendous amount of humor, the racism so prevalent in Brazilian society, also deals with Brazilian cinema and its modes of production. Early in the film is a scene in which Pena tries frantically to telephone Roberto Farias, then real-life director of Embrafilme, to arrange financing for his film. On the wall beside the telephone is a poster of a David Cardoso film entitled *Amadas e Violentadas* (*Loved and Violated*), a soft-core porn murder mystery released in 1976. This scene reflects an all-too-recent phase of Brazilian cinema in which the country's highly moralistic military government, through Embrafilme, was financing poor-quality pornographic films while more serious filmmakers, especially those linked to Cinema Novo, faced an unofficial blacklisting and extreme difficulty financing their film projects. Although the situation had changed by the time dos Santos made *Tent of Miracles* (which was partially financed by Embrafilme), the scene also spoofs Brazilian cinema's newfound dependence on the state: "What Embrafilme needs," mocks Pena, "is love."

Tent of Miracles is about filmmaking in Brazil in other ways as well. Self-referential moments resound throughout the film, including the stopping of an image of Pedro Archanjo on the movieola and Fausto Pena's final words that he will not finish the film because everybody has already seen it.

But even the self-referentiality goes much deeper. The actors often reveal a purposeful consciousness of the camera, as if they were playing dual roles, as actors and as fictional personages. As critic José Carlos Avellar cogently observes, the actors (often nonprofessional in accordance with dos Santos's idea that a film about popular culture should be marked by the presence of the people) seem to play with their characters in a continuous, gamelike activity. One scene, for example, presents the recently named police chief (a mulatto, played by Emanuel Cavalcânti) as he awaits a visit from Colonel Gomes, who is infuriated that his daughter Lu wants to marry Archanjo's son Tadeu (a light-colored mulatto). Alone in the room, the chief uses the camera as if it were a mirror, as he practices the best pose with which to receive the colonel: seated behind the table with his head uplifted, with and without glasses, standing with his hand Napoleon-like on his chest, leaning on a corner of the table. In this sense, Nelson Pereira dos Santos seems to be creating a new, nonformal mode of popular representation, modeled perhaps on the rather obscene puppet show Archanjo sets up in the Tent of Miracles. The film is so filled with disparate elements that combine different temporal moments and geographic spaces, that, in Avellar's words, it almost seems a "miracle" that such a brilliant film is the final result.[43]

With his most recent film, *Estrada da Vida*, the popular phase of Nelson Pereira dos Santos's cinema reaches its culmination. It is the most unpretentious, charming, and commercially successful film of his career. It succeeds in the director's proposal, stated since *O Amuleto de Ogum*, to adopt popular perspectives as the film's perspective, without condescension,

Plate 25. Milionário and José Rico, *Estrada da Vida (Road of Life)*

without intellectual justification, without a priori or a posteriori theorizing. The film is what it is: a simple, good-humored, playful story about a Brazilian "country" singing duo, Milionário and José Rico (Millionaire and Joe Rich), about their chance meeting in a cheap São Paulo hotel, about their tricksterish struggle for survival and success as artists. It tells their story from their own point of view. The screenplay, written by Chico de Assis, is based on hours of conversation and discussion with the duo. It preserves their penchant for mixing fantasy and reality in the recounting of their adventures and misadventures.

Estrada da Vida contains no critical vision, unlike the director's previous films. It is a film based on the *acceptance* of the protagonists' vision of life. Its critical elements derive from Milionário and José Rico themselves, not from any intellectual posturing imposed by the director; the critique is internalized.

Such a position on the part of Nelson Pereira dos Santos, however, is not without its ambiguity. Whereas on the one hand the director affirms that he has reached a point in his career where he attempts to avoid theorizing—perhaps in the sense that after thirteen films he no longer has to prove anything to anyone—at the same time he recognizes that he *is* an intellectual, that he does have esthetic concerns, that he is "colonized." His choice of subjects, in this case his choice of making a "popular" cinema, is a conscious decision to try to free himself from the bounds and constraints of the education that Brazil's social structure has imposed on him. By his social background and position, he and many other intellectuals and artists have been forced, or more precisely, induced, to have certain likes and dislikes, to favor certain things over others, to reject that which does not fit within a given "image" of correct ideological positioning. By means of his popular phase, Nelson Pereira dos Santos has rejected all a priori restraints or ideological demands on his filmmaking. Filmmaking for him is an activity, in his own words, based on "love and pleasure." In *Estrada da Vida* he chose to make a film about the country duo because he likes their music, although that music is widely rejected by urban middle-class audiences. *Estrada da Vida* frees him from such restraints and allows him to participate in the pleasure of making a film that will be seen *with pleasure* by vast numbers of the Brazilian population (and such has occurred since the film's release in February 1981). It is a film that takes dos Santos's popular phase to its limits (or to its goal) and that has led him to redefine popular cinema as "the cinema the people like."

If *Estrada da Vida* represents a culmination, it also represents a return. In *Tent of Miracles* the director was concerned with the roots of Brazilian culture and the African contribution to that culture. In *Estrada da Vida* he returns to his own roots. Although born and educated in São Paulo, *Estrada da Vida* is his first film shot in São Paulo (he did, however, serve as assistant director for Rodolfo Nanni's *O Saci*, 1951, and produced Roberto Santos's *O Grande Momento* in São Paulo in 1958). *Estrada da Vida* returns to the culture of the interior of the state of São Paulo, which, perhaps paradoxically, has also become the culture of the Northeast in São Paulo. The music of Milionário and José Rico is music made to a large extent by and for northeastern migrants to the large cities of the South. Both Milionário (Romeu Januário de Matos) and José Rico (José Alves dos Santos) are from interior regions of other states, the former from Minas Gerais, the latter from Pernambuco. Their music is essentially a rural form, but because of the extent of Brazil's internal migration, it appeals as well to an urban audience living on the periphery of São Paulo and other large cities.

São Paulo is the largest northeastern city in Brazil (i.e., it has the largest number of inhabitants from the Northeast), so dos Santos's return to São Paulo is also a return to the Northeast of *Vidas Secas* and, to a lesser degree, of *Mandacaru Vermelho*. It takes up themes originally discussed in *Rio 40 Graus* and *Rio Zona Norte* (marginal existence in the cities, the exploitation of popular musicians by the music industry). The influence of the *chanchada*, present in dos Santos's first two films, returns in this musical comedy. As in the *chanchada*, the plot of *Estrada da Vida* is often little more than a pretext to present musical numbers, which are frequently nonnaturalistic in presentation. Also like the *chanchada*, *Estrada da Vida* is family entertainment, perhaps Nelson Pereira dos Santos's first film ever to be released (by censors) for all ages.

Estrada da Vida also draws on a long tradition in São Paulo cinema, the *caipira* film, a film genre based on the culture of the rural inhabitants of the State of São Paulo. The *caipira* film was crystallized in the fifties by comedian/director Amácio Mazzaropi and raised to new levels in the seventies with Jeremias Moreira's *Menino da Porteira* and *Mágoa de Boiadeiro*, both starring popular "country" singer Sérgio Reis. Fortunately, dos Santos's film avoids the "cute," moralistic banality of Mazzaropi's films and aligns itself more with the authentic simplicity of Moreira's, which, by the way, specialized critics largely ignored but a broad public adored.

Milionário and José Rico, the subjects of *Estrada da Vida*, are one of the most popular of Brazil's *sertanejo* duos. As the film shows, they met by chance in a cheap hotel near São Paulo's bus station. To this date they have recorded ten long-plays, all of which are still in circulation. They sell an average of 1.3 million records per year, which places them among the top recording artists in the country, even though their recognition does not reach the "sophisticated" districts of Rio de Janeiro and São Paulo.

The duo got its start by performing in fleabag circuses in the outlying regions of São Paulo. This is reflected in the film, not only in the duo's first appearance (when the hole in his tennis shoe reveals José Rico's poverty) but also in the circus spirit the film adopts. Milionário and José Rico are natural actors—this is their first film—endowed with a clowning spirit. The film challenges their relegation to a secondary plane by "official" popular culture, that is, the music industry directed at urban youth. If Caetano Veloso, Gilberto Gil, and Elis Regina are considered true artists, so too then must Milionário and José Rico be so considered. On hearing agent Malaquias's denigrating remarks about circus performers, Milionário defends them by saying that "they are artists like us." The film equates the popular artist—the circus performers, the *sertanejo* duo—with more "sophisticated" artists, including the filmmaker himself.

The film's circus spirit is revealed not only in the circus sequences, but also and more importantly in its profound carnivalistic attitude. Like *Macunaíma* of Joaquim Pedro de Andrade's 1969 film, Milionário and José Rico are tricksters, surviving in the city on their own wits, struggling humorously against unscrupulous agents, construction foremen, and a record industry that refuses to pay the royalties due them. Their actions are a hilarious attack on the seriousness of the social structure. They turn their deceitful agent into a burro in a circus performance, they hail an expensive taxi only to have it stop some fifty yards later (to give the record company the appearance of their well-being), they turn a construction scaffold into a stage and the polluted city behind them into the green pastures of the country. Their devil-may-care attitude belies a seriousness of intent that brings them only respect from those they meet.

Their attitude is profoundly carnivalistic in other ways. In the carnivalesque, according to Bakhtin, actor and spectator—performer and audience, in this case—become one. As I have observed elsewhere in this book, the carnivalesque is profoundly subversive of the official, dominant ideology, since it abolishes hierarchies, levels social classes, and creates an alternative, second life, free from the rules and restrictions of official cultural life. In *Estrada da Vida* the workplace becomes a stage, the stage, a workplace, the "road of life" an eternal stage for singing and merrymaking.

When Milionário first appears in the film, arriving in São Paulo, he wanders through a park where he watches, as a spectator, an unseen popular artist. Likewise, when José Rico arrives at the cheap hotel he encounters many other migrant musicians like himself practicing in the hotel courtyard. He too is a spectator. After forming a duo, Milionário and José Rico rehearse in the courtyard. The other performers become spectators, and some even join in to become spectator and performer at the same time.

One of Milionário and José Rico's first official performances is in a circus in the interior of the state. Twice during their performance the camera focuses on a young man in the audience. The young man (the spectator) later becomes performer, as Milionário and José Rico, penniless, walk along a country road and hear him singing one of their songs. Milionário and José Rico are transformed once again into spectators, the spectator, into the performer. Similarly, in later performances, often before thousands of spectators, the camera alternates between the duo singing and spectators singing as well: despite the physical presence of the stage, the act of filming levels the performers and the spectators.

On film, all are performers, the distance between stage and audience is eliminated. The same relationship is repeated between the film itself and the film audience, as the latter is increasingly involved in the good-natured drama of the *sertanejo* duo. To reinforce this carnivalesque attitude, during the duo's final performance in the film, which takes place in Santa Fé do Sul in the state of Mato Grosso, Milionário and José Rico appear not on stage, but in the middle of the audience. As they walk singing toward the stage (never reached in the diegesis), fans surround and accompany them, as if there were no difference between them.

Although *Estrada da Vida* stresses the popular nature of Milionário and José Rico's art and their continued link to the people, it does not ignore the cultural industry that has permitted them such a wide following. Their first recording session is undercut with shots of the industrial process of record making, from the act of recording (a shot of a needle recording directly on a disk), of printing and reproducing, of the printing and folding of the record cover, of the vast publicity apparatus behind the industry, and, perhaps most importantly, of the radio stations that transmit their music to the public.

The success of Milionário and José Rico is due largely to the wide diffusion radio offers. As they tell it (and as dos Santos films it), they lived in poverty until one day, in desperation, they went to Aparecida do Norte (north of São Paulo) to ask their and Brazil's patron saint, Nossa Senhora de Aparecida (Our Lady of Aparecida), for help in making their music reach the people. As José Rico says in his prayer, their music is simple, it speaks of love, nature, and the people, and "the people's voice is the voice of God." As an offering to Nossa Senhora de Aparecida, they leave a copy of their record. The priest later finds it and takes it to the local radio station, where the disk jockey likes and plays it. Because of Aparecida's "miracle," requests pour in for Milionário and José Rico's music. (Milionário and José Rico now have a program three days a week on São Paulo's Rádio Globo.)

The most beautiful sequence of the film depicts their success following the miracle, and also characterizes São Paulo perhaps more precisely than any sequence in any other film about the city. As an early-bird radio announcer plays one of their records, the film registers the city and its people waking up: getting out of bed, opening windows, washing, drinking coffee, leaving home, waiting for the bus or train in the early morning fog, traveling to work in overcrowded transportation. The film establishes an audiovisual link between Milionário and José Rico's music and the daily lives of the people. The duo sings of their hopes, desires, frustrations. In the earlier construction-site sequence, work stops when they sing of the green fields of home, not necessarily because of the quality of their performance, but rather because their music emotionally touches the other workmen, who themselves have probably come to the city from a rural area and, like Milionário and José Rico, long to return. The collective is expressed through the individual. This is a natural feeling, idyllic or not, and is rendered superbly and poignantly by the duo's music.

Unlike earlier Cinema Novo films, *Estrada da Vida* does not challenge or question, but rather accepts and reinforces, the myths and beliefs held by Milionário and José Rico and the people they sing for. The singers attribute their success to Our Lady of Aparecida, their "boss," as José Rico says as he points to her medal around his neck during his performances. The film accepts their belief without question and even reinforces it near the end when, in answer to José Rico's prayer, a truck "miraculously" appears along the road and supplies them with gasoline so they can make their engagement in Santa Fé do Sul.

Myths often express the fundamental values of a people. To demystify or challenge the myth would be to impose an external, perhaps condescending, vision of the people; it would be to challenge the people from the outside, rejecting what is essential and important for them. Rejecting the myth would be a return to the paternalistic populism of the early days of Cinema Novo. *Estrada da Vida*, through its acceptance of the people's own ideology and its subversively humorous carnivalesque attitude of gay relativity toward the world, is indeed a popular film.

Conclusion: Cinema Novo, a Retrospective

It is not this book's intention to reduce Cinema Novo to the works of the five directors chosen for study, since many other filmmakers also contributed significant works to the movement. And yet there can be no doubt that the five discussed here are eminently representative of Cinema Novo's major concerns. Each has created a highly individual form of cinematic expression, but a certain unity underlies many of their films. Raquel Gerber has spoken, for example, of a dialectic that has always existed in Cinema Novo production between a "nuclear orthodoxy" and an "expressive heterodoxy."[1] In reality, a "nuclear orthodoxy" existed only briefly in the early 1960s, if at all, and only in the broadest of terms. In the words of Glauber Rocha, "Within the contradictions of Brazil, the initial Cinema Novo group, working with a lack of political discipline, defended something new, which was the creation of a cinema in Brazil. Each filmmaker worked within this program starting from his own individual and creative qualities, because . . . there was no such thing as a collective work."[2]

The idea, so often repeated by Carlos Diegues, was to create a "Brazilian cinema" in Brazil, a cinema that would not only reveal the true face of Brazilian society and all of its contradictions, but would also contribute in some way to its transformation. Despite the stylistic and thematic diversity of their work, a number of strategies and themes recur in many of the films studied in this volume. It is therefore necessary, in the guise of a conclusion, to come full circle and consider that which unifies the filmic production of the group known as Cinema Novo. I shall also refer to films by other Cinema Novo directors who do not appear in this volume but whose films share the general concerns of the movement.

In the introduction to this book I referred to the nationalism of the period in which Cinema Novo arose. Cultural and economic nationalism has been one of the mainstays of Cinema Novo, reflected not only in the choice of subjects for individual films, but also in the cinematic language used and in the industrial strategies of the movement. The roots of Cinema Novo's cultural nationalism are to be found in the political conjuncture of the late

1950s and the early 1960s, and also in the long Brazilian tradition of cultural and artistic nationalism, which dates back at least to nineteenth-century romanticism and, more recently, to the modernist movement of the 1920s. In their attempts to create a strong national cinema that would be recognized both as art and as a meaningful form of intellectual discourse, filmmakers continually stressed their ties to Brazil's literary traditions, specifically to modernism and the "social novels" of the 1930s. By anchoring themselves firmly to Brazil's literary traditions, they achieved "the first effective integration of cinema within the mainstream of Brazilian culture."[3]

The continued desire for cultural legitimation—reflected in critical and popular acceptance of their works—has resulted in a strategy of reliance on literary works as sources for their films. Looking at a Cinema Novo filmography is something like looking at a bibliography of modern Brazilian literature. Besides attempting to establish cultural credentials for the cinema, the high number of literary adaptations derives from a desire to take advantage of the original work's notoriety, not necessarily in a negative sense, to guarantee a priori a certain degree of interest on the part of the public and from the infrastructure of the cinematic production process itself. Only recently has there emerged in Brazil a reasonable number of screenwriters who provide raw material for film scripts. The lack of a qualified group of writers has resulted inevitably in the director being responsible for his or her own scripts, so that he or she is the *auteur* not only of the film, but also of the script itself.

The question of creating a national art form is perhaps more complex in the cinema than in literature or the other arts, since, as both a form of artistic and cultural expression and as an industry, it is faced with the tremendous pressure of foreign esthetic models, often deriving from the technological nature of the cinema itself, and also with a market occupied by foreign, largely American, film products. Ismail Xavier perceptively discusses the complexity of cinema's dilemma:

Whereas literature or painting are indirectly affected by colonization—as seen for example in the artist's imitations of linguistic or pictorial strategies—the cinema, by its very nature, entails a direct involvement with advanced technology. In cinema, the notion of "correct" technique assumes the legitimacy of "universal" rules embedded in the equipment and in the raw material, themselves products of advanced technology. And Hollywood can be taken as the model of film production in terms of management, technique, and language.[4]

At the outset, therefore, Cinema Novo faced a market dominated by foreign cinemas and the models of filmic expression they transmit, while at the same time it was forced to confront limitations deriving from the very nature of the cinematic instrument. It was also faced with Brazil's underdevelopment. Because of an extreme scarcity of finance capital for film production, Cinema Novo could not hope to equal the technical level of most foreign films. So rather than imitate dominant cinema, which would make their work merely symptomatic of underdevelopment, they chose to resist by turning "scarcity into a signifier."[5] The theoretical expression of this conscious resistance is to be found in Glauber Rocha's seminal manifesto, "An Esthetic of Hunger."[6]

The creation of a national cinema, in opposition to dominant cinema, also implies the development of alternate modes of filmic production and other means of cinematic expression. In both of these areas, Cinema Novo was well-served by the model of Italian neorealism and, to a lesser degree, of the French *nouvelle vague*. The idea of small production teams, location shooting, and the use of nonprofessional actors—all of this in opposition to large studios such as Vera Cruz—combined with collaborative financing strategies not only provided an alternate road of development for Brazilian cinema, but also provided the directors with authorial control over their films.

In more recent years, with the rapid growth of the film industry, such a model of production has shown its limitations, since industrial atomization has impeded capitalization and has assured that production financing would continue to be problematic and frequently dependent on the state. But in the early 1960s it was useful in challenging both dominant foreign cinemas and local imitations thereof.

Neorealism also served Cinema Novo well as an esthetic strategy, especially during the first phase of the movement, as filmmakers attempted to portray what they saw as the true face of Brazilian underdevelopment. The critical realism of films marked by the "esthetic of hunger" served an important tactical and political function by expressing the radical "otherness" of Brazilian cinema in relation to world cinema.[7] Later in the decade, realism gave way to a highly symbolic and allegorical, nonlinear discourse in the second and third phases, before returning, in a sort of pendular motion, to a more realistic mode of representation recently.

In part, political circumstances beyond the control of filmmakers frustrated the "realistic vocation" of early Cinema Novo. Government censors simply would not allow them to discuss certain issues directly. And yet, at the same time, the allegorical, metaphorical films of the late 1960s and early 1970s derive from filmmakers' recognition that Brazilian reality is too complex to capture with a realistic mode of discourse. The films of the third, or "tropicalist," phase of Cinema Novo attempt to provoke the liberation of Brazil's unconscious. As Glauber Rocha puts it, "The festival of metaphors, allegories, and symbols is not a carnival of subjectivity; it is the rejection of rational analysis of a reality deformed by European culture and stifled by American imperialism. A cinema that opposes the classifications of colonial anthropology. Its true dimension is that of 'irrational magic.' "[8] Such a stance on the part of Cinema Novo filmmakers in a sense took to an extreme the desire to create a "decolonized" cinematic language in opposition to the codes of dominant cinema.

The return to realism was foreshadowed in the late 1960s, as filmmakers became more concerned with reaching a broad public and, consequently, with the market potential of their films. Films began to be made in color in 1967 and, although alternatives to dominant cinematic codes were still attempted, particularly in the films of Glauber Rocha and experimental filmmakers such as Júlio Bressane, the mid-1970s saw an almost unanimous return to more conventional styles of filmmaking.

During the initial phase of Cinema Novo, the "esthetic of hunger" found resonance in the filmmaker's choice of subjects: urban slum dwellers (*Cinco Vezes Favela, Rio 40 Graus, Rio Zona Norte*); northeastern peasants (*Vidas Secas, The Guns, Black God, White Devil*); poor fishermen (*Barravento*), slavery (*Ganga Zumba*), migrants to the urban centers (*The Big City*, which fits both in the first and second phases of the movement, plus numerous documentaries). The idea behind these films was that the realistic portrayal of society's lumpen and the denunciation of social contradictions would be sufficient to raise the consciousness of the spectator, who would be spurred to action in the process of social transformation. These films, however, by and large did not reach the popular classes and thus remained discussions by and for a politicized middle-class audience.

Such an attitude, however, explains the didacticism of many of the films of the initial period of Cinema Novo, a didacticism that often resulted in a paternalistic attitude toward the people. Despite the narrative ambiguity and complexity of the film, in *Barravento* the catalyst of transformation comes from *outside* the poor fishing village, more specifically, from the city. In Diegues's *Ganga Zumba*, when Antão/Ganga Zumba looks at the camera and says, "We have to do something," he articulates the feelings of the young intellectuals who composed Cinema Novo. His trajectory serves as a perfect example of the didactic consciousness-raising strategy of the early phase of the movement. Rocha, in *Black God, White Devil*, is even more explicit when the film's theme song says at the end that "the land belongs to Man, not to God or the Devil," although the film itself transcends such a simplistic message. Guerra's *The Guns* and dos Santos's *Vidas Secas* also implicitly posit the necessity of political action for social transformation. And Joaquim Pedro de Andrade, in *Garrincha, Alegria do Povo*, paternalistically attempts to show that soccer, rather than being a source of national pride, is a factor in the people's alienation.

More recently, Carlos Diegues has criticized the didactic posture of early Cinema Novo. The mindreading sequence of *Bye Bye Brasil* clearly shows the limitations of artists who claim to have the answers to society's problems. In his campaign for a popular cinema, Nelson Pereira dos Santos, adopting without criticism (or apparently so) the people's vision of themselves, has come to reject the intellectual's view of society.

After the first phase of Cinema Novo, the directors began to use other filmmaking strategies, as the diversity of production increased dramatically. Comedy and satire became acceptable means of social criticism (*El Justicero, Macunaíma, How Tasty Was My Little Frenchman, Quando o Carnaval Chegar*) and have become even more fruitful in recent years with films such as *Xica da Silva, Bye Bye Brasil, Guerra Conjugal, Vereda Tropical, Tent of Miracles,* and *Estrada da Vida.* The humorless sobriety of early Cinema Novo has thus given way, over the years, to a salutary ability to laugh at itself while maintaining a critical attitude toward society. It was as if filmmakers suddenly realized that the function of cinema is not only to instruct, but also to entertain. Thus we have a comedy about slavery (*Xica da Silva*), another about the persistence of racism in Brazilian society (*Tent of Miracles*), and yet another dealing with cultural colonialism and the "decharacterization" of Brazilian society (*Bye Bye Brasil*). In response to other tendencies within Brazilian cinema, Cinema Novo directors have even produced "erotic" comedies (*Guerra Conjugal, Vereda Tropical*) that are both funny and critical of the sexual mores of the middle class.

With perhaps less frequency, Cinema Novo filmmakers have turned toward Brazilian history as a subject for their films. Carlos Diegues is the filmmaker most interested in historical topics, as evidenced by his two films on slavery, *Ganga Zumba* and *Xica da Silva* (he is currently filming what is in some ways a sequel to *Ganga Zumba,* about the slave Republic of Palmares), and his murals of modern Brazilian history and politics (*The Heirs* and, implicitly, *Joana Francesa*). Other historical films by Cinema Novo directors concern the struggle for liberation from colonial rule (*Os Inconfidentes*) and the process of colonization itself (*How Tasty Was My Little Frenchman*). In all of these films, the directors reject the official version of history, offering instead an alternative reading. Still other films concern an even more recent history: the struggle for land control and capital accumulation in the cacao region of southern Bahia (*The Gods and the Dead*), the history of Brazilian literature (*O Homem do Pau-Brasil*), and even the history of Brazilian cinema (*Quando o Carnaval Chegar*).

The concern with Brazilian cinema brings us to one of the central thematic motifs of Cinema Novo: the self-conscious discussion of the role of intellectuals and artists in contemporary Brazilian society. Initially, this concern arose as a form of anguished self-examination after the coup d'état of 1964. Films such as *O Desafio, Land in Anguish, O Bravo Guerreiro,* and *Hunger for Love* are starkly pessimistic views of leftist intellectuals and artists (Paulo Martins in Rocha's film) in post-1964 Brazil. They are uniformly unable to act, except in suicidal, individualistic fashion.

Later, in a historical context with explicit references to the then-current situation, Joaquim Pedro de Andrade's *Os Inconfidentes* looks once again at the role and responsibilities of intellectuals in a prerevolutionary situation and examines some of the contradictions therein (contradictions of race, class, privilege). Other films, such as *Quando o Carnaval Chegar, Bye Bye Brasil, Estrada da Vida,* and *O Homem do Pau-Brasil*, question the artist's role in society and create obvious parallels with the situation of the filmmaker in modern-day Brazil. The musical troupe's refusal to play for the "king" in *Quando o Carnaval Chegar* reflects Cinema Novo's refusal to mold its cinematic production to the conveniences of the military regime. *Bye Bye Brasil* sees the artist as one who must strive incessantly toward the creation of utopias, and *O Homem do Pau-Brasil* gives value to the impulsive, corrosive creativity of one of Brazil's greatest twentieth-century artists.

It is thus not surprising that many Cinema Novo films self-consciously discuss Brazilian cinema itself through implicit homage and explicit intertextual references to other films in the movement. In Saraceni's *O Desafio* we see posters of Rocha's *Black God, White Devil* on the wall. *The Big City* also includes veiled references to Rocha's film. *Quando o Carnaval Chegar* is not only an homage to the *chanchada*, with reconstructions of sequences from *Alô Alô Carnaval*, but also refers specifically to Rocha's *Antônio das Mortes*. *Macunaíma* also pays implicit homage to the *chanchada* in its choice of actors and its mode of representation. *Quem É Beta?* quotes sequences from *Hunger for Love*. *The Gods and the Dead* begins on the same highway where *Antônio das Mortes* ends. *O Amuleto de Ogum* makes veiled references to the director's own work, and *Tent of Miracles* wryly comments on the relationship of Brazilian cinema to the state and on the difficulty of making films in Brazil. *The Fall* incorporates entire sequences from *The Guns*. *O Homem do Pau-Brasil* pokes fun at the colonialist attitude of Blaise Cendrars, who plans to make a "100 percent Brazilian" film. The cinema, and more specifically, the trajectory of Cinema Novo, is also foregrounded in *Bye Bye Brasil*, as the director incorporates sequences from *O Ebrio*, provides an allegorical retrospective of the movement, and points toward new directions for filmmaking and popular artistic expression in an age of mass communications.

The films' discussion of Brazilian cinema is part of a broader concern, which appears in all of Cinema Novo's phases, with the nature of spectacle and of representation. The concern with spectacle and the tendency toward self-conscious narration finds resonances in many different aspects of the films: in the "Biography of an Adventurer" segment of *Land in Anguish*, a segment that in many ways parallels the encompassing film itself; in *Macunaíma*'s many self-referential moments; in *The Big City*'s recall of different cinematic genres and, especially, in *Calunga*'s final re-enactment of the film's action; in the explicit theatricality of *The Heirs, Quando o Carnaval Chegar*, and *Os Inconfidentes*, and in virtually all of Glauber Rocha's films; in the theater sequence of *Summer Showers*, and in much of *Bye Bye Brasil* ("the world is a stage") and *O Homem do Pau-Brasil*. What is at stake here is the nature of representation itself, as directors examine in different ways the most efficient means of communication with their audience and attempt to put into the foreground, to at least a limited extent, their own modes of filmic production.

One of the major areas of contention, especially in more recent production by Cinema Novo directors, is the nature of popular culture and the relationship of filmmakers to that culture. During the initial phase of Cinema Novo, perhaps because of the didactic proposals of the period, the question of the "popular" was not problematic. Filmmakers had not yet examined their own role vis-à-vis popular culture. They felt that transmitting a vision of the "people," seen always in mythic terms, was sufficient for the creation of a popular cinema. Filmmakers soon realized that, although the people were on the screen, they were not in the audience. During the second phase of the movement, the "people" continued to be absent from the audience, and were replaced on the screen by the middle-class, although the urban proletariat also began to make timid appearances in this phase (Saraceni's *O Desafio*, Geraldo Sarno's *Viramundo*, Luis Sérgio Person's *São Paulo S.A.*, and Diegues's *The Big City*, all 1965).

More recently, filmmakers connected with Cinema Novo see the question of the popular from at least three different perspectives. Since the success of *Xica da Silva* in 1976, Carlos Diegues has tended to define the popular in box-office terms. A popular cinema is one that the people like (or at least one that they pay to see). Arnaldo Jabor tends to echo this position. Nelson Pereira dos Santos has developed a different view of popular cinema, conceiving it not in terms of box-office success, even though success may be a result of his strategy, but rather in terms of a cinema that adopts the people's conception of their own culture. Since it is the people's conception, it must be right. *Estrada da Vida* is the apex of his concern with popular cinema; its values are the values of the musicians and music it portrays.

Ruy Guerra, on the other hand, rejects both of these views, and especially that of Nelson Pereira dos Santos; he asserts that there can be no popular cinema in Brazil without radical social transformations that would permit a direct relationship between that cinema and the potentially revolutionary classes. Simply being successful at the box office is not enough, nor is the idealistic posturing of an intellectual who, he claims, abdicates his critical role and becomes no more than a mouthpiece for "popular ideas."[9]

The urban proletariat has only recently become a major theme within Brazilian cinema, with such films as João Batista de Andrade's *O Homem que Virou Suco* (*The Man Who Became Juice*, 1980), Geraldo Sarno's

Coronel Delmiro Gouveia (1978), Arnaldo Jabor's *Tudo Bem* (*All's Well*, 1978), and, especially, Ruy Guerra and Nelson Xavier's *The Fall* and Leon Hirszman's *Eles Não Usam Black-Tie* (*They Don't Wear Black Tie*, 1981). Such a presence reflects the growing strength of the working class, evidenced in major strikes in São Paulo in 1979 and 1980.[10]

Cinema Novo has been successful in its initial proposal: to create a Brazilian cinema in Brazil. Its specific strategies have changed over the years, in part in reaction to political events beyond the control of filmmakers, and in part in reaction to the economic and social development of Brazil as a whole. Controversy and many on-going areas of contention have marked its trajectory, and yet its influence is difficult to underestimate. The new generation of Brazilian filmmakers, such as Tizuka Yamasaki and Ana Carolina, has been undeniably marked by Cinema Novo. The movement's insistence on thematic and stylistic diversity, supported in the last ten years by the state film enterprise, has decisively contributed to the development of Brazilian cinema and to its remarkable success both in Brazil and abroad.

Notes

Introduction: Cinema Novo, the State, and Modern Brazilian Cinema

1. See Maria Rita Galvão, "O Desenvolvimento das Idéias sobre Cinema Independente," *Cinema BR* (São Paulo), no. 1 (September 1977), pp. 15–19. The second part of this article is in *Cinema BR*, no. 2 (December 1977), pp. 10–17. Complete article reprinted in *30 Anos de Cinema Paulista*, Cadernos da Cinemateca 4 (São Paulo: Fundação Cinemateca Brasileira, 1980), pp. 13–23.

2. For a discussion of this period, see Thomas E. Skidmore, *Politics in Brazil, 1930–1964: An Experiment in Democracy* (New York: Oxford University Press, 1967), pp. 163–186; and Maria Victória de Mesquita Benevides, *O Governo Kubitschek: Desenvolvimento Econômico e Estabilidade Política* (Rio de Janeiro: Paz e Terra, 1976).

3. Information on the history of Brazilian cinema taken from Carlos Roberto Rodrigues de Souza, "A Fascinante Aventura do Cinema Brasileiro," *O Estado de São Paulo* (25 October and 2 November 1975); Alex Viany, *Introdução ao Cinema Brasileiro* (Rio de Janeiro: Instituto Nacional do Livro, 1959); Paulo Emílio Salles Gomes and Adhemar Gonzaga, "Panorama do Cinema Brasileiro," in Gomes, *Cinema: Trajetória no Subdesenvolvimento* (Rio de Janeiro: Paz e Terra, 1980), pp. 244–255; and Geraldo Santos Pereira, *Plano Geral do Cinema Brasileiro* (Rio de Janeiro: Borsoi, 1973).

4. For a discussion of Vera Cruz, see Maria Rita Galvão, *Burguesia e Cinema: o Caso Vera Cruz* (Rio de Janeiro: Civilização Brasileira/Embrafilme, 1981); and idem, "Vera Cruz: A Brazilian Hollywood," in *Brazilian Cinema*, ed. Randal Johnson and Robert Stam (Rutherford, N.J.: Fairleigh Dickinson University Press, 1982), pp. 270–280.

5. In Galvão, *Burguesia e Cinema*, pp. 204–206 (all translations are mine).

6. Galvão, "Cinema independente," p. 1:18.

7. Quoted in Galvão, "Cinema Independente," pp. 2:12–13. The "eight to one" proportion he refers to derives from a 1951 law providing Brazilian cinema with a screen quota of one film for every eight foreign films shown.

8. In Galvão, *Burguesia e Cinema*, pp. 204–206.

9. For legislation concerning the screen quota, see Alcino Teixeira de Mello, *Legislação do Cinema Brasileiro*, 2 vols. (Rio de Janeiro: Embrafilme, 1978).

10. "Produtores: Queremos Concorrer em Igualdade," *O Globo* (Rio de Janeiro) (29 October 1972).

11. Embrafilme provided information concerning these programs.

12. In 1982 Amorim was replaced by Roberto Parreira, but the basic situation remains the same.

13. The relationship between the state and the film industry is considerably more complex than here represented. It is the topic of my current research.

Chapter 1: Joaquim Pedro de Andrade: The Poet of Satire

1. "Joaquim Pedro Está Procurando um Herói Nacional," *Diário de São Paulo* (24 April 1970).

2. Jean-Claude Bernardet, "Com as Armas do Inimigo," *Opinião*, no. 127 (11 April 1975), pp. 20–21.

3. Joaquim Pedro de Andrade, "O Poeta Filmado," *Diário de Notícias* (n.d.). Reprinted in "O Cinema de Joaquim Pedro de Andrade," program notes of the Cineclube Macunaíma (Rio de Janeiro), August 1976.

4. *Jornal da Tarde* (22 November 1973).

5. Quoted by Ely Azeredo, "Garrincha," *Jornal do Brasil* (n.d.).

6. The poem is "O Padre, a Moça," published originally in Drummond's *Lição de Coisas* (1962), in *Reunião: 10 Livros de Poesia*, 10th ed. (Rio de Janeiro: José Olympio, 1980), pp. 246–278.

7. Joaquim Pedro de Andrade and Alex Viany, "*O Padre e a Moça*: Crítica e Auto-Crítica," *Revista Civilização Brasileira* 1, no. 7 (May 1966):255.

8. *The Priest and the Girl* did, in fact, provoke highly volatile political passions upon its release. Carlos Diegues relates that because of the film, he had a fist fight with Oduvaldo Vianna Filho, who had accused it of being "petit-bourgeois."

9. The following discussion of *Macunaíma* is adapted from my "Cinema Novo and Cannibalism: *Macunaíma*," in *Brazilian Cinema*, ed. Johnson and Stam, pp. 178–190. (Rutherford, N.J.: Fairleigh Dickinson University Press, 1982).

10. Andrade and Viany, "*O Padre*," p. 261.

11. Theodor Koch-Grünberg, *Vom Roroima zum Orinoco: Ergebnesse einer Reise in Nord Brasilien und Venezuela in den Jahren 1911–1913* (Stuttgart: Strocker und Schroder, 1924).

12. Quoted in "La cara fea," *Análisis* (Buenos Aires) (28 July 1970).

13. *Rabelais and His World*, tr. Helene Iswolsky (Cambridge: M.I.T. Press, 1968), p. 24.

14. "Sobre *Macunaíma*: Antropofagia y autofagia," *Hablemos de Cine* (Lima), no. 49 (September/October 1969), p. 10. English version in *Brazilian Cinema*, ed. Johnson and Stam, pp. 81–83.

15. Heloísa Buarque de Hollanda, "Heróis de Nossa Gente," (M.A. thesis, Federal University of Rio de Janeiro, 1974), p. 120.

16. Sérgio Augusto and Jean-Claude Bernardet, "A Guerra Conjugal de Joaquim Pedro," (interview), *Opinião*, no. 127 (11 April 1975), p. 20.

17. Ibid.

18. Johnson and Stam, eds., *Brazilian Cinema*, p. 40.

19. Augusto and Bernardet, "Guerra Conjugal," p. 20.

20. *O Globo* (24 March 1975).

21. Ibid.

22. "O Som e a Fúria," *Jornal do Brasil* (6 May 1975).

23. *Semiótica e Literatura* (São Paulo: Perspectiva, 1974), p. 134.

24. "Bibicos e Tataronas versus Pau Brasil," *Filme Cultura* 15, no. 40 (August/October 1982):78–80.

25. Ibid.

Chapter 2: Carlos Diegues: *Alegoria, Alegria*

1. "Cinema Novo," *Movimento 2* (May 1962). English translation in *Brazilian Cinema*, ed. Randal Johnson and Robert Stam, pp. 64–67 (Rutherford, N.J.: Fairleigh Dickinson University Press, 1982).

2. Ibid.

3. For a brief discussion of Cinema Novo's concept of *auteur*, see chap. 4, pp. 120–121.

4. *O Jornal* (1 March 1964).

5. Carlos Diegues, "Alguma Coisa Acontece no Meu Coração," *Folha de São Paulo (Folhetim)* (3 September 1978).

6. Federico de Cárdenas, "Diálogo con el cinema novo: Carlos Diegues," *Hablemos de Cine*, no. 36 (July/August 1967), p. 12.

7. Quoted by Cláudio Melo e Souza, *Jornal do Brasil* (12 March 1964).

8. Fred Estévez, "*Ganga Zumba*: Forms of Cultural Resistance," *Luso-Brazilian Review* 14, no. 1 (Summer 1977):49–52.

9. "Uma Estética da Fome," *Revista Civilização Brasileira* 1, no. 3 (July 1965):165–170. English translation in *Brazilian Cinema*, ed. Randal Johnson and Robert Stam, pp. 68–71 (Rutherford, N.J.: Fairleigh Dickinson University Press, 1982).

10. *Diário Carioca* (1 March 1964).

11. Jean-Claude Bernardet, *Brasil em Tempo de Cinema*, 2d ed. (Rio de Janeiro: Paz e Terra, 1976), pp. 132–136.

12. Ibid.

13. Ibid.

14. *Jornal do Comércio* (29 May 1966).

15. *O Estado de São Paulo (Suplemento Literário)* (24 December 1966); part 2 (7 January 1967).

16. Ibid.

17. "O Filme em Questão: *Os Herdeiros*, de Carlos Diegues," *Jornal do Brasil* (22 March 1970).

18. "Carlos Diegues: *Os Herdeiros* E o Testemunho de Minha Paixão pelo Brasil," *Jornal do Brasil* (n.d.).

19. Ibid.

20. Ibid.

21. Ibid.

22. See Umberto Eco, *Opera aperta* (Milan: Bompiani, 1962); Portuguese translation, *Obra Aberta* (São Paulo: Perspectiva, 1971).

23. "O Filme em Questão."

24. "Entretien avec Carlos Diegues," *Cahiers du Cinéma*, no. 225 (November/December 1970), p. 52.

25. Letter from Elia Kazan to Carlos Diegues, published in *Ultima Hora* (17 December 1969).

26. From distribution notes to *Os Herdeiros*.

27. From the press book of *Quando o Carnaval Chegar*.

28. Quoted by Pola Vartuk, *O Estado de São Paulo* (31 August 1973).

29. "Cinema Novo, O Delírio de um Gol por cima da Carne Seca," *Status*, no. 26 (September 1976), p. 128.

30. See Jean-Claude Bernardet, *"Joana Francesa*, um Filme Fechado?" *Argumento*, no. 2 (November 1973). Reprinted in *Trajetória Crítica* (São Paulo: Polis, 1978), pp. 231–234.

31. "A Crítica Esperava um That Night in Maceió. Eu Fiz *Joana Francesa*, *Status*, no. 2 (September 1974), p. 108.

32. The following discussion of *Xica da Silva* is a revision of my "Carnivalesque Celebration in Xica da Silva," in *Brazilian Cinema*, ed. Johnson and Stam, pp. 216–224.

33. "Nota Introdutória," in *Xica da Silva*, by João Felício dos Santos, p. xv (Rio de Janeiro: Civilização Brasileira, 1976).

34. The idea of Xica's disruption of official "solemnity" is developed by José Carlos Avellar in "Uma Grande Festa," *Filme Cultura*, no. 29 (May 1978), pp. 89–92.

35. Mikhail Bakhtin, *Rabelais and His World*, tr. Helene Iswolsky (Cambridge: M.I.T. Press, 1968), p. 34.

36. Ibid., p. 92.

37. "A Hierarquia do Poder dos Fracos," *Opinião* (15 October 1976), p. 19.

38. *Jornal do Brasil* (10 April 1978).

39. The following analysis is an abbreviated version of my "Film, Television, and Popular Culture in *Bye Bye Brasil*," written for the *Journal of Popular Culture* (Bowling Green).

40. *Folha de São Paulo* (15 February 1980).

41. *"Bye Bye Brasil*," *Cineaste* 11, no. 1 (Winter 1980–1981):34–36.

42. Décio Pignatari, "O Poder Global e o Fim do Improviso," *Jornal da Tarde* (5 January 1980).

43. Embrafilme, "Relatório da Diretoria," *Gazeta Mercantil* (25–27 April 1981).

44. "Lei Básica do Cinema Brasileiro," *Filme Cultura*, no. 33 (May 1979), p. 114.

45. "O Desenvolvimento da Televisão no Brasil," *Suplemento do Centenário, O Estado de São Paulo* (4 October 1975).

46. "Estatísticas 76," Cinemateca do Museu de Arte Moderna, Rio de Janeiro, n.d.

Chapter 3: Ruy Guerra: Radical Critique

1. "Ruy Guerra: Em Cinema ou em Teatro, o Importante É o Contato Humano," *O Globo* (3 July 1976).

2. Michel Ciment, "Ruy Guerra," in *Second Wave*, ed. Ian Cameron (New York: Praeger, 1970), pp. 99–109.

3. Rogério Sganzerla, "Revisão de 'Os Cafajestes,' " *O Estado de São Paulo* (4 January 1964).

4. Ely Azeredo, *"Os Cafajestes* na Justiça," *Tribuna da Imprensa* (16 April 1962).

5. "O Cinema e *Os Fuzis*," *Revista Civilização Brasileira* 1, no. 9–10 (September-November 1966):217–222. Reprinted in *Brazilian Cinema*, ed. Johnson and Stam, pp. 128–133 (Rutherford, N.J.: Fairleigh Dickinson University Press, 1982).

6. "Ruy Guerra on Os Fuzis," *Cinemantics*, no. 2 (March-April 1970), p. 10.

7. Schwarz, "O Cinema e *Os Fuzis*," p. 221.

8. "Ruy Guerra on Os Fuzis," p. 10.

9. Ibid.

10. Ciment, "Ruy Guerra," p. 104.

11. Ibid.

12. Michel Ciment, "Entretien avec Ruy Guerra," *Positif*, no. 116 (May 1970), p. 36.

13. René Capriles, "Los espectros interiores: Reencuentro con Ruy Guerra," *Hablemos de Cine* 13, no. 69 (1977–1978):31.

14. *New York Times* (19 June 1972).

15. She is the only one who holds rage and violence within her. In her womb is pus and all of the rottenness and weapons necessary to destroy the world she loathes. On the other hand, she is quite lucid and sees the dead who surround one of the colonels' daughters as gods who represent traditions, the presence of ancestors, the end of a race. She can see them with a critical vision the daughter does not have, . . . just as she sees those who are not yet dead but who are going to die. It is a lucidity of the future (Michel Ciment and Jacques Demeure, "Entretien avec Ruy Guerra," *Positif*, no. 123 [January 1971], p. 6).

16. Distribution notes to *Os Deuses e os Mortos*.

17. Cláudio Kahns and Inimá Simões, "Cinema Não E Festa," *Isto E* (31 August 1977).

18. Robert Stam, "*The Fall*: Formal Innovation and Radical Critique," *Jump Cut: A Review of Contemporary Cinema*, no. 22 (May 1980), pp. 20–21.

Chapter 4: Glauber Rocha: Apocalypse and Resurrection
1. "Ideology in the Third World Cinema: A Study of Sembene Ousmane and Glauber Rocha," *Quarterly Review of Film Studies* 4, no. 2 (Spring 1979):212.

2. Ibid., p. 213.

3. "Nota Breve: O Intelectual e o Cinema," *Jornal da Bahia* (25–26 January 1959).

4. "Experiência *Barravento*: Confissão sem Moldura," *Diário de Notícias* (Salvador) (25–26 December 1960).

5. *Revisão Crítica do Cinema Brasileiro* (Rio de Janeiro: Civilização Brasileira, 1963), pp. 13–14.

6. "Cinema novo y la aventura de la creación," *Hablemos de Cine* (Lima), no. 47 (May–June 1969), p. 25.

7. Piero Arlorio and Michel Ciment, "Entretien avec Glauber Rocha," *Positif*, no. 91 (January 1968), p. 19.

8. See Van Wert, "Third World Cinema," p. 214.

9. "A Narrativa Contraditória" (Ph.D. diss., University of São Paulo, 1979), p. 37.

10. Ibid., p. 214.

11. Van Wert, "Third World Cinema," p. 214.

12. René Gardies, "Glauber Rocha: Política, Mito e Linguagem," in *Glauber Rocha*, ed. Gerber, p. 54.

13. Xavier, "A Narrativa Contraditória," p. 36.

14. Ibid., p. 48.

15. Van Wert, "Third World Cinema," p. 216.

16. Ismail Xavier, "A Narrativa Contraditória," analyzes these two sequences in minute detail.

17. "Experiência *Barravento*."

18. Van Wert, "Third World Cinema," pp. 216–217.

19. Gardies, "Glauber Rocha," p. 72.

20. Xavier, "A Narrativa Contraditória," pp. 48–49.

21. Ibid., p. 39.

22. Ismail Xavier, "*Black God, White Devil*: The Representation of History," in *Brazilian Cinema*, ed. Johnson and Stam, pp. 134–148 (Rutherford, N.J.: Fairleigh Dickinson University Press, 1982).

23. In Glauber Rocha, *Deus e o Diabo na Terra do Sol* (Rio de Janeiro: Civilização Brasileira, 1965), p. 127.

24. Xavier, "*Black God, White Devil*."

25. For a discussion of music in the films of Rocha, see Graham Bruce, "Alma Brasileira: Music in Glauber Rocha's Films," *JumpCut: A Review of Contemporary Cinema*, no. 23 (May 1980), pp. 15–17; reprinted in Johnson and Stam, *Brazilian Cinema*, pp. 290–305.

26. Xavier, "*Black God, White Devil*," p. 138.

27. Ibid., p. 140.

28. Ibid.

29. Ibid., p. 137.

30. Ibid., pp. 141–142.

31. "Dialética da Violência," in Rocha, *Deus e o Diabo na Terra do Sol*, p. 212.

32. Luciano Martins, "Glauber Rocha em Transe," *Correio Brasiliense* (4 July 1979).

33. "*Land in Anguish*: Revolutionary Lessons," *JumpCut: A Review of Contemporary Cinema*, no. 10/11 (June 1976), pp. 49–51.

34. Maria Rosa A. Magalhães and Robert Stam analyze these two sequences in detail in "Dois Encontros de um Líder com o Povo: Uma Desconstrução do Populismo," in *Glauber Rocha*, ed. Gerber, pp. 148–156.

35. The link between *Land in Anguish* and *Citizen Kane* is discussed in depth by Barthélémy Amengual, "Glauber Rocha ou les chemins de la liberté," in *Le 'cinema novo' brésilien 2: Glauber Rocha*, ed. Michel Estève, pp. 63–65, Etudes Cinématographiques, no. 97–99 (Paris: Minard, 1973); and by Stam, "Land in Anguish."

36. Graham Bruce, "Alma Brasileira."

37. "Glauber Rocha," p. 62.

38. Miguel Torres, "Entrevista con Glauber Rocha sobre su película *Antônio das Mortes*," *Cine Cubano*, no. 60/61/62, p. 69, translated by Julianne Burton.

39. Burnes Hollyman, program notes to *Antônio das Mortes*, *CinemaTexas* (University of Texas at Austin) 12, no. 2 (13 April 1977).

40. Gardies, "Glauber Rocha," p. 49.

41. Ibid., p. 69.

42. Graham Bruce, "Alma Brasileira."

43. "Glauber Rocha, mystification ou lucidité," *Cinéma*, no. 150 (November 1970), pp. 88–89.

44. Quoted by Gerber, *Glauber Rocha*, p. 35.

45. "Glauber Rocha, mystification ou lucidité."

46. Gardies, "Glauber Rocha," pp. 48–49.

47. Ibid., p. 75.

48. Amengual, "Glauber Rocha," p. 78.

49. Quoted by Gerber, *Glauber Rocha*, p. 35.

50. Quoted in "O Leão do Apocalypse," *Veja* (24 December 1969).

51. Press book to *Der Leone Have Sept Cabeças.*

52. Quoted by Gerber, *Glauber Rocha*, p. 35.

53. Gardies, "Glauber Rocha," pp. 48–49.

54. The following example is provided and discussed in ibid., pp. 66–67.

55. "Glauber Rocha Lança 'A História do Brasil' no Festival de Pesaro," *Diário da Noite* (São Paulo) (20 September 1975).

56. Quoted in "Vaias, Assovios: Na Tela, Mais um Filme de Glauber," *O Globo* (22 November 1975).

57. From *Paese Seara* (Rome). Quoted in *Crítica* 2, no. 55 (25–31 August 1975):12.

58. See Mikhail Bakhtin, *Problems of Dostoevsky's Poetics*, tr. R. W. Rostel (Ann Arbor, Mich.: Ardis, 1973), p. 163.

59. "O Documentário que Poderia Ter Sido," *O Estado de São Paulo* (3 July 1977).

60. "Deus e o Diabo na Terra em Transe," *Jornal do Brasil* (25 November 1980).

61. *Jornal do Brasil* (19 November 1980).

Chapter 5: Nelson Pereira dos Santos: Toward a Popular Cinema

1. Randal Johnson, "Toward a Popular Cinema: An Interview with Nelson Pereira dos Santos," *Studies in Latin American Popular Culture* 1 (1982):228–229.

2. Federico de Cárdenas and Max Tessier, "Entretien avec Nelson Pereira dos Santos," in *Le 'cinema novo' brésilien*, ed. Michel Estève, pp. 61–62, Etudes Cinématographiques, no. 93–96 (Paris: Minard, 1972); translated by Julianne Burton.

3. "Manifesto por um Cinema Popular," Federação dos Cineclubes do Rio de Janeiro/Cineclube Macunaíma/Cineclube Glauber Rocha (Rio de Janeiro), 1975.

4. "Mandacaru Vermelho," *Jornal do Brasil* (11 November 1961).

5. In an interview in Ana Carolina Teixeira Soares's documentary *Nelson Pereira dos Santos Saúda o Povo e Pede Passagem* (1977), journalist Pompeu de Souza, who had led the struggle to release *Rio 40 Graus* from the censors in 1955, says that the myth is dos Santos's invention.

6. "Mandacaru Vermelho."

7. See Alex Viany, "Boca de Ouro: Nelson Rodrigues e o Cinema Novo," *Senhor* 5, no. 49 (March 1963):77–79.

8. *O Teatro de Nelson Rodrigues: Uma Realidade em Agonia* (Rio de Janeiro: Francisco Alves Editora, 1979), pp. 216–217.

9. Ibid., p. 107.

10. In an interview included in Soares, *Nelson Pereira dos Santos*.

11. The following analysis of *Vidas Secas* is a re-elaboration of Robert Stam's and my "The Cinema of Hunger: Nelson Pereira dos Santos's *Vidas Secas*," in our *Brazilian Cinema* (Rutherford, N.J.: Fairleigh Dickinson University Press, 1982), and of my "*Vidas Secas* and the Politics of Filmic Adaptation," *Ideologies and Literature* 3, no. 15 (January–March 1981):4–18.

12. Cárdenas and Tessier, "Nelson Pereira dos Santos," p. 64.

13. Paris: Gallimard, 1969, p. 144.

14. Telê Porto Ancona Lopez, *Mário de Andrade: Ramais e Caminho* (São Paulo: Duas Cidades, 1972), p. 133.

15. Mikhail Bakhtin, *Rabelais and His World*, tr. Helene Iswolsky (Cambridge: M.I.T. Press, 1968), p. 34.

16. For a discussion of this concept in the novel, see Affonso Romano de Sant'Anna, *Análise Estrutural de Romances Brasileiros*, 5th ed. (Petrópolis: Vozes, 1979), pp. 156–160.

17. Ibid., pp. 158–159.

18. Ibid., pp. 155–181.

19. "Manifesto por um Cinema Popular."

20. Cárdenas and Tessier, "Nelson Pereira dos Santos," p. 67.

21. Ibid., p. 66.

22. From the Difilme distribution notes to *O Bravo Guerreiro*.

23. João Luiz Vieira and Elizabeth Merena, "Hunger for Love," in *Brazilian Cinema*, ed. Johnson and Stam, pp. 162-168.

24. Cárdenas and Tessier, "Nelson Pereira dos Santos," p. 67.

25. *A Filosofia de Machado de Assis* (Rio de Janeiro: Vecchi, 1940), p. 56.

26. Cárdenas and Tessier, "Nelson Pereira dos Santos," pp. 67–68.

27. Ibid., p. 68.

28. "How Tasty Was My Little Frenchman," in *Brazilian Cinema*, Johnson and Stam, pp. 191–199.

29. Ibid., p. 194.

30. "Cinema: Trajetória no Subdesenvolvimento," *Argumento* 1, no. 1 (October 1973):55–67. English version in *Brazilian Cinema*, Johnson and Stam, pp. 244–255.

31. Peña, "How Tasty Was My Little Frenchman," p. 198.

32. Cárdenas and Tessier, "Nelson Pereira dos Santos," p. 72.

33. Ibid.

34. "As Memórias na Fumaça," *Jornal do Brasil* (13 June 1973).

35. "Who's Better?" *Ultima Hora* (27 June 1973).

36. See Bernardet's *Brasil em Tempo de Cinema*, 2d ed. (Rio de Janeiro: Paz e Terra, 1976).

37. From an article entitled "*O Amuleto* Mudou Tudo," included in "Manifesto por um Cinema Popular."

38. Johnson, "Toward a Popular Cinema," p. 229.

39. "Manifesto por um Cinema Popular."

40. Bernardet, "*O Amuleto* Mudou Tudo."

41. Joan Dassin, "Tent of Miracles," *JumpCut: A Review of Contemporary Cinema*, no. 22 (November 1979), pp. 20–22.

42. Johnson, "Toward a Popular Cinema," p. 234.

43. "Introdução a um Filme sobre o Verdadeiro Milagre Brasileiro," *Jornal do Brasil* (18 June 1977).

Conclusion: Cinema Novo, a Retrospective

1. "Glauber Rocha e a Experiência Inacabada do Cinema Novo," in *Glauber Rocha*, ed. Gerber, p. 11 (Rio de Janeiro: Paz e Terra, 1977).

2. Quoted by Gerber, "Glauber Rocha," pp. 11–12.

3. Ismail Norberto Xavier, "Allegories of Underdevelopment: From the 'Aesthetics of Hunger' to the 'Aesthetics of Garbage'" (Ph.D. diss., New York University, 1982), p. 27.

4. Ibid., p. 17.

5. Ibid., p. 18.

6. For an English version of Rocha's manifesto, see *Brazilian Cinema*, ed. Johnson and Stam, pp. 68–71 (Rutherford, N.J.: Fairleigh Dickinson University Press, 1982).

7. Xavier, "Allegories of Underdevelopment," pp. 18–21.

8. "Lumière, magie, action," *Positif*, no. 164 (December 1974), pp. 20–23.

9. Carlos Diegues's ideas are outlined in a series of newspaper articles published in Brazil starting in 1976. See, for example, *Jornal do Brasil* (9 March 1978). Nelson Pereira dos Santos first outlined his concept of a popular cinema in "Manifesto por um Cinema Popular," Federação dos Cineclubes do Rio de Janeiro/Cineclube Macunaíma/Cineclube Glauber Rocha (Rio de Janeiro), 1975. For Guerra's critique, see "Popular Cinema and the State," in Johnson and Stam, eds., *Brazilian Cinema*, pp. 101–103.

10. For a more detailed discussion of the working class presence in Brazilian cinema, see Jean-Claude Bernardet, "Operário, Personagem Emergente," in *Anos 70: Cinema* (Rio de Janeiro: Europa, 1980), pp. 29–47; also Bernardet's "Consideraçãoes sobre a Imagem do Povo no Cinema Brasileiro dos Anos 60 e 70," paper presented at the 44th International Congress of Americanists, Manchester, England, 5–10 September 1982.

Filmography

Joaquim Pedro de Andrade

1959—*O Mestre de Apipucos* (*The Master of Apipucos*; short documentary)
O Poeta do Castelo (*The Poet from Castelo*; short documentary)
1961—*Couro de Gato* (*Catskin*; short)
1963—*Garrincha, Alegria do Povo* (*Garrincha, Joy of the People*; documentary)
1965—*O Padre e a Moça* (*The Priest and the Girl*)
1967—*Brasília, Contradições de uma Cidade* (*Brasília, Contradictions of a City*; short)
1968—*Improvisiert und Zielbewurst* (short documentary)
1969—*Macunaíma*
1970—*Linguagem da Persuasão* (*Language of Persuasion*; short documentary)
1971—*Os Inconfidentes* (*The Conspirators*)
1975—*Guerra Conjugal* (*Conjugal Warfare*)
1977—*Vereda Tropical* (*Tropical Paths*; short)
1982—*O Homem do Pau-Brasil* (*The Brazilwood Man*)

Carlos Diegues

1960—*Fuga* (*Flight*; short)
Brasília (short)
Domingo (*Sunday*; short)
1962—*Escola de Samba, Alegria de Viver* (*Samba School, Joy of Living*; short)
1963—*Ganga Zumba*
1965—*A Oitava Bienal de São Paulo* (*The Eighth Biennial Exhibit in São Paulo*; short documentary)
1966—*A Grande Cidade* (*The Big City*)
1967—*Oito Universitários* (*Eight University Students*; short documentary)
1968—*Os Herdeiros* (*The Heirs*)
1970—*Un Séjour* (short; filmed in France)
1972—*Quando o Carnaval Chegar* (*When Carnival Comes*)
1974—*Joana Francesa* (*Joana the Frenchwoman*)
1976—*Xica da Silva*

Carlos Diegues (continued)
    1978—*Chuvas de Verão* (*Summer Showers*)
    1980—*Bye Bye Brasil*

Ruy Guerra
    1954—*Quand le soleil dort* (short; filmed in France)
    1962—*Os Cafajestes* (*The Hustlers*)
    1964—*Os Fuzis* (*The Guns*)
    1967—*Chanson pour Traverser la Rivière* (short; filmed in France)
    1969—*Sweet Hunters* (filmed in France)
    1971—*Os Deuses e os Mortos* (*The Gods and the Dead*)
    1977—*A Queda* (*The Fall*; with Nelson Xavier)
    1978—*Mueda Memória Massacre* (*Mueda Memory Massacre*; filmed in
        Mozambique)

Glauber Rocha
    1958—*O Pátio* (*The Patio*; short)
    1960—*A Cruz na Praça* (*The Cross in the Plaza*; short)
    1962—*Barravento* (*The Turning Wind*)
    1964—*Deus e o Diabo na Terra do Sol* (*Black God, White Devil*)
    1966—*Amazonas Amazonas* (documentary)
        Maranhão 66 (documentary)
    1967—*Terra em Transe* (*Land in Anguish*)
    1968—*Câncer* (finished in Cuba, 1973–1974)
    1969—*O Dragão da Maldade contra o Santo Guerreiro* (*Antônio das
        Mortes*)
    1970—*Der Leone Have Sept Cabeças* (*The Lion Has Seven Heads*; filmed in
        Brazzaville, Congo)
    1971—*Cabezas Cortadas* (*Severed Heads*; filmed in Spain)
    1974—*História do Brasil* (*History of Brazil*; with Marcos Medeiros;
        documentary produced in Cuba and Italy)
    1975—*Claro!* (filmed in Italy)
    1978—*Di* (short documentary)
    1979—*Jorjamado no Cinema* (short documentary)
    1980—*A Idade da Terra* (*The Age of the Earth*)

Nelson Pereira dos Santos
    1950—*Juventude* (*Youth*; short documentary)
        Atividades Políticas em São Paulo (*Political Activities in São Paulo*;
        short documentary)
    1955—*Rio 40 Graus* (*Rio 40 Degrees*)
    1957—*Rio Zona Norte* (*Rio Northern Zone*)
    1958—*Soldados do Fogo* (*Soldiers of Fire*; short documentary)
    1961—*Mandacaru Vermelho* (*Red Cactus*)
    1962—*Boca de Ouro* (*Gold Mouth*)
        Ballet do Brasil (*Ballet of Brazil*; short documentary)
    1963—*Vidas Secas* (*Barren Lives*)

Nelson Pereira dos Santos (continued)
    1963—*Um Moço de 74 Anos* (*A Young Man of 74 Years*; short documentary)
    1965—*O Rio de Machado de Assis* (*Machado de Assis's Rio*; short documentary)
    1965—*Fala Brasília* (*Speak Brasília*; short documentary)
    1966—*Cruzada ABC* (*ABC Crusade*; short documentary)
    1967—*El Justicero* (*The Enforcer*)
    1968—*Fome de Amor* (*Hunger for Love*)
        Abastecimento, Nova Política (*Provisioning, a New Policy*; short documentary)
    1970—*Azyllo Muito Louco* (*The Alienist*)
    1971—*Como Era Gostoso o Meu Francês* (*How Tasty Was My Little Frenchman*)
    1973—*Quem E Beta?* (*Who Is Beta?*)
    1974—*O Amuleto de Ogum* (*The Amulet of Ogum*)
    1977—*Tenda dos Milagres* (*Tent of Miracles*)
    1980—*Estrada da Vida* (*Road of Life*)

Index